LEADING
FROM BEHIND

OTHER BOOKS BY RICHARD MINITER

The Myth of Market Share:
Why Market Share Is the Fool's Gold of Business

Losing Bin Laden:
How Bill Clinton's Failures Unleashed Global Terror

Shadow War:
The Untold Story of How America Is Winning the War on Terror

Disinformation:
22 Media Myths That Undermine the War on Terror

Mastermind:
The Many Faces of the 9/11 Architect, Khalid Shaikh Mohammed

ABOUT THE AUTHOR

Richard Miniter is the author of two top-10 *New York Times* bestsellers on foreign affairs, *Losing bin Laden* and *Shadow War.*

He writes the "national security" column for *Forbes.com.*

Miniter's articles have appeared in *The New York Times, The Wall Street Journal, The Washington Post* as well as *The Atlantic, Newsweek, Reader's Digest, The New Republic,* and *National Review.*

Previously he was an editorial writer for *The Wall Street Journal* in Brussels, a member of the investigative team of the *Sunday Times* of London, and editorial-page editor and vice president of *The Washington Times.*

He regularly appears on CNN, C-SPAN, Fox News, and MSNBC as well as nationally syndicated radio programs. He has won journalism awards from the National Press Club, the Institute for Humane Studies, and International Society of Investigative Journalists.

www.RichardMiniter.com

Twitter: @minitermin

facebook.com/RichardMiniter

LEADING
FROM BEHIND

THE RELUCTANT PRESIDENT AND THE ADVISORS
WHO DECIDE FOR HIM

RICHARD MINITER

ST. MARTIN'S GRIFFIN ☙ NEW YORK

LEADING FROM BEHIND. Copyright © 2012 by Richard Miniter. All rights reserved. Printed in the United States of America. For information, address St. Martin's Press, 175 Fifth Avenue, New York, N.Y. 10010.

www.stmartins.com

The Library of Congress has cataloged the hardcover edition as follows:

Miniter, Richard.
   Leading from behind : the reluctant president and the advisors who decide for him / Richard Miniter. — 1st ed.
           p. cm.
   ISBN 978-1-250-01610-2 (hardcover)
   ISBN 978-1-250-01629-4 (e-book)
   1. Obama, Barack.   2. Obama, Barack—Political and social views.
3. Obama, Barack—Friends and associates.   4. Presidents—United States—
Staff.   5. Political leadership—United States.   6. United States—Politics and
government—2009–   7. United States—Foreign relations—2009–   I. Title.
   E908.3.M56 2012
   973.932092—dc23

                                                            2012024080

ISBN 978-1-250-03138-9 (trade paperback)

St. Martin's Griffin books may be purchased for educational, business, or promotional use. For information on bulk purchases, please contact Macmillan Corporate and Premium Sales Department at 1-800-221-7945 extension 5442 or write specialmarkets @macmillan.com.

First St. Martin's Griffin Edition: May 2013

10 9 8 7 6 5 4 3 2 1

To Nina Rosenwald, who, as usual, had an idea . . .

CONTENTS

The Perspective ix

Introduction 1

1. The Women 9

2. Health Care, by Hook or Crook 45

3. Nothing Is Sure but Debt and Taxes 77

4. Killing bin Laden Loudly 115

5. Israel's Dilemma 169

6. Fast and Loose and Furious 201

7. What Kind of Leader Is Obama? 233

Acknowledgments 247

Notes 249

About Sources and Methods 273

Bibliography 275

Index 277

THE PERSPECTIVE

This book is about presidential leadership at a particular historical moment, and is the first book of its kind in the Obama years. *Leading from Behind* is solely concerned with the six pivotal decisions of the Obama years and how and why the president decided as he did. It is a book about leadership and decision-making, grounded in history, fact, and direct observation. The quality of the president's leadership is the essential question of the year 2012.

It is important that this question be answered fairly. In that spirit, I have relied extensively and exclusively on President Obama's admirers and advisors, allies, and associates. Democrats all. The stray few Republicans, who were interviewed for this book, were consulted solely to gather their eyewitness accounts of President Obama in private meetings. All of the secondary sources, newscasts, and newspapers, are mainstream outlets that, if anything, tend to favor the president over his critics and rivals.

LEADING
FROM BEHIND

INTRODUCTION

For we are strangers before them, and sojourners, as were all our fathers.

—Exordium chosen by Barack Obama for *Dreams from My Father,* drawn from I Chronicles

The Unanswered Question

What kind of a leader is Barack Obama?

Strangely enough, for a president in his fourth year of office, this remains an open question.

So far the press has been uncharacteristically reluctant to probe the nature of Obama's leadership abilities. Part of the reason is that ideology colors the coverage and obscures Obama, the real leader. Instead the media presents an empty screen on which are projected the hopes and fears of partisans, Left and Right, leading his enemies to overestimate him and his friends to misunderstand him.

On the Right, Obama is seen as an evil genius with a dark, complex plan to ruin America. On the establishment Left, he is portrayed as a man dealing with immense problems inherited from his unpopular predecessor, who, through it all, somehow has racked up historic achievements.

Bill Keller, a *New York Times* columnist, writes that Obama's critics overlook his "real accomplishments, achieved despite a brutally divided government. Lost in the shouting is the fact that Obama pulled the country back from the brink of depression; signed a health care reform law that expands coverage, preserves choice, and creates a mechanism for controlling costs; engineered fairly stringent financial regulatory reform; and authorized the risky mission that got Osama bin Laden." All true enough, but misleading and avoid the issue of Obama's leadership abilities.

Both of these dueling media narratives—Left and Right—fail to consider Obama, the leader. They embody opinions only about the outcomes of Obama's decisions, not the process that made those decisions. They tell us the media's take on his decisions, not the quality of those decisions.

So the question remains: What kind of a leader is Barack Obama?

Evaluating Obama's leadership abilities means investigating his signal successes, those banner-headline moments he will campaign on in 2012 to make the case for his reelection. Hidden in each success (and in some dangerous failures) is a case study in how Obama makes presidential decisions. The only way to probe his leadership abilities is to interview participants and eyewitnesses in the White House, in Congress, in the Pentagon, and in several foreign capitals. This is what I set out to do in the pages that follow.

The Mystery

Barack Obama is the most mysterious manager of our age.

He appeared suddenly, like a meteor dropping from the night sky. Within four years of his first, fleeting appearance on the stage at the Democratic National Convention in 2004, he became president of the United States. He had moved so quickly that his 2008 presidential campaign felt compelled to repeatedly reintroduce him, to tell his life story in flickering videos and campaign speeches. When his autobiography was reissued during the campaign, it became a No. 1 *New York Times* bestseller. Its sales were driven by curiosity, an urgent desire to know: Who is he?

The mystery did not burn away in the heat of the presidency, the most public office in the world. As president, he has remained surprisingly aloof, distant, and private. He stands apart in our joined-up, interconnected, social-networked world. In a hint of self-criticism in his autobiography, he writes: "I had grown too comfortable in my solitude, the safest place I knew."[1] Indeed, Obama may be the most solitary man to hold the office of president.

Social circles usually widen as presidents build alliances and recruit the public to their side. Strangely, Obama's circle shrank. State dinners, public receptions, and private moments with the barons and baronesses of Washington, were few. His disdain for official Washington was not a campaign pose, but a genuine feeling, welling from a deep inner spring.

It is not that he dislikes power or the perks that come with it—his elated explanation to Oprah Winfrey about the joys of having White House butlers, servants, guards, and other attendants testifies to that. But he dislikes the public give-and-take of politics. He distrusts the idea that political decisions are supposed to be a collaborative enterprise involving experts and executives with conflicting interests, similar to making a movie or running a corporation. Instead he wants the presidency to be more like writing a book or commanding a battalion, a lone decider who hands down commands. He retreats from people, aside from a small trusted circle, because he believes power is sullied when it is shared.

As a result, even old friends found themselves marooned. Christopher Edley Jr., the dean of the University of California at Berkeley's law school had been a friend and informal advisor to Obama for years. Often he would phone or text ideas or mild critiques to Obama while he was on the campaign trail. When he wrote the president a short note to take issue with a public statement in 2010, he received a call from Obama's most powerful and influential advisor, Valerie Jarrett. She said the president did not appreciate his remarks. The abruptness surprised the mild-mannered scholar. The president no longer tolerated even moderate criticism from a friendly liberal source.

And the president famously said he didn't want any "new friends." There is no evidence that Obama has added many "new friends" since he moved to the White House, except for a handful of Secret Service agents. One trusted friend, presidential "body man" Reggie Love, has even left his position at the White House to earn his master's degree.

Isolation—more than previous presidents—seems to be the rule in the Obama White House.

Informal moments paint the picture. When watching his beloved Pittsburgh Steelers win the 2009 Super Bowl, Obama didn't mix much with the guests packed in the yellow-walled Oval Room in the White House residence. (The White House staff, not the president or first lady, had invited most of the guests.) Obama sat directly before the television, positioned in the front of the room, with an empty seat to his right. To his left sat a longtime pal, Marty Nesbitt, an African American from Chicago who plays no formal role in national politics. Behind the president were clustered other longtime Chicago friends, with Attorney General Eric Holder leaning confidently against a wall. Virtually everyone physically close to the president was African American and linked to Chicago. Farther back sat Congressman Mike Doyle, a reliable white Democrat from Pittsburgh, where the Steelers hail from. Farther back still were other political supporters. The Washington insiders were packed into the outer reaches of the room, like Pluto elliptically orbiting a distant sun.

In a telling photo, Obama is shown pumping his two arms in the air, the nearby faces of his friends alive with joy. The mood fades, though, as you move away from the president. In the back of the room, the Washington crowd is almost out of focus and seemingly unsure of what is expected of them. Only two people are cheering along with the president.[2] Pluto is a cold planet.

The photo, taken by Obama insider Pete Rouse, was snapped during the ascendant, triumphant period of the first Obama years. It was 2009, when Democrats controlled all the elected branches of the federal government, the country overwhelmingly supported the new president, and many hopeful changes seemed possible. The Steelers were winning. Yet Obama seemed almost alone.

Obama's solitary style shows up during the workday, too. Even West Wing staffers—people who in any other presidency are the president's "inner circle"—say the president rarely makes a decision in their presence. He may announce decisions that he has already made, but he doesn't wrestle with dilemmas in front of his staff or demand additional options from them, as Presidents Clinton and George W. Bush often did. When he collects opinions in staff meetings, he rarely gives his own. Indeed, after extensive briefings with the president, staffers say, they often have no hint as to what his eventual decision will be. Or, whether he will decide at all.

Instead, he prefers to retreat to a makeshift private office on the White House's third floor—the Treaty Room, near the Lincoln Bedroom— where, at a paper-stacked antique table, with ESPN droning from a television near the fireplace, he ponders and weighs. He does his best thinking after he has had dinner with his wife and daughters. Usually, he is there at night, when no moving traffic is visible in the ornate window frame. He is, almost always, alone.

His solitariness, an unusual quality in a politician or public figure, is a lifelong feature. As a boy in Indonesia, he often played and studied alone. He confesses in his first autobiography that, as a student and a young man, he was "prone to see other people as unnecessary distractions."[3]

It is a habit of mind encouraged by his mother, who raised him nearly alone. His father disappeared to Harvard and then Nairobi when Barack Obama Jr. was two. His adoptive father rarely spent time with him.

Obama's mother herself was often described as "solitary and bookish."[4] He is very much his mother's son.

What critics call his "aloofness," or even "arrogance," is actually a brooding nature common to writers and scholars. While nineteenth-century voters might have prized this quality, Obama's seeming coolness in today's hotter age actually slowed his political rise during the 1990s. Voters have come to demand less Calvin Coolidge and more Oprah Winfrey. While Obama is a gifted public speaker, his private coolness led his colleagues in the Illinois legislature to complain that he was cold and "thought too much."[5]

The counterpart to this brooding isolation is often a paralyzing caution. He voted "present"—rather than "yea" or "nay"—more than eighty times in the Illinois statehouse and in the U.S. Senate, sometimes when his Democratic colleagues sorely needed his vote.

Barack Obama brought both of these character traits to the presidency.

Usually the arc of a president's prior career guides how he makes decisions. Ronald Reagan, we now know, made decisions like a Hollywood director, orchestrating events and ruling out options quickly.

Like the former governor he was, Bill Clinton liked to debate the details with his staff, constantly turning an issue around to look at its different facets. Clinton's advisors said he saw the presidency as a "contact sport," always trying to determine the equilibrium between what he hoped to achieve and what the balance of political forces would *allow* him to achieve. He liked to brainstorm with staff, deep into the night.

George W. Bush ran the presidency like the Harvard MBA that he was, having earned it in his formative years. He preferred a well-defined bureaucratic process with a managed gauntlet of deadlines before approaching a winnowed set of options, which his advisors would present to him. He preferred things to be orderly and deliberate; rarely were decisions made on the fly and always in concert with staff.

Obama's decision-making style is harder to describe. Asked for one adjective to sum up the president's leadership style, P. J. Crowley, the former State Department spokesman for Hillary Clinton in the Obama years, and National Security Council spokesman in the Clinton years, settled upon this phrase: "very corporate."[6] He means that the Obama White House is much less freewheeling than in the Clinton days, his point of comparison. Pushed a bit, Crowley conceded that once decisions reach the president's desk, no one knows what happens. Aides are consulted, memos scribbled on, questions asked, but in the end Obama decides alone, in an upper room where even the West Wing staff dare not intrude.

Bush and Clinton were isolated in the sense that leaders usually are and presidents always are. But, still, they were highly engaged in a communal decision-making process that was specified and styled to their own personal needs.

By contrast, Barack Obama, a former constitutional scholar and lawmaker, has no executive or managerial habits to guide him. Throughout his career, he was always at a lectern or a committee table. Importantly, he never ran a major committee in the Illinois or U.S. Senate. He alone could choose what to teach or what vote to take. He never led a campaign to pass a controversial piece of legislation. He rarely, if ever, had to compromise, coach, or cajole. In his entire career he flew solo, with the counsel of a handful of trusted associates.

Nor does his life story tell us about his qualities as a leader. We know the bare facts of his biography: raised by a single mother in Hawaii and Indonesia; a community organizer; a state lawmaker, a U.S. Senator. We know the historic results attributed to him: first black president; health care reform; killing bin Laden. But we simply don't know what kind of a leader he is.

The most important things we need to know about any leader are: Is he decisive or dilatory? How does he manage people and priorities? What *are* his priorities? Can he inspire in private and in public? What does he do when he fails? What is his vision? Are his goals important and realistic?

These questions matter because 120 million voting Americans will soon have to choose the next president in what will be the most consequential national election in a generation.

Answering the Question

The case for reelecting Barack Obama rests on four pillars: victories in Congress (principally health care reform); victories in war (mainly dispatching Osama bin Laden); management of global financial and security crises; and maintenance of key foreign alliances (with Israel and the Arab world). Two other crises are also key measures of Obama's management abilities: the national debt crisis of 2011, and Operation Fast and Furious, a Justice department sting that killed at least one U.S. Border Patrol agent, funneled more than 1,000 guns into the hands of lethal Mexican drug cartels, and led Attorney General Eric Holder to stonewall and mislead investigators in both houses of Congress.

By investigating each of these consequential decisions in the coming six chapters, we can map out how the president manages in crises. In the process, we will discover just what kind of a leader Barack Obama is.

In the end, we will at last be able to answer the question first raised by Hillary Clinton in the 2008 Democratic nomination fight: how does Obama respond as a president whom he gets a crisis-call at 3 A.M.?

CHAPTER 1

THE WOMEN

You can be stylish and powerful, too. That's Michelle's advice.

—Barack Obama speaking to graduates at Barnard College,
May 14, 2012

Every examination of a president should begin with the people and events that shaped him. In the case of Barack Obama, four strong-minded women, who intertwined their lives with his, were the most formative: his mother, Stanley Ann Dunham; his wife, Michelle LaVaughn Robinson; his mentor, Valerie Jarrett; and his secretary of state, Hillary Clinton. Nancy Pelosi, the former House Speaker, also has a starring role, as we will see in chapter 2.

Each continues to play an important part in presidential decision making—though, in his mother's case, an indirect and perhaps unconscious one.

Stanley Ann Dunham

Her first name was Stanley because her father wanted a boy.

Or perhaps, as Obama's mother later said, she was named after a

Bette Davis character that her mother liked.[1] Like many details of Stanley Ann Dunham's life, the truth is hard to pin down.

Barack Obama's mother was born in Kansas and moved through a series of American suburbs, from the Midwest to the West and Northwest, throughout her childhood. She inherited her father's gypsy ways.

Stanley Ann's father, a difficult man who often forced the family to move, only stayed in one place for the years when he fought in World War II. He had no real career, but a string of unrelated jobs. By contrast, her mother later rose from bank clerk to executive—a role model for her young and increasingly independent daughter.

In high school, Stanley Ann was "bookish" and prone to disappear with fast-driving boys who were willing to drive from Washington State to California for a weekend lark. Obama, himself, would later become an avid reader with a penchant for mysterious adventures, such as his 1981 trip to Pakistan. It wasn't an official college trip and was not connected to any course of study. He had no friends there and the war-torn, poor country was hardly a tourist destination. He likely went for the same whimsical reasons his mother took sudden and strange trips in her teens and twenties: a desire for dramatic personal adventure.

Swept up in the progressive causes of the early 1960s, Stanley Ann attended Russian language classes at the University of Hawaii, where she met a foreign student from Kenya. His name was Barack Obama. He was interested in Soviet economics, smoked a beloved pipe, and spoke with a British-colonial accent. She found him romantic and exotic.

Shortly after John F. Kennedy's election, Stanley Ann and Barack Sr. conceived a baby, Barack Jr., but they never lived together.

The union didn't last. Barack Sr. went on to study at Harvard and later married an American woman he met there. They settled in Nairobi and had several children together. His career as civil servant ended abruptly when he published an article in an African academic journal, in which he faulted Kenya's revolutionary leader, Jomo Kenyatta, for failing to adopt a consistent Maoist line on economic policy. (Kenyatta was initially fonder of Soviet thinking, as Barack Obama Sr. had been in his university days. And, the new leader of an independent Kenya didn't tolerate criticism.)

Stumbling drunkenly, Obama's father was struck by a car on a crowded street in Kenya's capital city. As a result of his injuries, a surgeon amputated both of his legs. Two decades later, the gifted student of languages and economics died penniless. He did not live to see his son's rise.

Meanwhile, Stanley Ann had moved on and had married another foreign student whom she met at the University of Hawaii, Lolo Soetoro. Within a year, the new family had decamped to Indonesia. Barack Jr. was just six years old.[2]

On that island archipelago, Muslim radicals and Maoist revolutions clashed while seeking to topple Indonesia's iron-fisted dictator.

There was a clash inside Obama, too. He simply didn't fit in there. Native children taunted him and sometimes threw stones. He was new, and his grasp of their language was poor.

The few strangers he could speak to in English were American oil executives who would come to his adopted father's house to discuss deals over dinner. His mother didn't like them and said they were shallow and materialistic. While they lived in compounds with servants, hers was a small house on a busy street in a native neighborhood. Young Obama was not encouraged to befriend the children of the American executives. He grew without the company of his countrymen or his extended family.

No part of his identity was solidly locked in place. He was neither white nor black; neither American nor Asian nor African; neither Christian nor Muslim. His adoptive father didn't practice his own religion (Islam) and his mother (nominally Christian) mocked all religions. Obama's former teacher in Indonesia, Israella Pareira, said: "His mother was white, his father was Indonesian, and here was a black, chubby boy with curly hair. It was a big question mark for us."[3]

And it was for him, too, as Obama later wrote.

The little guidance he received from his mother about Christianity was dismissive. First, he attended a Roman Catholic school, an experience he later recounted: "When it came time to pray, I would close my eyes, then peek around the room. Nothing happened. No angels descended. Just a parched old nun and thirty brown children, muttering words."[4] The irreligious views of his mother were stamped on him early, and firmly.

He then moved to a Muslim neighborhood and attended a Muslim school.[5] Obama sometimes attended the local mosque with his stepfather. Some of the president's critics, both Democrats and Republicans, have focused on the fact that Obama's school registration card, at both the Catholic and Muslim schools in Indonesia, identified him as a "Muslim." They miss something more important: Obama was given no distinctive religious identity, nothing to hold on to. "Muslim" was assumed by form-fillers because his father was Muslim and nearly everyone else in Indonesia was.

Life in Indonesia was always changing. Obama shared a home with tropical birds, monkeys, and small crocodiles. When one pet died, another of a different species replaced it. Nothing continued or endured, except his mother.

When not in the care of his mother or stepfather, a nanny cared for him—one who was every bit as exotic as Obama's pets.[6] He was openly gay, dated the local butcher, and played street volleyball with a team of transvestites named the Fantastic Dolls.[7]

Soon, the nanny was fired. Nothing lasted.

Still, Obama tried to make a home there, and imagined a larger life for himself. When a visitor asked what he wanted to be when he grew up, he said, "Oh, prime minister."[8]

But that was not to be. Stanley Ann Dunham's marriage to Soetoro dissolved after barely seven years. She never remarried.

Obama returned to the United States in 1971, but not to any sort of stability.[9]

Stanley Ann Dunham and young Barack Obama returned to Hawaii and, briefly, moved in with her parents. She earned a master's degree, in anthropology, at the University of Hawaii in 1974. She wanted to write a dissertation about iron-working techniques of rural Indonesians, though she had no plans to teach, and the esoteric subject had no commercial applications.

Yet, to complete her PhD, she had to return to Indonesia—without her son, who was just entering his combustible teen years. She later said leaving her son was the single hardest thing she had ever done.[10]

Still, she wanted to be alone with her books and her thoughts. After an internal debate, she left.

• • •

This decision undoubtedly shaped young Barack Obama. The only constant in his ever-changing life, in which people and countries suddenly disappeared in the oval-shaped window of a jet plane, had been his mother. Now she, too, was gone. He was barely ten.

Dunham's biographer was an enterprising *New York Times* contributor named Janny Scott. "When people learned that I was working on a book on the president's mother the question I encountered most often was: 'Do you like her?' Sometimes people asked, 'Was she nice?' The line of questioning puzzled me: Why were these the first things people wanted me to know? Gradually, it became apparent that those questions were a way of approaching the subject of Ann's decision to live apart from her child. They were followed by ruminations on how a mother could do such a thing. As many Americans see it, a mother belongs with her child, and no extenuating circumstances can explain the perversity of choosing to be elsewhere. Ann's decision was a transgression that people thirty-five years later could neither understand nor forgive."[11]

Did this intensify Obama's inclination to stand apart from people? Strangely, his mother's biographer doesn't consider the question. But it undoubtedly did.

Stanley Ann's other child is Barack's half sister Maya. "It was one of those things where she [Stanley Ann] felt like, 'Well, life is what it is.' She gained a great deal" in terms of personal discovery and intellectual development. "The transition may have been difficult, but look . . ."[12]

So Obama learned to live in his own head. It was safer there.

In Hawaii, he lived with his grandparents, whom he called "Gramps" and "Toot," from the fifth grade until he graduated from Punahou, a private prep school, eight years later.[13]

Obama learned early that connections matter. He later wrote that "Gramps" had given him some advice, that "the contacts I made at Punahou would last a lifetime, that I would move in charmed circles and have all the opportunities that he'd never had."[14]

It was a vital lesson and one that he never forgot. He soon became a natural networker.

• • •

A devoted husband and father, the president has said that he wanted to raise his children to have the family life that he never had. He didn't want to leave his family the way his mother left him. His mother-in-law, Marian Shields Robinson, lives in the White House; he makes a point of attending his daughters' school functions, and enjoys vacations with them and Michelle; with rare exceptions, he has breakfast and dinner with his family every day.

Stanley Ann's other legacy in his life is his preference for private reflection over public debates among his staff. Obama diligently studies the briefing books he is given—alone in a private, hideaway office. He has banned jokes in his presence unless he is the one telling them. He reminds his staff that he is "no-drama Obama," that he dislikes disagreement among his staff and loathes any comment that implies criticism. The penchant for avoiding conflict—for leaving contentious issues to others—is a hallmark of his leadership style.

Obama admirer David Brooks wrote in *The New York Times,* a few months before the 2008 elections, "Obama lives apart. He put one foot in the institutions he rose through on his journey but never fully engaged."

Obama learned that a certain aloofness could be combined with networking to give many different people the idea that he shared their views and values. Even ideological adversaries saw part of themselves reflected in his remarks. It was a valuable skill. When he was one of three remaining candidates for the presidency of the Harvard Law Review, the minority of conservative law students comprised a crucial swing voting bloc. They saw in Obama a willingness to listen and amend his views after hearing them out. They backed him and Obama won.

The other side of this trait is that it means that he can confide in almost no one, because opening up would break the spell that he has managed to cast over people with opposing views, making opponents believe he secretly agrees with each of them. The exceptions are his wife, Michelle, and his mentor, Valerie Jarrett.

Valerie Jarrett

While Valerie Jarrett's official White House biography lists her as a "senior advisor and assistant to the president for Intergovernmental Affairs and Public Engagement,"[15] it hides her true institutional importance and significance in Obama's life.

In the press, longtime friends and advisors to Obama offer other descriptions, which are more personal but also seem to fall short: "First Friend," "big sister," "the other half of Obama's brain,"[16] "Barack's secret weapon," and even "a female version of Barack."[17] *Consigliora* is the term that might best capture Jarrett's power, range, and trust.

The president himself says he talks to Jarrett several times a day and that he rarely makes a major decision without consulting her. While every Nixon has his Kissinger, one of the things that make Jarrett unique in presidential history is that she is also the first lady's mentor. Indeed, she has guided the careers and lives of both Obamas for twenty years.

Barack Obama and Jarrett have a lot in common. Like him, she spent her childhood in a Muslim country far from home, both in miles and in culture. When the Obamas first met Jarrett, this point of commonality as well-traveled strangers among a less-mobile majority was the first building block in a life-changing relationship.

In 1991, Jarrett was working for Chicago mayor Richard Daley, which was the avenue that led her to the Obamas. Jarrett's colleague Susan Sher handed her a letter from a young attorney named Michelle LaVaughn Robinson. Sher remembers saying to Jarrett something like, "This woman is no longer interested in being at her law firm. She wants to be in government and give back."[18] (Sher would later become first lady Michelle Obama's chief of staff.) In fact, Michelle Robinson had complained repeatedly about the "boring" work given to first- and second-year associates in her law firm and sought a more interesting career. Jarrett, meanwhile, was on the hunt to recruit more African American women with prestigious degrees to join the Daley administration.

Jarrett phoned her immediately. "I was just unbelievably bowled over by how impressive she was," Jarrett later said. She offered Michelle a job, sight unseen, over the phone. Michelle was more cautious. She said that she would not make a decision until Jarrett met her fiancé, Barack. They scheduled a dinner.

Walking between the two large wolf statues guarding the entrance to Le Loup Café on a warm Chicago evening in July 1991, Jarrett soon spotted Robinson and her slim companion. Michelle Robinson had shrewdly chosen the place for its mix of French and Middle Eastern cuisine, a sign of sophistication that she hoped would resonate with Jarrett. After Barack was introduced to Jarrett, he began to softly but persistently pepper her with questions. Jarrett spotted a political comer and, more importantly, discovered a kindred spirit.

They held surprisingly similar views about America's place in the world. She told the perceptive *New Yorker* editor David Remnick, "Barack felt extraordinarily familiar. He and I share a view of where the United States fits in the world, which is often different from the view of people who have not traveled outside the United States as young children."[19] Jarrett added that she "had come to see the United States with greater objectivity as one country among many, rather than as the center of all wisdom and experience."[20] It was a view that Obama shared.

Jarrett had an edge on the worldly Obama in both global travel and social position. Unlike him, she was actually born abroad, in the ancient Silk Road city of Shiraz in southern Iran. The old caravan city is known for its distinctive carpets, crumbling mud-brick walls, green-domed mosques, and sharp business practices. The Jarretts lived in Iran until she was five. Throughout her childhood she would travel to Africa, Asia, and Europe. The family traveled widely as Jarrett's father roamed the world to collect blood samples for his work on sickle-cell anemia and other blood disorders.[21]

Unlike Obama, Jarrett's family hailed from the top of the African American meritocratic elite—a place both Obamas urgently wanted to vault themselves into. This made Jarrett's friendship desirable and valuable. The Shah of Iran invited Jarrett's father, Dr. James Bowman, the world-renowned expert in blood disorders, to open the Department of Pathology at the new Nemazee Hospital in 1955.[22] Jarrett's mother, Barbara Taylor, was the daughter of Robert Taylor, the first black graduate of the Massachusetts Institute of Technology and the first black chairman of the Chicago Housing Authority.[23] Both sides of Jarrett's family had strings of first African American achievements, and Jarrett herself was on her way to racking up a few more.

Jarrett's family and social connections were formidable. When the family resettled in Chicago in 1962, her father became an assistant professor of pathology at the University of Chicago and ran the blood bank at the University of Chicago Medical Center, the hospital at which Jarrett would later hire Michelle Obama in a key administrative position.

As a teenager, Jarrett attended a private Ivy League feeder school, Northfield Mount Hermon in Massachusetts, and earned a bachelor's degree in psychology from Stanford University and a law degree from the University of Michigan. While the upper reaches of the preceding generation of African Americans had concentrated on science, medicine, and engineering, Jarrett, like many African Americans of her generation, gravitated to law, business, and politics. Returning to Chicago in 1981, Jarrett joined the top law firm of Sonnenschein, Carlin, Nath & Rosenthal.[24]

She married another African American aristocrat, Dr. William Robert Jarrett. The marriage ended after the birth of her daughter, Laura. The one time she discussed her marriage publicly, she summed up the experience to Don Terry of the *Chicago Tribune* without emotion, saying, "Married in 1983, separated in 1987, and divorced in 1988. Enough said."[25] There is nothing else on the public record about Jarrett's first and only marriage. Her husband died a few years after the divorce, having said nothing about their union to the press.

Jarrett also told the *Chicago Tribune* that the birth of her daughter inspired her to make major professional changes. "I wanted to do something she'd be really proud of me for."[26] For Jarrett, that meant politics.

The Obamas, of course, were also interested in politics. And they shared a perspective on politics as a way of creating a personal identity while transforming the nation.

When Chicago elected its first-ever black mayor, Harold Washington, Jarrett quickly joined his administration. She hints that her corporate law firm associates disapproved of her shift into politics. While they may have thought she was recklessly giving up a promising career in the private sector, she made a point of telling *The New York Times* that the "nearly

all-white firm" treated her departure with "polite silence."[27] Clearly, despite her many successes, she saw herself as a racial outsider. In his books,
Obama takes a similar view.

Jarrett found her niche at City Hall. She had the skills and the influence to stay on through the changing of administrations and to join Chicago mayor Richard Daley's team as deputy chief of staff. While Daley
was a new Democrat, distinct from his father, Jarrett's move required
considerable dexterity. Daley's father, as mayor, famously ordered the police to arrest countercultural protestors at the 1968 Democratic Convention. The men in blue were equally unpopular among politically active
members of the black community at the time because of law-enforcement
practices they believed to be racist. Given the historical animosity between
the new mayor's family and Chicago's black political class, some saw Jarrett's
transition as bold, shrewd, or ambitious. Still, she thrived.

In years following that fateful dinner with the Obamas, Jarrett's
power and influence would continue to grow—both in the wider world
and in the lives of the Obamas. It was a start of an alliance that would
propel the Obamas to the top of Chicago and Illinois politics, and later
the nation's. Jarrett was present at every pivotal moment in their political
lives from that night forward.

Shortly after their dinner, Jarrett took control of downtown Chicago's urban renewal and business development projects as commissioner of
the Department of Planning and Development.[28] Michelle Obama followed her, as one of her deputies. Jarrett became known as "the deal
buster," because she often used her near-absolute power over real-estate
transactions involving city approval to quash multimillion-dollar development efforts.[29] Cynics privately complained that Jarrett often seemed
to kill deals in which friends or allies did not share an opportunity to
profit. She thought the failed deals lacked a social conscience.

With that power came influence and, later, money. "She is like a god
in Chicago, an icon," said Adrienne Pitts, a lawyer at Michelle Obama's
former law firm, Sidley Austin.[30] "She knows everyone in Chicago. She may
be one of the most plugged-in people in the United States," Obama advisor Anita Dunn said.[31]

Jarrett left the city government in 1995 for a role as CEO of The

Habitat Company, which developed housing projects under city con-tracts.[32] There she was paid an annual salary of $300,000 with another $550,000 in deferred compensation.[33] In addition to what she earned at Habitat, Jarrett also served on for-profit boards of real estate and building-materials firms,[34] pocketing another $346,000 per year.[35]

Soon she joined nearly every influential board in Chicago. She was first a member, then the chairman of the Chicago Stock Exchange, chair-man of the Chicago Transit Board, vice chairman of the Board of Trust-ees of the University of Chicago, director of the Federal Reserve Bank of Chicago, trustee of Chicago's Museum of Science and Industry, and chair-man of the Board of Trustees of the University of Chicago Medical Cen-ter.[36] And she shared her ever-growing network with both Michelle and Barack Obama.

Like Obama, Jarrett trumpets her concern for the plight of the poor and shares a view of government as the principal uplifter of the downtrodden. She explained in September 2011: "We are working hard to lift people out of poverty and give them a better life, a footing, and that's what government is supposed to do."[37] This was said as simply a fact, not a political opinion.

But her record as a manager of low-income housing tells a different story. As CEO of The Habitat Company, while her firm received tens of millions in government subsidies to manage public housing, many of the properties under her care became slums. *The Boston Globe* described one such Habitat property, Grove Parc (located in Obama's Illinois state sen-ate district), as a symbol of "the broader failures of giving public subsidies to private companies to build and manage affordable housing."[38] Grove Parc raises troubling questions about Jarrett's management abilities, for the project was worse than the slums it replaced: "About ninety-nine of the units are vacant," *The Boston Globe* reported, "many rendered unin-habitable by unfixed problems, such as collapsed roofs and fire damage. Mice scamper through the halls. Battered mailboxes hang open. Sewage backs up into kitchen sinks. In 2006, federal inspectors graded the condi-tion of the complex an 11 on a 100-point scale—a score so bad the build-ings now face demolition."[39]

Indeed, Chicago's new mayor, Rahm Emanuel, Jarrett's former White House colleague and Obama's chief of staff, announced in August 2011 that the city has received some $30.5 million in federal stimulus money to "revitalize" Grove Parc by tearing it down.[40]

Yet, in spite of Jarrett's shoddy record as caretaker for the poor in his district and state, Obama never publicly criticized her either in his capacity as Illinois state senator or as U.S. senator. Perhaps he didn't feel free to criticize her. After all, his wife's job depended, in some measure, on Jarrett's favor, as did his own in the state senate. Or perhaps he made his own personal triangulation between ambition and idealism. One thing his decision to remain silent unquestionably reveals is that Obama is not the blind idealist his critics like to imagine; rather, he is perfectly capable of real-world calculation.

Nor was Jarrett's tenure as chairman of the Board of Trustees of the University of Chicago Medical Center an example of compassionate management. Working with Michelle Obama, who was hired as executive director of community outreach, Jarrett launched an initiative called the "South Side Health Collaborative."[41] This program "redirected" poor patients—those who were a profit drag on the medical center—to other hospitals and clinics. The program pushed hospital intake specialists to determine the personal finances of potential patients, after which they advised low-income patients to seek treatment elsewhere and then put them on a bus to that somewhere else.[42]

Critics call this "patient dumping." The practice had been outlawed by the Emergency Medical Labor and Treatment Act during the Reagan years.[43] Illegally dumping indigent patients on other hospitals or refusing transfers of poor patients from other hospitals can be profitable. For patients, the consequences can be death.

At the U.S. Department of Health and Human Services, the Office of Inspector General's fraud database contains this entry from May 8, 2006:

> The University of Chicago Hospitals (UCH), Illinois, agreed to pay $35,000 to resolve its liability for CMPs under the patient dumping statute. The OIG [Office of Inspector General] alleged that the hospital failed to accept an appropriate transfer of a sixty-one-year-old male who presented to another emergency de-

partment with a complaint of flank pain. UCH had specialized capabilities not available at the transferring hospital and allegedly refused to accept transfer after learning that the patient did not have insurance. UCH then later agreed to accept transfer of the patient only if he provided proof of funds in a bank account. The patient was transferred to [yet] another hospital where he died.[44]

In plain English, the hospital refused to take a patient unless he could prove that he had either the insurance or the cash to cover his likely hospital expenses. When he was turned away, he died.

Sadly, this was not an isolated, tragic case. As Chicago newspapers discovered, there were more like it. Many more indigent patients were forced to endure agonizing journeys to distant clinics and hospitals. Most of the victims were poor African Americans, who lived near the hospital that turned them away.

When the patient-dumping scandal erupted, Michelle Obama was executive director of community outreach at the hospital and Valerie Jarrett served on its board. While the two were not the sole decision makers involved, they played an essential part in what some euphemistically called a "management crisis."

That dozens of critically ill people were turned away in the patient-dumping scandal did not make the Obamas question Jarrett. There was no public comment from Barack Obama, and Michelle Obama continued to work with her friend and mentor. They were in it together and apparently adopted a "see no evil" faith in Jarrett.

Far from doubting her, the Obamas' predominant attitude toward Jarrett appears to be gratitude. They had much to be grateful for. Jarrett would find Michelle a series of jobs and help Barack rise from the University of Chicago Law School, where he was a part-time lecturer, to the Illinois State Senate, the U.S. Senate, and, ultimately, the White House.

She began by introducing Barack to powerful players in Chicago and encouraged him to earn some favors by registering black voters for Carol Moseley-Braun's Senate campaign in 1992.

From voter registration drives to Hyde Park social circles, she helped him win election to the Illinois State Senate in 1995. Jarrett arranged for Obama to announce his candidacy for the state senate at the same Hyde Park hotel where Chicago's first black mayor, Harold Washington, had announced his historic campaign.[45]

By 2000, Jarrett was indispensable to the Obamas. She tried to talk Barack out of running for a U.S. congressional seat. Her political advice was prescient. Bobby Rush, a Democrat with deep roots in the black and liberal communities, eventually won the seat. "I don't think either of them made major decisions without talking to her," Susan Sher said.[46]

When Obama first raised the idea of running for the U.S. Senate in 2004, Jarrett told him it was "a lousy idea."[47] Still he persisted and asked her to invite "friends" to her home to hear him out. Jarrett and Michelle had already talked and were determined to disabuse him of his reckless musings. Let him have his say and then we will have ours, Jarrett told Michelle Obama.

Barack Obama stood up to speak in Jarrett's living room, knowing the stakes. If he couldn't persuade Jarrett, his chances of raising money and winning endorsements would be slim. Equally important, Jarrett's enthusiasm would be needed to overcome Michelle's objections. His wife wanted him to forget electoral politics and hold a "normal" job that would allow him to spend more time at home.

He spoke calmly, slowly, and logically. He began with their shared ideals and principles, and then quickly pivoted to explain, in specific terms, why he could win the Democratic primary.

By the end, Jarrett was nodding. He had won her over. Michelle Obama changed her mind after talking to Jarrett in the kitchen.

Once again, Jarrett agreed to connect him with donors (one of whom was developer Tony Rezko, who was sentenced in November 2011 for extorting money from companies seeking help with state regulatory approvals).

At every turning point in Obama's career, Jarrett was there to introduce, to solve or resolve, to console or confirm. She was in the room when Obama decided to run for president. And she was there on a warm summer night in July 2007 when Obama was afraid he was losing to Hillary Clinton.

His campaign was floundering and seemed out of control. Three key players were gaming it out: Obama, Jarrett, and Pete Rouse, U.S. Senate Majority Leader Tom Daschle's former chief of staff, who had signed on to run Obama's senate office after Daschle lost his seat in a surprise upset. Rouse's role, still underappreciated by much of the media, was essential for transforming Obama from a freshman senator with no clout into a reasonable contender for the presidency in a few short years.

Obama looked to him for guidance. "Pete," he said, "what can I do that I'm not doing?"

"Barack," Rouse said firmly, "you need to take ownership of this campaign. You need to leave your comfort zone and directly manage your own campaign."[48]

Obama seemed unsure. He didn't like hands-on management. He preferred to set a strategic direction and have a chief of staff work with key personnel. Now he was hearing that he needed to personally take charge.

Eventually, he found a way to return to his aloof ways. Penny Pritzker, then Obama's finance chairman, gave him the out he was looking for: "You need another smart, capable, really close advisor involved who could play a bridging role."[49] She meant, of course, Jarrett.

He knew she was right; he couldn't manage alone. Obama began a nightly call with his senior staff and gave Jarrett a bigger role.

That role was essentially limitless, which soon caused trouble among the campaign staff. Barack Obama explained Jarrett's role in the 2008 presidential campaign and, indirectly, in his own life: "She participates in every conversation we have in the campaign. She is involved in broad strategic decisions about our message and how we approach the campaign, and she's involved in the details of managing the organization. She's really a great utility player."[50]

Jarrett soon became a source of friction and had frequent run-ins with campaign manager David Plouffe. Decisions made by the campaign staff would frequently be upended when Jarrett got involved. Still, Obama backed her without question. Rouse complained: "In the campaign, she was sort of outside and free-floating; it complicated things at times."[51] Classic Washington understatement.

Jarrett didn't have an official title on the campaign, yet seemed to insert

herself into every decision that interested her. This pattern would continue at the White House.

When Obama was elected president, campaign insiders angling for
an administration role encouraged the idea that Jarrett should take Obama's
soon-to-be-vacant Senate seat. It seemed an ideal solution. She would be
busy in the Senate and far from the White House. And she had the resources and Chicago connections to win and hold the seat.

Having heard enough stories from people who crossed swords with
Jarrett during the campaign, Emanuel, like other White House insiders,
tried to eliminate her as a potential rival by suggesting she take Obama's
vacated Senate seat.[52] Perhaps she would take the bait. His gambit failed.
Why be the most junior member of a hundred-person body when she
could have a large say in running the powerful executive branch?

Yet Michelle Obama insisted that Jarrett have a White House role.
During the presidential transition, Obama made his preference clear, telling Rahm Emanuel, whom he'd tapped to be his chief of staff, "I want her
inside the White House."[53]

When Emanuel showed up for a tour of the West Wing, he was annoyed to learn that Jarrett had gotten there first and had already put dibs
on the relatively large suite of offices, formerly occupied by Karl Rove,
George W. Bush's "architect."[54] Did she plan a Rove-like role for herself,
he wondered?

Pete Rouse suggested to Jarrett that she take on a specific and official
function to avoid becoming a disruptive and amorphous presence, as many
thought she had been during the campaign: "If you don't have line responsibility, you tend to wander, swim outside your own lane, and get into other
people's work and irritate people and complicate things."[55] It was good
advice.

But it was not advice she wanted to take. Still, Rouse's words proved
to be prescient.

Jarrett's White House role is unprecedented. She meets privately with
the president at least twice a day with no one else present. Her influence is
enormous and wide-ranging. She wields informal power, like a first lady;
scheduling power, like a chief of staff; and power over policy, like a special
envoy. She has the unusual freedom to put herself in any meeting she

chooses and to set the priorities as she sees fit. When *The New York Times*'s Robert Draper asked Obama if he "runs every decision past her," the president answered immediately: "Yep. Absolutely."[56]

Every decision?

Yes, Jarrett's scope is as unlimited as it sounds. She has "wide latitude over how she spends her day"[57] and that makes her "close to omniscient."[58]

Though the highly anticipated Jarrett-Emanuel feud never materialized, Emanuel, not known for reticence, has had little positive to say about her. In fact, he pointedly has said almost nothing at all about her.

While White House staffers may be displeased, it is a measure of Jarrett's influence that they dare not say so. A prominent Obama supporter and big-time donor told *The Washington Post,* on the condition of anonymity, of course: "I have always thought she was a liability. I've talked to people in the White House about it, and they have agreed with me, but they are scared to say anything."[59]

White House staffers were wise to fear her retribution. Jarrett has sometimes consciously misused her power, using her unique access to manipulate and unsettle other staffers, particularly those whom she and Michelle Obama mistrust.

Press Secretary Robert Gibbs was one of the people in her crosshairs. She repeatedly said that the president "needed a less abrasive press secretary."[60] While some of Jarrett's efforts to submarine Gibbs are well known, it is the postscript of one tale that reveals both her power and her mercurial streak.

Early on the morning of September 16, 2010, Robert Gibbs noticed the blinking red light on his BlackBerry. The news alert meant he was about to have a very tough day. Carla Bruni, the wife of French president Nicolas Sarkozy, had written a book that included some caustic remarks about first lady Michelle Obama. The English tabloids were having a field day. By 11 A.M. (EST), Gibbs had persuaded both the French and American governments to issue official denials—a real achievement given that he had to get the French government to contradict the wife of the French president. Gibbs thought it was a textbook case of responding inside the news cycle to stop a hurricane of a story before it landed on American shores. A victory, he thought.

The next day, Jarrett dropped in on Rahm Emanuel's 7:30 A.M. staff meeting. She hinted that the first lady was not happy.

In her book *The Obamas,* Jodi Kantor reports what happened next:

> All eyes turned to Gibbs. Emanuel grew alarmed at the expression on the press secretary's face and reached out to take him by the hand, "don't go there, Robert, don't do it," another aide later remembered him saying. Years of tension between Gibbs, Jarrett, and an absent Michelle Obama, exploded, the other aides watching in shock or staring down at the table.
>
> "Fuck this, that's not right, I've been killing myself on this, where's this coming from?" he shouted. Months of anxiety about Michelle Obama and resentment of Jarrett's curious role as senior adviser and First Friend came to a boil. "What is it she has concerns about? What did she say to you?"
>
> Jarrett answered vaguely.
>
> "What the fuck do you mean?" Gibbs said. "Did you ask her?"
>
> Jarrett said something about the denial not being fast enough.
>
> "Why is she talking to you about it? If she has a problem she should talk to me!"
>
> "You shouldn't talk that way," Jarrett said.
>
> It was Jarrett's tone, calm to the point of condescension, that finally undid Gibbs, others said later. He shook with rage, so frustrated one colleague thought he was going to cry. "You don't know what the fuck you're talking about," he hurled back.
>
> "The first lady would not believe you're speaking this way," Jarrett said, still composed.
>
> "Then fuck her, too!" He rose and stormed out. The rest of the group sat stunned.
>
> Emanuel grew very still for once. "Everyone knows Robert has done a really good job on this," he said.[61]

What makes this story so revealing is what happened next, the key bit that hasn't been so widely reported.

Gibbs quickly recovered himself and decided to mitigate the damage. He sent an e-mail to Michelle Obama's other longtime Chicago friend, Susan Sher. Gibbs asked Sher for specifics about the first lady's displeasure with his performance. Sher said that Michelle Obama had no complaint. Gibbs was dismayed. "Valerie made the story up. Valerie went into the meeting to convey what Michelle was angry about when they actually hadn't talked about it."[62]

Still, Gibbs's career at the White House was effectively over and staffers had new reasons to fear Jarrett.

That isn't the only example of Jarrett's misuse of her extraordinary access. Jarrett's control of the president's agenda has led to questionable use of his time at taxpayer expense. After weeks of saying he would not get involved, Obama finally yielded to Jarrett's pleas to fly to Copenhagen to personally pitch Chicago as host city for the 2016 Olympic games.[63] Critics complained that the president's agenda should have centered on the country's challenges: the then-9.8 percent unemployment rate, the raging health care reform debate, escalating wars in Afghanistan and Iraq, and Iran's successful test of a nuclear-capable mid-range missile.[64]

No matter. Lobbying for Chicago to be chosen as host city for the Olympics was a major focus for an administration filled with Chicagoans and it was a top priority for Jarrett, who was in charge of the Olympic initiative. Jarrett made sure that she kept the issue on the front burner with her daily meetings with the president, as she told *Bloomberg News:* "We talk about it every single morning together as we meet."[65]

For Chicago, which had never hosted the Olympics, winning the bid would be a coup. Jarrett was especially interested because many of the planned Olympic events and the Olympic "village," which would house the world's best athletes, would be located in the predominantly black South Side of Chicago.

Jarrett saw a big role for herself in the 2016 Olympics. She admitted to an Olympics movement newsletter, *Around the Rings,* that she would be personally involved in the Olympics, despite her commitments in the administration: "I will look forward to working with the Chicago 2016 team, and coordinating at the federal level."[66]

Jarrett was aboard Air Force One as it carried the president and a delegation of Olympic athletes, cabinet secretaries, Chicago luminaries, corporate leaders—and even Oprah Winfrey—to woo International Olympic Committee members.[67] Jarrett predicted victory, adding that when Michelle Obama finished her pitch, "there won't be a dry eye in the room."[68]

It didn't work. The city of Chicago came in dead last in the balloting and was eliminated in the first round, winning just eighteen of ninety-four votes.[69]

It was the first time an American president was directly and personally involved in an Olympic bid, and it illustrates Jarrett's unusual power with the Obamas.

More importantly, this humiliating snub illustrates the pitfalls of investing the prestige of the presidency in such high-risk ventures. Usually arms control summits and other international presidential trips are carefully negotiated before the president departs and a clear achievement is waiting in the wings for the president to trot on stage and trumpet. In this case, it was a jump ball. Jarrett put the president in a situation in which victory would look routine and defeat would be devastating.

Make no mistake: It was a defeat of Olympic proportions.

Yet, strangely, the Obamas and Jarrett remain as close as ever. She remains President Obama's most powerful advisor—the only administration official he talks to every day, usually alone. Jarrett also played a large and unreported role in the mission to kill Osama bin Laden, in the health care reform battle plan, and on virtually every major issue facing the Obama administration.

One West Wing staffer, with a sense of history, compares Jarrett to President Woodrow Wilson's wife, Edith. When he lapsed into an illness, she controlled access to the president and brought out messages from him. "People say that she pretty much ran the government for a year, while Valerie has been doing it for four."[70]

Michelle Obama

Sitting across from Valerie Jarrett at the wolf-themed Le Loup Café in 1991, and alongside her then-fiancé Barack Obama, Michelle Robinson had traveled further than either of them, if you measure in money, not miles. She had never lived outside the United States and indeed had lived precious few years outside of her native Chicago. But she had climbed from one of the poorest sections of Chicago's South Side to one of the richest sections, known as Hyde Park.

It was a very American story. The Robinsons lived in a small apartment, up a narrow staircase on the top floor of a two-family bungalow, near public housing projects and defunct plants. The nighttime sounds in the overwhelmingly black neighborhood alternated between crickets, cars, and police sirens. Michelle and her brother, Craig, shared a room, separated only by a sheet that hung across the middle.[71] Both of them eventually went to Princeton.

Her parents worked hard, in different ways, to prepare their children to live a better life than they had.

Her father, Fraser Robinson, worked at a city water treatment plant and was active in local Democratic Party politics. Nearly every night of Michelle's childhood, her father sat at the head of table as the family shared dinner together. He exuded a quiet strength that Michelle would later insist that her husband learn to embody.

Her mother, Marian, quit her job as a secretary at Spiegel's, a local chain store, to stay home with Michelle and Craig, and she urged them on academically. Money was tight, but the family managed. With workbooks and cassette tapes, she had both of her children reading by age four. The homework didn't stop when Michelle and Craig attended a nearby public school; the Robinson children earned higher marks than other students, who came from less demanding homes. As a result, both children were allowed to skip second grade.[72]

While Michelle worked hard in school, she never thought of her high-crime neighborhood as hazardous. "We knew the gang-bangers— my brother played basketball in the park. Home never feels dangerous."[73]

In 1981, she arrived at the Princeton campus and into another world: Gothic stone and grillwork, a march of tall trees, a dorm window overlooking a tranquil quadrangle. On a later visit, her father drove through the night to see his children. He was then in a wheelchair, which promptly sank into the gravel of the parking lot. He ground forward, uncomplaining. He was proud of her finding a place in that alien world.

She was one of ninety-four black students at Princeton, a world within a world. While she had worked very hard to make it to the Ivy League, she did not join any of its unique social institutions. Princeton is famous for its "eating clubs," private student-run associations that do not select on the basis of race, sex, or creed.

Curiously, Michelle instead immersed herself mainly in campus organizations that defined themselves on a purely racial basis, including the Organization of Black Unity and the Black Thoughts Table. She spent a lot of time at seminars at the African American Studies department, and much of her free time at the Third World Center.[74] While such self-segregation was typical of black students at elite schools in the 1980s, her pattern of scholarly and social activities suggests that she shared a feeling of isolation from students of other backgrounds at Princeton. Her thesis, written in her senior year, suggests that her sense of exclusion continued throughout her entire time in college. She wrote about the pain of being always a stranger in what she saw as a white world: "My experiences at Princeton have made me far more aware of my 'blackness' than ever before. I have found that at Princeton, no matter how liberal and open-minded some of my white professors and classmates try to be toward me, I sometimes feel like a visitor on campus; as if I really don't belong. Regardless of the circumstances under which I interact with whites at Princeton, it often seems as if, to them, I will always be black first and a student second."[75]

In her thesis, she was deeply skeptical of integration. "Many 'integrated Blacks' have lost touch with the Black culture in their attempts to become adjusted and comfortable in their new culture—the White culture. Some of these Blacks are no longer able to enjoy the qualities which make Black culture so unique or are unable to openly share their culture with other Blacks because they have become so far removed from these experiences and, in some instances, ashamed of them as a result of their integration."[76]

After interviewing dozens of black Princeton graduates, she was disappointed. "I hoped that these findings would help me conclude that despite the high degree of identification with Whites as a result of the educational and occupational path that Black Princeton alumni follow, the alumni would still maintain a certain level of identification with the Black community. However, these findings do not support this possibility."[77]

She concludes that integration may not be desirable for her: "further integration and/or assimilation into a White cultural and social structure that will only allow me to remain on the periphery of society; never becoming a full participant."[78]

While she may have sincerely felt the pain and alienation evident in her thesis, critics tend to miss the intellectual conformism it suggests. Quite simply, professors at elite liberal-arts universities were rewarding theses like hers with high marks in the 1980s. It was the kind of thing that they were looking for: skepticism about the benefits of integration, the loss of identity when joining the mainstream, and so on. She wrote her thesis less than a generation after landmark civil-rights legislation had transformed the country, and her instructors liked to point out that the transformation was still incomplete.

It is one of the oddities of American life that concerns about racism crested on liberal campuses almost two decades after the tide of intolerance began to ebb in society as a whole. In short, beyond Michelle's personal feelings of estrangement, it is risky to draw too many conclusions from a college thesis she wrote in 1985.

She was quickly admitted to Harvard Law School, where she played a significant role in black student groups.[79] Though she may not yet have been the bridge-builder that her future husband aimed to be, she graduated with honors.

Upon graduation, Michelle joined the mostly white Chicago law firm of Sidley Austin Brown & Wood. But she was not intimidated. Andrew Goldstein, a fellow associate at the firm, said, "You didn't want to underestimate her." In disagreements, he said, she didn't hesitate to "push back."[80]

Much of her pushing back was directed against her direct supervisor, Quincy White: "She wanted significant responsibility right away and was not afraid to object if she wasn't getting what she felt she deserved."[81] He recounted to a *Washington Post* reporter that Michelle was "perennially dissatisfied" and frustrated by the hard work and "tedium" that first- and second-year law associates faced.[82] He tried giving her "glamorous assignments" like working for the legendary promoter Don King, but it failed to satisfy her. Did she work so hard for so long to be a glorified clerk?

White said: "She at one point went over my head and complained that I wasn't giving her enough interesting stuff, and the [human resources] person came down to my office and said, 'Basically she's complaining that she's being treated like she's a second-year associate,' and we agreed that she was a second-year associate. I had eight or nine other associates, and I couldn't start treating one of them a lot better."[83]

Quincy White is now dead and cannot elaborate. And, of course, Michelle Robinson's feelings were not unique. Many people in the early parts of their legal careers find the work to be a dull chore.

In the end, White eventually gave up. "I couldn't give her something that would meet her sense of ambition to change the world."[84]

While Michelle worried and wondered about her future, her life began changing around her. Her father died in 1991. She remained exceptionally close to her mother—unusually so for an adult woman, one friend said—and took her father's death very hard. A cornerstone of her foundation had been removed and the whole idea of her mission in life began to shift. She began to look at familiar things in new ways as she reconsidered her life. "I looked out at my neighborhood and sort of had an epiphany that I had to bring my skills to bear in the place that made me. I wanted to have a career motivated by passion and not just money."[85]

She began to think seriously about leaving Sidley Austin and the for-profit world.

Yet the law firm proved to be a turning point in two important ways: It persuaded her to seek a career outside of law, and it introduced her to a summer associate whom she was asked to mentor, Barack Obama.

At first, she wasn't impressed. "I had dated a lot of brothers who had this kind of reputation coming in, so I figured he was one of these smooth brothers who could talk straight and impress people. So we had lunch, and he had this bad sport jacket and a cigarette dangling from his mouth, and I thought, 'Oh, here you go. Here's this good-looking, smooth-talking guy. I've been down this road before.'"[86]

Over time, he won her over with his community activism. It was the kind of thing she had been thinking about doing in her own neighborhood. During a February 2008 *CBS Evening News* segment, she talked about Obama arriving in her life just when she was weighing her options. "He took me to a training that he was doing. And there were mostly single parent mothers, mostly African Americans on the South Side." It was that experience that captivated her: "And I knew then, there's something different about this guy."

Michelle was inspired. Barack reminded her of her idealistic school days: "It was impressive. And his message was moving. I mean, it touched me."

Obama came into her life just as she was rethinking it. "It made me think differently about what am I doing with my life. And how am I adding to the notion of getting us to the world as it should be? Am I doing it in my law firm? You know? So he made me think in ways that I hadn't before."[87]

Eventually, she brought him home to meet her family. "He was very, very low-key," Craig said. The two played basketball together and her brother reported back that Barack wasn't a show-off. Craig said, "I was thinking: 'Nice guy. Too bad he won't last.'"

It did last, and within a year she was the one pushing for marriage. He resisted. He hated making a life-altering decision, any move that would foreclose options. Instead, he talked about the meaninglessness of marriage as an institution and that love is all that mattered. At that point, he wasn't sure about marriage: His mother had married and divorced twice.

In the end, Michelle's pressure worked. The story of his 1991 proposal offers insight into Obama's leadership style. Over dinner, he repeated his earlier speeches about marriage. She became frustrated; it was the same old story.

Then he produced the ring. She was completely surprised.

This suggests two things about Obama's leadership style: He can be doctrinaire, resisting logical next steps, preferring to stay in his comfort zone; and she (and a very few others) can sway him to change his mind.

They began to build a life together. Sometimes she would push him, sometimes he would tug her. But they were always a team, just like her parents were. It was exactly their shared, impatient ambition that led them to that 1991 dinner with Valerie Jarrett.

That year began Michelle's transformation. Her father died, she became engaged to Barack Obama, she left the law firm, and, with the help of Valerie Jarrett, she became assistant commissioner of planning and development for the city of Chicago. By the end of the year, she was Michelle Obama.

From then on, Jarrett played a major role in Michelle Obama's career in both government and the nonprofit sectors. From city hall, she became executive director of Public Allies, a liberal nonprofit, and then associate dean of student services at the University of Chicago. Later, until Obama was sworn in as president, she served as executive director for community affairs at the University of Chicago Medical Center.[88] She also sat on numerous boards, including the Board of Directors for TreeHouse Foods,[89] the Chicago Council on Global Affairs, and the University of Chicago Laboratory Schools.[90]

Thanks to Jarrett, Michelle Obama's public-spirited career also paid well. By 2006, the Obamas had a declared joint income of $991,296.[91] During every year of their marriage, Michelle earned more than Barack—until he was sworn in as president and she stopped working in Chicago.

The transition to first lady was difficult for her. Initially she didn't want to join her husband at the White House until June 2009, when her daughters had completed the school year in Chicago. There were other reasons: She had spent virtually all of her life in Chicago and didn't want to leave her mother and her friends. When Barack agreed to let her bring her mother to live with them at the White House, she still wasn't sure. For nearly a month after he won the 2008 election, she was still hinting to friends and government officials that she wanted to stay in Chicago. She had to be persuaded that the presidency wasn't a job like being a U.S. senator or state senator; she would actually hurt Barack politically if she didn't move into the White House with him on Inauguration Day.

Some of her Chicago friendships were falling apart: She was sensitive to any hint of exploitation, and certain old friends, she felt, had crossed the line, using her name to try to get jobs. Like her husband, her social circle shrank shortly after she moved into 1600 Pennsylvania Avenue.

Used to being an executive in her own right, she found the traditional role of first lady to be stuffy and limited. As one aide put it, "She was very frustrated that so much of the strategy was president-driven. There was no consideration of how she fit in the broader Obama narrative."[92]

Hillary Clinton also found the role difficult, but it doesn't appear the two ever discussed the tribulations of being first lady. This is surprising, given that Hillary Clinton is often in the White House as secretary of state and one of only two living former first ladies from the Democratic Party. (Rosalynn Carter is the other.) Nor did Michelle Obama ever reach out to Laura Bush, who was friendly and gave her an extensive tour of the residence in January 2009, a few weeks before Inauguration Day. Instead, she decided to figure the job out on her own.

That isn't easy to do. The first lady may be the last of the eighteenth-century ceremonial posts remaining in American life. The transition for any modern woman can be surprisingly difficult. The closest equivalent may be found in British culture: Becoming first lady is like becoming Princess of Wales. Diana Spencer, a modern woman, famously found the transition difficult—as did those around her.

To compound matters, the role seems alien to a woman used to being an executive. A first lady's job description is actually a series of ancient and courteous virtues: modest, attractive, enterprising, charitable, and, above all, apolitical. A first lady can skirt the corners of politics by charming an ambassador's or a senator's wife, or by taking up a high-minded cause (promoting literacy as Mrs. Bush did, fighting drug dependency as Mrs. Reagan did, combating litter and billboards as Mrs. Johnson did). But for wives who played active roles in their husbands' political campaigns, as Mrs. Clinton and Mrs. Obama did, the transition to political Siberia can leave them cold. When they use their political experience to make political decisions, however, the public tends to react negatively—as Hillary Clinton learned when she worked on what critics derided as "HillaryCare," the Clinton administration's attempt to establish a national health care system.

Michelle Obama grew increasingly frustrated with her role's limitations. When touring a public school, a little girl told her that she wanted to be first lady one day. Her response, in earshot of the press, was caustic: "Doesn't pay much."[93]

Soon she became a political target for her costly clothes and trips. This, too, tells us something about President Obama's leadership style: He appears either unable to anticipate the predictable reaction of the press or unable to rein in the first lady.

During a 2009 visit to France, the U.S. Embassy was asked to arrange a shopping outing for Michelle and her daughters on a Sunday, a day when French law requires stores to remain closed. The press was quick to notice that she chose to shop at expensive stores. One store she visited was Bon-point, which sells clothes for children, where a small girl's sundress goes for more than $250.[94] With U.S. unemployment then approaching 10 percent, the move seemed tone-deaf.

Michelle Obama's use of designer clothes for magazine shoots also drew fire, as did her wardrobe for her Hawaii vacation during the 2011 Christmas holiday, which garnered nearly as much media coverage as America's sputtering economy and the withdrawal of troops from Iraq. Whatever the merits of these stories, expecting the press not to cover them is unrealistic in any president.

Her trips also sparked controversy. To keep a promise to the first lady, the president took her to New York for dinner and a Broadway show. The famous "date night" in New York drew fawning coverage at first. "Even cooler-than-thou New York allowed itself a bit of excitement over their arrival," *The New York Times* wrote.[95]

The backlash came quickly. Tallying the cost for crew and fuel for three airplanes, secret service, police overtime, street closures, and other expenses, the total was estimated to range as high as $250,000.[96] Again, the president seemed unable to say no to his wife or to develop a strategy for a predictable press response: "The notion that I just couldn't take my wife out on a date without it being a political issue was not something I was happy with."[97]

The controversial trips continued. During their first summer vacation in 2009 on Martha's Vineyard, the Obamas stayed at the Blue Heron Farm, which rents for upward of $50,000 per week.[98] That Michelle and her daughters flew up separately added to the cost for taxpayers—a detail that cable-news outlets soon focused on.

Then there was Michelle's multimillion-dollar trip to Spain with her daughters and girlfriends, which reignited media fascination with her clothes and travel budgets. When she stepped out of her $2,500-a-day hotel room in the Ritz-Carlton's Hotel Villa Padierna, female reporters noted that she was wearing a top by Jean Paul Gaultier. Though the White House was at pains to explain the trip was private and that Michelle was covering her own expenses, the security expenses—costing far in excess of her personal travel expenses—were covered with taxpayer money.[99]

And, in June 2011, Michelle took family and friends on a "goodwill mission" to South Africa, which was counterproductive diplomatically since the South African president refused to meet the first lady. The cost of the air travel alone was more than $400,000.[100]

Suddenly Michelle Obama was becoming a political liability.

In stepped Valerie Jarrett with a makeover campaign. Jarrett's approach was simple and somewhat effective: a montage of typical, family-friendly first lady activities. Jarrett made arrangements for Michelle Obama to co-host *The View* in the hope of winning over women. Then came a cuddling Michelle and Barack on the cover of *Us Weekly* and a friendly profile in *The New York Times*.

Next, Jarrett urged her to take on a cause. Together they selected supporting military families, with Michelle Obama making appearances and speeches on their behalf.[101]

Meanwhile, President Obama stayed in the background, neither defending his wife in public nor urging her to change in private. As his wife was maligned, he remained aloof.

Hillary Clinton

Hillary Clinton struggled with her role from her early years. In a series of letters she wrote to high school friend John Peavoy, while he was at Princeton and she was at Wellesley, she writes about trying on different identities, like hats or hairstyles. "Since Xmas vacation, I've gone through three-and-a-half metamorphoses and am beginning to feel as though there is a smorgasbord of personalities spread before me. So far, I've used alienated academic, involved pseudohippie, educational and social reformer, and one half of withdrawn simplicity." This is Hillary Clinton, as we now know her: keenly observant, self-analytical, changing as circumstances require. Even in her student days in the 1960s, she had a sense of her destiny, and would say with a sigh that she had "not yet reconciled [herself] to the fate of not being the star."[102]

In her career with Bill Clinton, and later with Barack Obama, she would have to grapple with this reality.

Hillary arrived at Wellesley a "Goldwater Girl," having campaigned for the archconservative Barry Goldwater in 1964. But the Vietnam War, the assassination of Martin Luther King Jr., and the feminist movement had a profound effect on her. By her senior year, she was campaigning for Eugene McCarthy and writing her senior thesis on radical organizer Saul Alinsky. She interviewed him for her thesis and he was impressed enough to offer her a job.[103]

Hillary was tempted, but, as she later explained, "we had a fundamental disagreement. He believed you could change the system only from the outside. I didn't."[104]

Hillary was all for fighting the revolution, but she wanted to use the power of government, not replace it. She also noted the contradiction in Alinsky "living a comfortable, expenses-paid life," while "he considers himself a revolutionary."[105]

Still, she learned the power and pull of a star by dwelling on Alinsky's ability to connect with people. Barbara Olson, in her analysis of Hillary's college thesis, wrote, "Hillary had come to recognize the potential power of a man of exceptional charm."[106]

That charm was something Hillary initially lacked. In *Hillary's Turn*, Michael Tomasky described her as being the kind of Midwesterner "who men tend to regard as unapproachable and a little scary."[107] Bill Clinton's outsize personality could open doors and win over people. But he couldn't help but hog the spotlight.

No matter what Hillary's achievements are, she has had to deal with the aerodynamic drag of the men around her. Her younger brothers Hugh (often called Hughie) and Tony were a constant presence. She even took them with her on her honeymoon with Bill Clinton.[108] "You are not doing enough for your brothers," Hillary's mother told her shortly after Bill Clinton won the presidency.[109] Former Clinton staffers said that you never wanted to hear their names unless it had something to do with golf.[110] Otherwise, it was trouble.

One time Hugh got into a screaming match with Hillary on Air Force One. He had wanted her to give one of his clients a ride on the president's plane and she had said no. He slammed doors, was rude to staff, and yelled at Hillary. When he stopped, it was Hillary who apologized to the room. "I'm sorry. My family can be very demanding," she said.[111]

When Hillary married Bill Clinton and moved to Arkansas in 1975, she went by "Hillary Rodham" in a show of feminist independence. That gesture didn't change the fact that she owed her clout to her husband being the Arkansas attorney general and later governor.[112] She joined the Rose Law Firm in 1977 and almost immediately made partner, despite billing relatively few hours.[113] The firm was an ideal perch for the governor's wife, as the government of Arkansas was the law firm's largest client.[114]

When Bill lost his reelection bid for governor in 1980, Hillary assumed a new identity. Gone were the dowdy dresses, mousy hair, and thick glasses of Hillary Rodham. Instead, voters met "Hillary Clinton," blonde, sleek, and wearing contact lenses.[115]

When her husband ran for president, she was again eager to show she was a liberated woman with her own achievements.

During the 1992 presidential campaign, she told *60 Minutes,* "If you elect Bill, you get me."[116] Bill Clinton dutifully echoed those sentiments with his constant refrain of "Buy one, get one free."[117] She explained that she looked down on the traditional role of supportive wife: "I suppose I could have stayed home and baked cookies and had teas, but what I decided to do was to fulfill my profession which I entered before my husband was in public life."[118] It didn't play well with the public.

Shortly after these campaign gaffes, a reporter asked Hillary to respond to the people who thought she was "the overbearing yuppie wife from hell." *The New York Times* noted that "a look of annoyance glittered through Mrs. Clinton's blue eyes, but she was on a mission to soften her image."[119] Hillary showed admirable discipline through the end of the campaign. Indeed, going to teas and baking cookies is exactly what she did. She addressed a tea given in honor of congressional wives and announced she had entered a recipe in *Family Circle*'s candidates' wives' cookie competition. She asked the tea-sipping ladies to get behind her recipe: "Try my cookies. I hope you like them, but like good Democrats, vote for them anyway."[120]

Stymied in her desire for a cabinet position of her own by the so-called "Bobby Kennedy law" that barred the appointment of family members to jobs in the executive branch, Hillary's informal influence was felt throughout the White House.[121] She took an office in the West Wing, near the president's senior advisors.[122] And she was instrumental in choosing some of those advisors.[123]

She was soon put in charge of the President's Task Force on National Health Care Reform.[124] After some eighteen months of political combat, Congress refused to even vote on her proposal. Instead, it was quietly shelved. Still, her plan to create a government health care monopoly was so unpopular that it handed the Republicans control of both houses of Congress in the 1994 elections. It was the first time in forty years that the GOP had run the entire legislative branch.

Hillary spent much of the next six years either campaigning for her husband or defending him in the press. At the end of the Clinton administration, she decided to seek public office in her own right. She soon announced she was running for the U.S. Senate from New York.[125] Harold Ickes told Hillary biographer Gail Sheehy that for Hillary, "This is a race for redemption. It's really that simple."[126]

She won easily.

Once in the Senate, Hillary's legislative achievements were virtually nonexistent. In the eight years she served, she introduced only twenty bills that became law. These laws were slight: the creation of the Kate Mullany National Historic Site; lauding the goals and ideals of Better Hearing and Speech Month; creating the Ellis Island Medal of Honor; naming one courthouse after Thurgood Marshall and another after James L. Watson; naming a post office after John A. O'Shea and another for Sergeant Riayan A. Tejeda, creating a National Purple Heart Recognition Day; a measure honoring Alexander Hamilton on the bicentennial of his death; one congratulating the Syracuse University Orange Men's Lacrosse Team on winning a championship and another for the Le Moyne College Dolphins Men's Lacrosse Team on winning theirs; launching the 225th anniversary of the American Revolution Commemorative Program; honoring Shirley Chisholm and firefighters John J. Downing, Brian Fahey, and Harry Ford for their service to the nation.

The liberal *Huffington Post* concluded, "It's a track record of legislative failure and futility."[127]

The only real mark she made on the U.S. Senate is telling. Early in her tenure there, she went to see Majority Leader Tom Daschle. She suggested creating a "war room" in the Senate, similar to the rapid response communication center at the Clinton White House. She wanted to "pound the Republican attack machine."[128] Daschle declined. But after the loss of four Senate seats in 2004—including Daschle's own—Hillary's war room became a reality. *The Hill* reported that Hillary's legacy made the Senate far more partisan, creating "a permanent campaign atmosphere in a chamber that has long prided itself on collegiality and across-the-aisle relationships."[129]

After winning a second Senate term, she launched an epic battle for president. The campaign for the 2008 Democratic nomination was long and bitter. Virtually all of the memorable attacks against Barack Obama began with the Hillary Clinton campaign, including questions about his birth certificate.

She had anticipated an early victory. Before the Iowa caucuses, she told ABC's George Stephanopolous, "I'm in it for the long run. It's not a very long run. It'll be over by February fifth."[130]

As polls began showing Barack Obama was gaining strength, though, she went into fight mode. She said, "Well, now the fun part starts."[131]

Hillary fought it with her signature style. She adopted macho bravado, claiming to be "the only candidate with the testicular fortitude to be president."[132]

Before the voting in the Iowa caucuses, her campaign produced a copy of Obama's second-grade essay about wanting to be president. She questioned Obama's motivation. "You gotta ask yourself, 'Who's really committed here [and] who's doing it just for political reasons?'" Answering a question about Obama having a character problem when he said he had only recently thought about being president, she said, "It's beginning to look a lot like that. You know, it really is."[133]

She lost in Iowa.

When asked about the difficulty of campaigning in a Portsmouth, New Hampshire, coffee shop, she choked up when she said, "It's not easy, it's not easy . . . This is very personal for me." Reporters, as cruel as second-graders, were snickering among themselves that she was "feeling her own pain."[134]

Still, she won the New Hampshire primary.

Hillary continued on offense, not quite realizing she could come off as offensive. In a January 22 debate, drawing a chorus of boos, she said, "You know, Senator Obama, it is very difficult having a straight-up debate with you, because you never take responsibility for any vote, and that has been a pattern."[135]

Hillary's problems quickly mounted. She was supposed to be the star, but her husband was a liability. One fund-raiser said, "Bill Clinton was out of control . . . even the night she won in New Hampshire. Even Hillary couldn't control him."[136]

Then the former president made a series of racially charged remarks in South Carolina. Just before the January 26 primary there, he said that black support for Obama "is understandable, because people are proud when someone who they identify with emerges for the first time."[137] It came off as patronizing.

Behind the scenes, Bill Clinton kept making gaffes. When trying to talk Senator Ted Kennedy out of endorsing Obama, he said, "a few years ago, this guy would have been getting us coffee."[138] Kennedy endorsed Obama.[139]

By the March 4 primary in Texas, Hillary had already lost Super Tuesday and was on the wrong side of the delegate count. Yet she soldiered on, hoping to be "another comeback kid."[140]

Five days before that primary, she went on the air with a direct attack on Obama's fitness and readiness to be president. It began with an ominous voice-over: "Inevitably, another national security crisis will occur. And when it does, voters shouldn't have to wonder whether their president will be ready. As president, Hillary will be ready to act swiftly and decisively."[141]

By April 2008, Hillary's supporters launched the Obama birth-certificate issue. Desperate to carry Pennsylvania, the campaign sent out an anonymous e-mail: "Barack Obama's mother was living in Kenya with his Arab-African father late in her pregnancy. She was not allowed to travel by plane then, so Barack Obama was born there and his mother then took him to Hawaii to register his birth."[142] The tactic didn't help much: Clinton won the primary by a small margin and split the delegates.[143]

By June 3, when the final state had voted in the Democratic primaries, Hillary had lost. She didn't suspend her campaign until June 7, after making frantic efforts to get unelected "super delegates"—roughly one thousand party and union officials—to back her. Party leaders repeatedly told her to concede defeat. Even then, she was forty-five minutes late to her own press conference at the National Building Museum, prompting rumors of second thoughts.[144]

She only appeared to quit. Almost immediately after the primaries ended, Hillary began campaigning for the vice presidential spot through intermediaries.

The Obama campaign never seriously considered her for the vice presidency. The wounds were too fresh. In a bid for party unity and to keep Hillary Clinton from attacking him from the outside, Obama eventually offered her the role of secretary of state.[145]

In November 2011, the presidential speculation and arguments resurfaced. Hillary supporters Pat Caddell and Douglas Schoen published a plea in *The Wall Street Journal* called "The Hillary Moment." In it, they said Obama "should step aside for the one candidate who would become, by acclamation, the nominee of the Democratic Party: Secretary of State Hillary Clinton."[146]

Nevertheless, Clinton forged a constructive role inside the Obama administration. Indeed, she would play a defining role in Obama's finest foreign-policy victories: from killing bin Laden and ousting Libyan leader Muammar Qaddafi to staving off the world financial crisis and maintaining key alliances that were under threat. But she often achieved these historic goals by battling Valerie Jarrett, Michelle Obama, and sometimes the president himself.

Meanwhile, the president has sat at the center of a triumvirate of powerful women: Jarrett, Clinton, and Michelle Obama. They were educated, experienced, and decidedly liberal—as were most of the powerful men in the Obama administration. But each of the women brought two qualities that the men largely did not bring: an ability to read Obama's subtle and complex moods as well as a willingness to work with often ambiguous guidance from him.

Obama did not usually think in sharp edges or bright lines. He simply wasn't that kind of leader.

But he was about to tangle with a woman who did, a leader who imposed her vision on the world with clarity and boldness. The contrast was going to be difficult for him. It would challenge his ability to lead.

CHAPTER 2

HEALTH CARE, BY HOOK OR CROOK

We will go through the gate. If the gate is closed, we will go over the fence. If the fence is too high, we will pole-vault in. If that doesn't work, we will parachute in.

—House Speaker Nancy Pelosi, talking about health care reform[1]

President Obama's greatest and most controversial achievement wasn't his idea, at least, at first. And, in the earliest days of the Obama administration, his chief of staff and his senior officials did everything they could to stop it, shift it, or sideline it.

It was really the work of a different relentless and ruthless leader with a vision—Nancy Pelosi.

Meanwhile, in the beginning, the president looked on efforts to revolutionize health care in America with a kind of detachment. He didn't order his inner circle to back the reform plans. He took a wait-and-see approach, as congressional leaders shaped the historic legislation.

Critics soon called it "ObamaCare," just as an earlier generation of critics had derided President Clinton's proposed health care reforms as "HillaryCare." Yet in the spring of 2009, it hardly seemed destined to be Obama's signature issue, despite the name that critics had appended to it.

The president had not campaigned on transforming health care financing and delivery in the United States (although reform promises were made in both the Democratic Party platform, as they had been for decades, and in Obama campaign documents). He didn't have a particular sense of ownership on the issue. He had not advocated legislative change in the health care sector either as a U.S. senator or as an Illinois lawmaker.

On Election Day 2008, few Americans would have thought that re-engineering health care's one-seventh of the U.S. economy would soon be the president's highest priority. Fewer still would have wagered that comprehensive health care reform would be the president's signature domestic accomplishment.

And, apparently, neither did the president himself. He barely touched on the subject in his Inaugural Address or during his early presidential press conferences.

Certainly, President Obama supported the goal of universal health care for all Americans, free at point of service (though paid for by a mix of insurance and taxpayer contributions), just as all progressives and liberals did. Nor was his staff united in support of health care reform. "In the first two years of the administration," a former senior Obama White House official told progressive journalist David Corn, "there was a split between those who believed in fighting for things even if you know you're going to lose and those who said, get the best thing possible passed. As for the president, he really is a stone-cold progressive. But he believes you have to get stuff done."[2]

But was it something that he could get done? Obama's chief of staff, Rahm Emanuel, and other senior domestic policy officials who had served in the Clinton White House weren't so sure. They had seen this movie before and knew that it ended in tears.

Other advisors, who had not served in the Clinton White House, were more hopeful. They saw large Democratic Party majorities in both houses of Congress, a supportive media, and a demoralized opposition party—the perfect alignment of stars that may not come again in their lifetimes.

The president, at first, could not decide between these warring factions. He saw both sides and saw strong arguments for each position.

Why were the White House and the Congress fighting about revolutionizing health care at all?

After all, unemployment was starting its long upward march, housing prices were sinking, mortgage defaults were rising, and everywhere the specter of economic despair haunted ordinary Americans. Health care did not even make the top-ten list of public concerns in any major poll conducted in the spring of 2009.

Yet, the issue was already devouring thousands of man-hours, measured in meetings and memos, in the White House and Congress.

To understand why the war over health care policy broke out in the first few months of the Obama administration, it helps to understand the history of the progressive movement in American politics and the weak grasp many Democrats believed they had over a growing number of independent voters.

Universal health care had been a top priority of America's progressive movement and its labor unions since the late nineteenth century. Progressive Republican Teddy Roosevelt repeatedly called for universal health insurance. Franklin Delano Roosevelt also supported universal coverage, though he excluded it from Social Security legislation lest it doom his landmark retirement insurance plan. Then, the American Medical Association was adamant in its opposition. (When the association later backed health care reform in the Obama years, it cost the organization more than 5 percent of its members, who resigned in protest.) Universal health insurance had been an official part of the National Democratic Party agenda since Harry Truman called for a national health care program in a special address to Congress on November 19, 1945.[3]

But no president had been able to pass it. Truman couldn't even get a vote on his health care plan in both houses of Congress. Lyndon Baines Johnson, whose "Great Society" program ushered in more progressive programs than any other administration since FDR, was only able to enact federal health programs for the poor (Medicaid) and the aged (Medicare). A broader bill providing coverage for the whole population would have to wait—until President Bill Clinton. Starting in January 1993, the Clinton administration tried for almost two years to get Congress to adopt government-funded universal health insurance coverage. *Newsweek's* Eleanor Clift compared it to being lashed to the bow of a ship, heading for the rocks.

After more than eighteen months of public debate and media criticism, President Clinton had to fight to even get a vote on the measure. The Democratic-led Congress reluctantly brought it to the floor in August 1994 (by which time it provided less than universal coverage), where it was promptly voted down.[4] As usual, the bill floundered over the questions of who would pay for it and how much it would actually cost. Medicare, created in 1965, had cost many times more than was projected and is now one of the federal government's most costly entitlements. "HillaryCare" would have cost far more.

If Obama could succeed where Truman, Johnson, Clinton, and both Roosevelts failed, some officials contended he would have an historic legacy. He would accomplish a goal that the progressives had dreamed of, debated for, and demanded for more than a century. He would be the greatest progressive in American history. He would forever be the one who got it done.

Another powerful factor was the future of the Democratic Party, America's oldest political party. Certainly, many believed that increasing entitlements—especially providing free health care to the millions of uninsured—would make for a better, fairer society. But the assumption also reigned that expanding entitlements would increase the ranks of reliable voters for the Democratic Party.

This view had emerged from the nation's labor unions. In the late nineteenth century, unions provided unemployment, life, and health insurance. The migration by which union benefits became government programs began with unemployment insurance—once seen as one of major reasons to join a union in the first place. As the expense of these unemployment programs became too heavy to be borne by union dues, union leaders succeeded in persuading state governments to take up the burden. Eventually, however, even states with their immense taxing power could not bear the costs, so the federal government was entreated to pick up part of the tab.

Old-age insurance made a similar migration, ultimately becoming what we know as Social Security, in both its retirement and disability programs. In both cases, unemployment insurance and Social Security brought in grateful voters for a generation or more. The Democrats were able to run Congress, with only a few brief interruptions, from 1932 to 1994—largely due to popular entitlement programs.

Health care stubbornly failed to make the usual, expected migration from private to public burden. Some states, including Tennessee, Oregon, and Massachusetts, had adopted universal health care plans but had to either scale them back or raise taxes to cover the ever-growing tab. And, so far, the federal government had failed to put the weight on its own massive shoulders.

If the Congress could adopt universal health care, the theory went, a new generation of grateful voters would give the Democrats another long reign in running Congress and perhaps the White House. Of course, this is precisely what the Republicans feared.

Hence their implacable opposition. Many had begun their careers in the political minority and endured decades of powerlessness in Congress. They had personal aversion to returning to that loathsome Siberia.

Among Democratic Party skeptics, there was also a sense of history and party politics. History showed that attempts to reform health care at the federal level consistently lost and that voters tended to punish parties that pushed health care reform. In 1994, the Republicans won control of the House of Representatives for the first time in fifty years, largely due to the Clinton administration's failed plans to reform health care. Changing health care at the national level was a dangerous "fool's errand," in the words of one participant. Yet for most, the errand was a long-awaited rendezvous with destiny.

So in the spring of 2009, progressive history and party politics fed views on both sides of the health care war in the Obama White House.

Then the president chose sides, making "ObamaCare" his own. Its journey into law is a window into Obama's abilities as a leader and manager.

The story behind Barack Obama's most historic and consequential legislative victory is one of backroom deals, last-minute threats, desperate bargaining, secret White House meetings, shadowy interest group trades, and a complex but daring set of stunning legislative moves. In the popular press President Obama is lionized as a dogged marathon runner, relentlessly going the distance to pass national health care reform. Behind the scenes, it was a far different picture.

The dogged marathoner who risked political fortunes, and paid a steep political price for universal health insurance coverage, was actually House Speaker Nancy Pelosi.

Far from feeling empowered by the president's support, Pelosi had to overcome his constant interference, which repeatedly brought health care reform to the brink of destruction.

Near the end, Pelosi was on the verge of saving it through an unusual legislative move to pass exactly, word-for-word, the measure that had already passed the Senate through a simple majority vote—followed by a package of "fixes" to be voted on separately—when Obama summoned her to the White House.

The president was furious. He opposed this legislative move—the one that would ultimately lead to historic passage of health care reform.

Obama, far from being a leader, dithered, delayed, and distanced himself from deals that might have enabled passage of health care reform much sooner. There were many moments in which he chose the policy ideal over the politically doable—and nearly torpedoed the entire effort. At other times, he raged at Pelosi uncontrollably, and yet when his presence was vitally needed, he refused to meet with congressional Democratic leaders.

Meanwhile, White House chief of staff Rahm Emanuel and the White House staff charged with working with Congress, along with Health and Human Services secretary Kathleen Sebelius, simply ignored the president and made their own covert deals and private plans. Sometimes they acted as if they had the complete backing of the president when, in fact, he had no clear idea what policy they were pursuing; other times they secretly pledged fealty to the House Speaker, pleading with her to stay the course irrespective of the president's views, telling her, "I am on your side."

During the fifteen-month fight over health care reform, more factions and plans developed inside the Obama administration than in the two houses of Congress. Self-described "realists" wanted a scaled-down plan that would be acceptable to the health care industry (which they knew had halted HillaryCare years earlier), while the "idealists" sought to bring into being the very legislation Democrats had dreamed of for more than a century: government-funded health care, free of charge to all Americans at point of service.

As the months tolled on, feuding inside the Obama administration became savagely sharp-edged. The realists pointed out that it wasn't 1945 anymore. Americans had observed more than fifty years of nationalized health care programs in Canada, in Britain, and elsewhere in Europe, and had heard the horror stories: Denied treatments. Long waiting lists. Crowded waiting rooms. Outdated equipment. Poorly paid doctors.

The only reason Canada's health system worked, critics said, was because Canadians had universal access to American health care—by driving across the border. Trying to pass a program modeled on designs from 1940s Europe, they said, would not fly in Congress or with the public. (The opposition of the courts on constitutional grounds was even considered, at the time.) Instead, the realists said, we need to do something "scaled down and sensible"—an incremental improvement.

When the idealists said Obama wasn't elected to make small changes when large reforms were needed, the realists responded that if the increment in an "incremental change" is big enough, it can be packaged and branded as "revolutionary."

The idealists believed that the realists had been captured by insurance companies, pharmaceutical giants (whom they dubbed "big Pharma"), greedy doctors, and other defenders of the medical status quo. The idealists simply couldn't understand how anyone could oppose health care that was free at point of service. They saw health care as a basic human right, akin to equal opportunity in housing or employment. It had been the No. 1 public policy goal for all of their political lives and they simply couldn't imagine that anyone, especially in the Obama White House or the Democratic precincts of Congress, would want to throw away a once-in-a-lifetime chance to pass what eventually became known as "The Patient Protection and Affordable Care Act." Since they believed the realists had no moral basis for disagreement, arguments about cost or complexity seemed more like pointless hostility than real concerns that needed addressing in order to refine reform and make it acceptable to a majority in Congress.

The line between realists and idealists was somewhat fluid. On particular points, some idealists might shift toward the realist position in order to pick up congressional supporters, while some realists would at times balk at proposed concessions on grounds that it took the legislation too far from the ideal. The realists were not simply hard-bitten cynics, eager to do a deal at any cost, and the idealists were not merely starry-eyed utopians. Instead, they were policy professionals and political veterans who, depending on their perspective, put their emphasis either on simply passing a bill or on achieving landmark legislation embodying a long-held liberal dream.

Despite this fluidity, the head of the realist school was generally Rahm Emanuel; Pelosi headed the idealist camp. Obama floated between the two.

Over and above their differing blends of pragmatism and principles, Emanuel and Pelosi distrusted and disliked—even despised—one another.

Their rivalry began within weeks of Obama's historic election. In a makeshift transition office near the White House, Pelosi sat down to meet with Emanuel.[5] It was not a social call.

They already had a lot of history together, not all of it positive.

That history began when Pelosi tapped Emanuel, then an Illinois congressman who had proven adept at raising money for his colleagues, to head the Democratic Congressional Campaign Committee in 2005. Emanuel had done an incredible job raising a then-record amount of money for Democrats and leading them out of the political wilderness by helping his party recapture the House majority. After twelve years in the minority, victory was sweet.

Prior to the defeat prompted by opposition to HillaryCare in 1994, the Democrats had held the majority for half a century.

But Rahm's techniques and tactics rankled Pelosi and some other older members of Congress. He could be brash and bullying, supremely self-confident, and overwhelmingly determined to get his way. He seemed to speak in an overcaffeinated bark of four-letter words and political jargon. He would sometimes hang up during long phone calls without saying good-bye, leaving people talking to dial tones. He would order around even experienced candidates, insisting he knew best. To his critics, he cared only about results, not relationships. To his allies, he was a can-do guy who delivered incredible results and shrugged off complaints with bromides like "nice guys finish last." And, his friends and colleagues would say, he was extremely loyal.

Emanuel delivered the majority in 2006 that allowed Pelosi to become the first woman Speaker of the U.S. House of Representatives in American history. Yet she didn't exactly go out of her way to reward him. When Emanuel said he was considering running for Majority Whip, the No. 3 post in the Democratic Caucus, she didn't back him. Instead, she supported Rep. Jim Clyburn, an African American from a safe seat in South Carolina, who had done little to elect Democrats in swing states. Pelosi probably feared angering the Congressional Black Caucus, but friends say Emanuel saw it as a stab in the back for a loyal lieutenant.

Clyburn easily won his election as Majority Whip. Emanuel never forgave her.

As an opening gambit in that 2008 meeting in the transition offices, Emanuel offered Pelosi some advice on her upcoming campaign for speaker. Pelosi was in no mood for small talk or olive branches. "It's an internal House Democratic Caucus matter," she said firmly, "and we'll handle it."[6]

She was there to deliver a message. She had long demanded that Senate Majority Leader Harry Reid alert her to communications with any members of her caucus. Emanuel probably already knew that, but he could see where she was going. She wasted no time in getting there. She would not tolerate any attempts to go around her by allowing the White House to work with "moderate New Democrats or conservative Blue Dogs."[7] She wanted to know about *any* contact between anyone at the White House and any Democrat in the House of Representatives. Period.

She called her communication doctrine "no surprises," but it amounted to "no triangulation."[8] No Clinton-style "third way" strategies that went around the liberal leadership of the House.

Pelosi had seen how President Clinton had used moderate Democratic lawmakers to pass legislation that she did not favor, and she wasn't going to let another Democratic president use that technique on her. More importantly, she wasn't going to tolerate any interference with her ability to run the House of Representatives as she saw fit. She was a strong leader and knew how to defend her turf.

Rahm wasn't happy. Pelosi was tough to deal with even before the inevitable crises came. He coolly said he would pass on her request to the appropriate White House staff.

To underscore her hardline position, Pelosi allowed her aides to leak the story of her meeting with Emanuel to *Politico,* a newspaper that covers Capitol Hill. The headline said it all: "Pelosi Lays Down the Law with Rahm." This warning was directed not only at Emanuel, but at every Democrat in Congress that he might try to phone or meet.

Even if Emanuel and Pelosi had had a better relationship, the political architecture of their new roles would have put them at odds. One top Democrat who knows them both told *Politico,* "Look, they have different goals now. Her job is to protect her members; his job is to protect Obama. Those can't always be the same thing. I think they will do what they can to work together, but these are two strong-willed people who are used to getting their way. There's bound to be some areas of disagreement."[9]

In fact, as one person who has known both Pelosi and Emanuel for years said, Pelosi wanted to be in charge. One of the reasons she backed Obama over Hillary Clinton was because she thought Obama was more pliable.

The House legislative session of 2009–2010 would be Pelosi's first test of her abilities to steer the president; she wasn't going to let Obama's chief of staff get in her way.

Pelosi wasn't afraid to take on Obama. During a private meeting in January 2009, Obama mentioned that he had campaigned on reducing the special requests for spending known in Washington as "earmarks." He wanted her support for a poll-tested and popular measure to ban them.

To almost any other politician, the logic of Obama's suggestion would seem obvious and compelling. An earmark ban was popular and harmless.

Still Pelosi quickly dismissed any idea about eliminating or even limiting earmarks. Those special spending orders were a valuable tool for rewarding loyal members and punishing others.

They were part of her power. Firmly, she said no.

Obama was actually right about the political appeal of reining in spending that was not approved in the normal appropriation process. Every poll showed strong public support for ending earmarks. Republicans would successfully campaign on the issue in 2010.

But it didn't matter. She did not want the president to have too many big ideas.

Pelosi also had a tortured personal history with Hillary Clinton. When Clinton was running neck-and-neck with Obama in one of the longest running and closely fought nomination fights in Democratic Party history, Pelosi was supposed to remain neutral and allow rank-and-file Democrats to pick the nominee. But many Hillary campaign aides felt Pelosi was taking every opportunity to favor Obama at their expense.

The rift widened when Pelosi tapped Kansas governor Kathleen Sebelius to respond to President George W. Bush's 2008 State of the Union address. The very next morning, Governor Sebelius endorsed Obama. Hillary's aides saw it as a slap, and it was.

It wouldn't be the last. Unlike the Republican Party in 2008, which decided its nominations solely from the votes received in each state, the Democrats had an additional 2,000 "super delegates." These convention-goers were largely leaders of local chapters of teachers' unions and other unions, big-city mayors, and activists of all stripes. Super delegates were supposed to be independent. Since many of them were believed to favor Clinton over Obama, Pelosi said repeatedly and publicly that the super delegates should not vote according to their consciences but according to the popular vote of the states that they hailed from. Of course, this would mean they would have to vote as ordinary delegates do and, since Obama had won more states (but at that point fewer delegates), Pelosi's rule would help Obama.

In April 2008, almost two dozen major Democratic Party donors signed an open letter to Pelosi, asking her to remain neutral with respect to the candidates and the super delegates. Pelosi was furious. A Pelosi aide acidly told *The New Republic*, "It was a mistake on their part."[10]

Ultimately, the April 2008 letter backfired: She worked even harder for Obama behind the scenes.

Pelosi was a political animal from birth. Born in 1940 in Baltimore's Little Italy, she was the only daughter (and seventh child) of Thomas "Big Tommy" D'Alesandro Jr., who was first elected to the Maryland House of Delegates at age twenty-two. He went on to serve for nearly a decade in the U.S. Congress and was mayor of Baltimore for three terms. Big Tommy's oldest son, Thomas D'Alesandro III, also served as mayor of Baltimore. "The D'Alesandro home operated like a field office, with the children serving as auxiliary staff," writes Michelle Cottle in *The New Republic*. "Constituents streamed through the door starting at 10:00 A.M., and whoever was manning the front desk—a post at which every child served several hours a week starting at age thirteen—handled requests ranging from finding a family public housing to bailing someone's husband out of jail. 'It was quite the education,' says Tommy D'Alesandro, [Pelosi's brother]. 'We dealt with human nature in the raw.'"[11]

Pelosi made sure that Obama adopted health care reform as his top policy agenda. She personally lobbied the new president on the issue. It was essentially her idea.

Obama was not so sure. He went to see Emanuel.

When Obama told Emanuel that he planned to put comprehensive health care reform atop his legislative agenda, all the chief of staff saw was a sea of red flags. Emanuel had been inside the Clinton White House during the 1993–1994 "HillaryCare" debacle and didn't want to repeat the experience. "I begged him not to do this," Emanuel told Jonathan Alter.[12]

The chief of staff had good reason to worry. Giving health care such priority came as a surprise to many of the White House's senior staff. The economy was in the throes of its greatest crises since the Great Depression; public polls consistently listed the economy or jobs as Americans' top concern.

Obama dismissed Emanuel's concerns that the initiative would fail and would be viewed as irrelevant at a time when most Americans were desperately afraid of losing their jobs, homes, cars, and retirement savings. He had come to believe what Pelosi had been telling him for months. "I wasn't sent here," Obama said, "to do school uniforms."[13]

This was a dig at Rahm's former boss, President Clinton, who was forced to advocate small incremental measures, such as uniforms for public school students, after his party lost control of Congress midway through his first term. Of course, pushing health care reform is one of the main reasons his party lost control of Congress, but Rahm wasn't about to point that out to President Obama. "Rahm is incremental," one veteran Democratic strategist said. "A school uniform strategy only gets you so far; at some point there needs to be a bigger vision."[14]

Emanuel met with Nancy-Ann DeParle, another veteran of the Clinton White House, and discussed the president's surprising new priority. As the conversation progressed, their enthusiasm slumped. "Both of us had been through the Clinton experience together," DeParle said. "So we made a promise to each other that we weren't coming out of this with nothing."[15]

Thus were the dividing lines being drawn between "the realists" and "the idealists."

In the realist camp were Emanuel, DeParle, and Vice President Joseph Biden. In the idealist camp were Pelosi, some of the ultra-liberal "old bulls" who chaired key House committees, plus David Axelrod, Jarrett, and other Obama aides from Chicago.

By the summer of 2009, Obama was leaning toward the "idealist" camp. Though Emanuel had begged Obama not to push health care reform, once the president had firmly made up his mind, he asked Obama, "Do you feel lucky?"

Obama smiled. "My name is Barack Hussein Obama and I'm sitting here. So yeah, I'm feeling pretty lucky."[16]

Passing health care reform would take more than luck. The American Medical Association, a massive national doctor's group, and the health care insurance industry as well as medical device makers, pharmaceutical companies, hospital chains, and so on, were expected to be well-funded foes. Indeed, some version of this opposition coalition had defeated every other attempt at national health care reform during the past century. Obama and Pelosi agreed that something would have to be done to defang these likely opponents.

They developed a multipronged strategy in early 2009. The biggest reason for most opposition was not principle, but payment. Requiring insurers to take all comers regardless of preexisting conditions would boost demand for health services without a matching increase in revenue for providers. The difference between the new costs and existing revenues could easily amount to billions of dollars per year. Adding some 40 million people to the health care sector (without an increase in doctors or hospitals) would push demand over supply. Prices could only rise in such a situation. If health insurance premiums couldn't also rise, insurers and others would be stuck with bankrupting losses.

Progressive health care reformers had long recognized this problem and had hit upon a solution: requiring everyone to buy health insurance that met certain minimum government standards. Suddenly, projected revenues would exceed potential surges in demand. (The new revenues, in turn, would eventually increase the supply of health care services.) The health care sector would actually make money from the reforms, or so the reformers claimed.

The industry coalition was divided on the idea. Some believed health care reform was, indeed, a moneymaker while others suspected government projections were more rosy than realistic. They worried not just about the increased demand from some 40 million uninsured (many of whom were young and healthy and wouldn't demand much more health care), but about how health care reform would affect the behavior of the industry's best customers: middle-aged, middle-class people, who were actually well positioned to demand more services.

Copayments exist largely to reduce demand. If medicine were free at point of service, existing customers might decide to get "value for their money" and demand more services. Plus, the proposed reform would require health insurers to cover many costly treatments and tests that some policies may not have previously covered, such as mental-health counseling and anti-addiction medication.

While the industry groups debated among themselves, a series of private side conversations revealed what Pelosi and Obama wanted in return: If you want a seat at the table while we reform health care, you will cease lobbying and advertising efforts opposing the reforms.

That summer, it worked.

Instead of the industry groups, the main opposition to ObamaCare in mid-summer 2009 came from progressives. As soon as the word got out that Pelosi and Obama were jettisoning the "public option" (direct government control of health care in a Medicare-like program) in order to compromise and cut a deal with industry groups, a new war began.

Rahm never wanted to be in this fight, but once in, he was all in. The Obama White House used various daily conference calls and weekly meetings to coordinate with its ideological allies in liberal interest groups, much as Republican presidents did with conservative organizations. In the Obama years, there was a daily 8:45 A.M. conference call (getting the call's pass code was considered a status symbol among Northwest D.C. liberals), a weekly meeting formerly called "Unity 09," and one called the Common Purpose Project.

Common Purpose held weekly invitation-only meetings at the Capital Hilton Hotel, a few blocks from Pelosi's Capitol Hill office. The location was no accident: The meetings were held more than fifteen minutes away from the White House by taxi, and yet near the Democratic Party's longtime center of gravity, the Pelosi-run House of Representatives. Senior White House officials, including the chief of staff and occasionally the president himself, were expected to make the trek.

The Common Purpose Project meeting had, and still has, power. Obama used a catchphrase from its January 2011 meeting in the closing line of his 2011 State of the Union speech. The meeting is often run by Erik Smith, an activist who started the progressive forum to counterbalance the power of weekly Wednesday meetings led by anti-tax powerhouse Grover Norquist at Americans for Tax Reform. Norquist's weekly meeting convenes a few blocks from the White House. Like Norquist, Smith aimed to use his meeting to coordinate interest groups' media statements with those of their allies in the White House and in Congress, to forge coalitions to pass legislation, and to put ideas onto the political agenda. The Common Purpose Project also has its liberal critics, including FireDog-Lake blogger Jane Hamsher, who refers to it as the Obama administration's "veal pen"—a way to discipline independent groups and get them to toe the administration's line.

The Common Purpose Project became a key battleground in the internal war over the shape of health care reform. In August 2009, the war went from sniper shots to blitzkrieg. Rahm Emanuel led the attack.

In the room was every interest group that the White House would need to push reform through Congress: an array of unions (including the AFL-CIO), Rock the Vote, the Sierra Club, Americans United for Change, the Center for American Progress, Media Matters for America, MoveOn .org, and the Campaign for America's Future, among others.

They were not happy with Rahm before he started speaking and they were angry when he finally stopped.

Many of the liberal leaders at the table wanted "single payer," a plan that would essentially eliminate all private-sector health plans and replace them with a single Canada-style, government-run plan. This had long been the progressive dream. Now that Democrats held large majorities in both houses of Congress and had a progressive as president, they argued, it was time to go for it.

Rahm saw the situation differently. The key, he repeatedly said, was to write a bill that could become law. That meant concessions to the moderate "Blue Dog" Democrats, who largely hailed from Southern and Midwestern swing districts. The Blue Dogs said they couldn't support "single payer"—it simply terrified the people who voted them into office in 2006 and 2008. Liberal leaders, who thought moderates were squandering an historic opportunity, largely ridiculed those concerns.

Rahm sided with the Blue Dogs. He had helped deliver a congressional majority to the Democrats by recruiting and fund-raising for these moderates in swing districts. He was incensed that some liberal groups were developing online and broadcast videos that were critical of these moderates. Without them, he cautioned, the Democrats would lose the Congress in 2010.

Now Rahm put it more succinctly: Liberals who disagreed were "fucking retarded."[17]

"We are 13 and 0," Rahm said, explaining that Congress had passed thirteen pieces of progressive legislation. But health care reform was the big one. We are "going to fuck up" if we don't pass this, he said, which meant passing a bill that commanded a majority in each house of Congress, and they needed Blue Dog votes to do that. There was no mathematical way to do it without them, he said. That meant no "single payer," but instead the state-run "insurance exchanges" favored by both the insurance industry (which liked the cartel-like aspect) and the moderates (who liked the idea that it sounded private).

When the four-letter-word barrage ended, the room was restive. No one liked Rahm's tone or his message. After a few days of private complaints and political calculations, most of the groups in the Common Purpose Project meeting decided to back the Obama administration's plan. They would support a bill that could actually become law, while vowing to fight more when the time was right.

MoveOn.org, which began as an online activist group formed to defend President Clinton from allegations (later proved well-founded) made by Monica Lewinsky, organized an e-mail letter-writing campaign that urged Obama to rein in his chief of staff. It didn't work.

Rahm was right to worry. That month, Democratic lawmakers were shocked that their informal "town hall" meetings were drawing large crowds of constituents, many of whom were angry about what they called "the government takeover of medicine." Congressmen were being shouted down. Some in the Obama administration tittered over protest signs that told the federal government to keep its "hands off my Medicare."

Rahm and his team weren't laughing. It reminded them of the summer of 1988, when the powerful Chairman of Ways and Means, Rep. Dan Rostenkowski (D-Illinois), was chased by angry constituents, who pounded on his car, for passing the Medicare Catastrophic Coverage Act, which would have increased costs by as much as $1,600 per elderly couple. Congress repealed Rostenkowski's health care measure in November 1989.

The ObamaCare changes were much larger—and so was the building public anger.

The tide was turning. Rahm knew the president was losing independents. Without them, he would lose Congress. They were running out of time. It was now or never. Unless something else went wrong.

Then, down the hill from a stone Roman Catholic Church, in a rain-stained shingle house overlooking Hyannis Port, the brother of President John F. Kennedy and Attorney General Robert F. Kennedy slipped away into eternity. It was August 25. Sen. Ted Kennedy had succumbed to a brain tumor.

At first, Kennedy's passing fueled support for comprehensive health care reform. It was a "win one for the Gipper" kind of moment. The Liberal Lion had been calling for a national health care program for decades. Why not finally make it law as a posthumous gift to him?

Nearly everyone expected Kennedy to be replaced by another Democrat. The special election was considered over when Martha Coakley won the Democratic Party nomination. Other than as a talking point in favor of massive health care overhaul, Kennedy's death initially seemed to have no connection to the eventual passage of the measure. Once again, official Washington had miscalculated.

(Oddly, President Obama did not interrupt his Martha's Vineyard vacation for Kennedy's internment at Arlington National Cemetery, even though Kennedy's endorsement—just prior to the critical Super Tuesday contests—propelled Obama to the Democratic presidential nomination.)

Opposition continued to grow. As ordinary people became more vocal in swing districts, their leaders began to follow. Republicans were uniting in opposition and many Democrats were wavering. Public opposition, reflected in polls, was climbing. And a new force was being felt, a giant emerging from the landscape that became known as the "tea party."

While Obama was speaking at a joint session of Congress on September 9, 2009, the gale force of the tea party reached into the hall through the voice of Rep. Joe Wilson (R-South Carolina). Channeling the emerging conservative faction's rage, the congressman shouted, "You lie!" right in the midst of Obama's speech.

The president continued as if nothing had happened and the congressman later apologized. But it was a sign of things to come.

Health care reform was not unifying, as some progressives had hoped. It was polarizing.

Obama made it clear to Emanuel that he would not relent. He didn't come to the White House to do "small things."

Emanuel phoned Senate Majority Leader Harry Reid. It was time to make some deals in order to move the bill through committee and to the floor of the U.S. Senate. If they waited much longer, even stalwart supporters might change their minds. Congressional support was like a melting ice cube in a hot hand.

But deals were hard to secure. Every senator seemed to have a different plan. The dominant Senate version contained funding for abortion, which Emanuel saw as a "poison pill" that would kill the prospects of final passage. Special "carve-outs" that exempted certain states from certain provisions—such as the "Cornhusker Kickback" that exempted Nebraska—cluttered the main bill and were about to explode in controversy.

The situation, if anything, looked worse in the House of Representatives. Pelosi still supported "single payer." Emanuel and his White House team still worried about the Blue Dogs, who had not budged in their opposition to a single-payer proposal. And the tea-party protests had only elevated concerns of both the moderate Democrats and Emanuel's White House team.

Obama dithered. He didn't back any of the Senate or House plans. The tactics were left up to Emanuel and, increasingly, to Pelosi. The strategy, the overall vision of where the president wanted to end up, was left unspoken. Obama seemed to be waiting to see what would turn up on his desk, and then he would decide whether or not to sign it.

To the frustration of Democratic leaders—from lowly members of committees to the leaders of the House and Senate—there was no personal guidance from Obama. In the summer and fall of 2009, Democrats received from the White House only the brutal certainty on certain spe-cifics from Emanuel and the wispy abyss of platitudes from the president himself.

Obama seemed unwilling to even decide between a single-payer sys-tem and insurance exchanges. To some, he seemed uninterested or aloof; to others, he was a wily tactician who kept his cards close to his vest.

Previous presidents, when working on landmark legislation, submit-ted a draft of the proposed law for Congress to use as a starting point. Obama did not. Congress had to begin on its own and run the risk that the president might veto its laborious efforts. Earlier presidents issued cri-teria and checklists for items that final legislation must include or exclude. The lists that did arrive came from Emanuel.

When Obama was asked about items on Emanuel's lists, he would present the case both for and against an item—like a professor enumerat-ing policy options. He didn't seem to have an opinion.

Eventually, Pelosi and Reid decided to work with their key commit-tee chairmen and cut what deals they could. They were on their own.

By October 2009, Obama grew restless. The danger of complete failure loomed. A grim feeling spread, a fear that Obama's effort at health care reform was going to fail just like Clinton's, Truman's, and Roosevelt's. An historic opportunity was moving just out of reach, and failure would cast a pall over the entire administration.

If Emanuel was thinking "I told you so," he was wise enough to keep that thought to himself. He knew the political perils of failure as well as anyone. He and DeParle redoubled their efforts to save ObamaCare.

Angry and frustrated, Pelosi told the president they "can't twist one hundred arms." She had done her part. She had allowed a vote on the single-payer framework, which promptly failed on the House floor. Then she forced through a phone book-sized piece of legislation. The more than 1,000 densely printed pages were too much for any member of Congress to read, and they weren't even given time to try. The problem was that the House and Senate versions of health care reform, which hadn't even been passed by this time, were wildly incompatible. The current iteration of the

Senate version was wholly unacceptable in the House. Since neither legislative body could pass the other's bill, the result was a stalemate.

Pelosi angrily told the president that the House had done virtually all the heavy lifting for his agenda: Stimulus spending. "Cap and trade" environmental legislation. New regulations on banks and brokerages. Now health care. And much of the House Democrats' work died in the Senate.

As usual, she had a solution in mind. The president should get behind either the House or the Senate version and use his "bully pulpit" and formidable powers of persuasion to move the other chamber to act. Naturally, Pelosi wanted Obama to back the House's version. But, at the very least, she wanted him to choose one or the other.

Obama said he needed time to think. He didn't want to decide immediately. And certainly not while he was talking to her.

A week later, on advice from Emanuel, Obama slighted Pelosi by backing the Senate version. At least Obama had made a decision. But Pelosi was not happy. She knew she might have to sacrifice much to save her legislative baby.

The rift deepened when Emanuel declined to attend a fund-raiser for the Democratic Congressional Campaign Committee, which recruits donors for Democratic congressmen's reelection efforts.

Now Pelosi had a decision to make. She could insist on the House version and, likely, end up with no bill at all. Or she could try either to twist enough arms to win passage of the Senate bill or to devise a legislative maneuver to ease its passage. Either attempt to pass the Senate version could cost the Democrats seats in the House and perhaps even their majority itself.

It was a big gamble. Should Pelosi roll the dice? Obama didn't say. It was up to her.

Moving forward would take guts. Pelosi didn't hesitate.

She told her fellow Democrats in the House that she was prepared to lose seats in the 2010 midterm elections "if that's what it takes" to get health care reform done. The members knew it was dangerous to argue with Pelosi when she had made her mind up. Many feared it would cost them control of the House and perhaps even their own seats. But they admired her guts.

Critics might call it ObamaCare, but at that moment it was really PelosiCare. If she had decided to avoid one of the hardest political fights of her career, health care reform would die. If it became law, it would be almost solely on the back of her hard work.

Just as Pelosi was about to take the biggest risk of her career, insurance industry groups panicked as Emanuel and DeParle predicted they would.

The industry group had researched and studied the projected costs of the health care plan that had already passed the House. The results were sobering: "Between 2010 and 2019, the cumulative increases in the cost of a typical family policy under this reform proposal will be approximately $20,700 more than it would be under the current system." Once again, it seemed that the industry was about to torpedo reforms because of their elephantine compliance costs.

Pelosi knew better than to get into a deadening debate about costs and benefits. It would provide too much cover for wavering congressmen to shift from support to opposition.

Pelosi played her hole card. She said she had "tremendous interest" in revoking the industry's decades-old antitrust exemption. That exemption allowed health insurers to share information.

This was no empty threat. The House Judiciary Committee promptly passed a bill to revoke the exemption.

What a difference a season made. In the summer, the industry was willing to play ball and stay silent, thereby protecting themselves against retaliation. Once the industry believed that it had been betrayed on costs, and objected, it became the object of what George Orwell in *1984* called the "Two Minutes Hate."

The insurers got the message.

Meanwhile, a health care bill was finally lumbering through the Senate. On Christmas Eve a key Senate vote finally moved the bill. Once the full Senate could vote, sometime in January, Pelosi would have something to work with. Hope had appeared on the horizon, if ever so briefly.

Few realized that in the early days of January 2010, the U.S. Senate was actually in a race against time.

On the night of January 19, Democrats were shocked that state senator Scott Brown, a Republican, had won his special election in Massachusetts to replace the recently deceased Ted Kennedy. A Republican victory had been unthinkable in Massachusetts—a shocking and symbolic loss for the Democrats. Few had seen it coming.

Even more surprising was that Brown had won by campaigning against health care reform in supposedly deep-blue Massachusetts. On election night, Senator-elect Brown made the meaning of his election evident by saying, "One thing is clear: Voters do not want the trillion-dollar health care bill that is being forced on the American people."

Was health care reform dead? Without a sixtieth vote to end a filibuster in the Senate, Republicans could literally talk the bill to death—denying a vote that would give Pelosi something to pass.

Obama, after talking to Pelosi, emerged with a sudden steel spine. "We are this close to the summit of the mountain," he said. "We need to try one more time."[18]

Senate Majority Leader Reid was told that he had to have a vote on the health care bill before Scott Brown was sworn in as the new senator from Massachusetts. Interestingly, Obama didn't tell him. Pelosi did.

Some dispute the timeline. Sen. Tom Harkin (D-Iowa) insisted that Pelosi and Reid had reached agreement on a deal four days *before* Scott Brown's victory. In other words, it wasn't an attempt to get around the verdict of the voters, but simply coincidental timing. He said negotiators had an agreement in hand on Friday, January 15. "We had an agreement, with the House, the White House, and the Senate," he said. "We sent it to the CBO [Congressional Budget Office] to get scored and then Tuesday (January 19) happened [Scott Brown won] and we didn't get it back."[19]

This may be true, but Harkin was also misleadingly Jesuitical. In the final week before the January 19 special election, polls had shown that the race was surprisingly close. The prospect that the Democratic nominee might lose, the whip hand of fear, drove party leaders to urgently hammer out a deal before the new senator could be seated.

Strangely, Obama was not the main force behind the historic bargain, but a bystander.

•   •   •

That second week in January, Democrats had made a Herculean three-day push to reach agreement. But there was a stark reminder during that time of the differing styles, House versus Senate, and how that divide would define the endgame in the next two months for passage of health care reform.

On the second day of that push, Obama asked House and Senate leaders to return to the White House after dinner with some $70 billion in suggested cuts from the bill. The projected costs of the Senate and House bills had to be equal, or close to equal, or under long-standing legislative rules the Senate bill would have to be amended in the House—a procedure that could undermine the entire effort.

With the cuts in mind, a group of senators gathered in the office of Sen. Max Baucus (D-Montana), ate pizza, and talked turkey. Each senator gave up something, aides said.[20]

Later that night, back at the White House, the House presented its approach: They would cut nothing. It was the Senate's mess and they could fix it.

Obama's eyes flashed in anger. He asked the representatives of the House and Senate to go to different rooms and reconsider. It was as if he had called a time-out on unruly children.

Eventually, the senators whittled the gap down to $20 billion, and Obama made his own suggestions. Rep. Henry Waxman (D-California), chairman of the House Energy and Commerce Committee, seemed pleased. "I don't speak for the House, but you have put forward a serious set of numbers," he said to Obama, according to a person present.[21]

Pelosi was not so impressed. "Mr. President, I agree with Henry on two points," she said, before turning to Waxman. "The president put out a set of numbers, and you don't speak for the House of Representatives."[22]

Pelosi knew she needed help from Obama. But she wasn't going to let him run the show.

Pelosi told the president that she was unhappy because "Obama had yet to state publicly, in crystal clear terms, what he wanted to see in a health bill."

She wasn't going to fight alone. Obama needed to publicly back her efforts.

Obama's response was defensive: "I'm not a stupid man."

He was, in turns, angry and despondent. He said "dammit" a number of times, hoping that would make him sound more powerful.

Then Obama got up and walked out.

As he was gliding out of the room, Obama told his aides, over his shoulder, to work out a deal with the Speaker of the House. Left unsaid, Pelosi was in charge. It was her baby.

Obama literally walked away. If health care reform was going to have a future, it was out of his hands.

Pelosi's people left the meeting with the sense that the president had no plan and no idea what to do next. And that was frightening.

Obama's version of this meeting is unpersuasive. He said that he faked his tantrum:

> Apparently Obama can fake emotion, and to great effect. He admits . . . he was acting when he stormed out of a meeting with Democratic leaders in the House and Senate after Nancy Pelosi shot down the Senate's proposed $15 billion cut to the health care plan. "I wasn't really that frustrated," Obama said of the scene, in which he sputtered, "Dammit, folks, this is history," and stormed out of the room, telling Rahm to "clean it up." "The truth was we were very pleased that it was going as well as it was. There are certain points during negotiations where the big issues have really been settled. Everybody knows where the agreement is going to be, and people are then dickering over stuff that is not worth another hour or two of lost sleep."[23]

To some in the meeting, Obama was abdicating his role and his responsibility at a pivotal time. Or, maybe, he was simply "leading from behind."

It was up to Pelosi now.

Even before the Massachusetts election electrified Washington, D.C., Ron Pollack, the executive director of the pro-health-care-reform organization Families USA, began canvassing health care and legislative experts for ways to keep the bill alive without sixty votes in the Senate. The most

promising option was something he called the "two-step": the House
would pass the Senate bill, followed immediately by a package of fixes that
could move through the Senate through the reconciliation process, a legislative maneuver not subject to a filibuster.

A day before the January 19 Massachusetts election, Pollack sent a
memo to senior congressional and White House staffers. It quickly leaked.
"I felt it was predictable that if (Brown) did win," Pollack said, "it would
have a major impact in terms of what the perceptions would be about the
future of the health reform effort."[24]

Pelosi and her staff liked the idea. It was bold and unprecedented for
a major, controversial piece of legislation. But, in Pelosi's mind, it was nec-
essary. It was the only way to save the baby.

The morning after the Brown blowout, Obama seemed unnerved. A loss
in Massachusetts? Was Pelosi leading the Democrats off a cliff?

Rahm Emanuel renewed his push for a simpler, slimmer bill. Obama
agreed.[25]

Later, in an interview with ABC News, Obama said he wanted "to
coalesce around those elements in the package that people agree on."[26]

Senate Majority Leader Reid was also wavering. The Massachusetts
election result was still echoing in his mind.[27]

With no clear direction, Obama kept sending contradictory statements. In the first weeks of January 2010, *Politico* noted: "Publicly, the
White House seemed to send a different signal each day. In the space of two
weeks, Obama or his top advisors suggested breaking the bill into smaller
parts, keeping it together in one comprehensive package, putting it at the
back of legislative line and needing to 'punch it through' Congress, as
Obama himself said at one point."[28]

Obama's meandering on health care reform was also noted by *The New
York Times*: "At that moment, the president did not know whether, or how,
to proceed. The House and Senate had passed different versions of the bill
and could not come to terms. Republicans were unified in their resistance.
He considered his options, including Mr. Emanuel's 'skinny bill.' Whatever
the course, aides said, Mr. Obama was insistent that health care not be put
into a 'time capsule,' never to be opened again in his tenure."[29]

Obama was not leading the health care reform efforts, according to all mainstream news accounts at the time. He was trying to find a way to vote "present," to stay out of harm's way during the biggest political fight in decades.

There are many words for this, but "leadership" is not one of them.

The leader was Pelosi, not Obama.

She had put health care on the agenda in the first few months of the Obama administration—over the tepid objections of the president himself, initially—and doggedly fought to save it from every snare over the next eighteen months. And she often took on her own party, fighting for something she considered big and meaningful. "My biggest fight," she told reporters, "has been between those who wanted to do something incremental and those who wanted to do something comprehensive."

In other words, her biggest fight was with Obama's chief of staff.

Pelosi still needed what help she could get from Obama.

In a series of telephone and in-person conferences, she implored the president to get personally involved. Pelosi and Reid were taking huge political risks. He needed to join them.

Obama wasn't sure he wanted to commit himself. Can you actually pass it? Obama only wanted to bet on a sure thing.

Pelosi was cool under fire. "We're in the majority," she said. "We'll never have a better majority in your presidency in numbers than we've got right now. We can make this work."[30] She was confident and bold; he was unsure and uncommitted.

By Thursday, January 21, Obama had adopted Pelosi's position as his own and was now supporting the "two-step" plan: pushing the Senate bill through the House, and then getting the Senate to pass a series of "fixes."

But House committee chairmen were not convinced. Even in the wake of Scott Brown's election and months of protests at town hall meetings and on courthouse lawns, some liberal barons still thought they could pass "single payer." They largely hailed from "safe" House districts, where the majority of voters had easily reelected them for decades. They were also largely first elected in the 1960s or 1970s, when liberal solutions both sounded new and enjoyed greater popularity. They had been waiting for their entire congressional careers to pass Canadian-style health insurance. They didn't want to give up.

Now Pelosi wanted the more liberal House to adopt the Senate version, which denied government direct control of the health care infrastructure. Obama was enlisted to phone wavering liberals, who had to be persuaded that half a loaf was better than none.

The president gamely tried to persuade Rep. Barney Frank (D-Massachusetts). That should have been easy—Scott Brown had just won the majority of votes in Frank's congressional district (along with a majority statewide). But Representative Frank was reluctant to yield. Obama ended up promising him that somehow the Senate would pass "fixes," which would address Frank's concerns. As canny a calculator as ever, Frank agreed to think about it.

Other influential Democrats were harder to persuade. "You have to let my colleagues work through their stages of grief," said Rep. Robert Andrews (D-New Jersey). The first stage of grief is denial and the second is anger. As for Andrews, in January 2010, what stage was he in? "Still in denial," he said.

More than a week after Scott Brown's shocking victory, House Democrats were still fighting for a complete government monopoly of health care. Pelosi had a tough time persuading them. "Herding cats" is how one Democratic staffer described it.

Meanwhile, moderate Democrats were increasingly worried as they learned more about the Senate measure. For one thing, it included subsidies for abortion providers. To many liberals, abortion was just another health care service; to most moderates, it was a deal-killer.

Abortion itself had been growing more unpopular for the past decade— by 2008, support for abortion fell below 50 percent for the first time—and paying for other people's abortions with tax dollars had always had minority approval in public polls. In Southern and Midwestern swing districts, this was the kind of thing that defeated Democrats. The abortion provision had to come out, the moderates said, or they couldn't vote for it. Rep. Bart Stupak (D-Michigan) led this clutch of Democratic opponents.

Obama's lobbying of House Democrats soon tapered off. It was a dull and thankless task, and it didn't appear to be working. So he reverted to form: he retreated and disappeared. If the House was going to pass the Senate bill, it would be up to Pelosi now.

Pelosi sought out Senate Majority Leader Harry Reid with an unusual request: She wanted a letter, signed by a majority of Senate Democrats, agreeing to pass the menu of "fixes" demanded by the House leaders. It was Friday, January 22—four days after Brown's victory. She wanted the letter by Monday.

Reid didn't like the idea. It wasn't how the Senate did things. And senators hate to sign on to things before the legislative details had been fully spelled out. The House's menu of "fixes" was just a few pages of bullet points, not a carefully drafted legal document vetted by career Senate staffers.

There was no time for that. Pelosi, one Senate staffer who was briefed on the meeting said, was "like that union general on the third day of Gettysburg, who sees the confederates coming, and rallies his guys, saying 'we've only got ten minutes to save the union.' "[31]

Reid reluctantly agreed. He wasn't going to take the blame if the biggest initiative of the Obama years exploded on the launch pad. Somehow, he would have the letter signed by Monday.

Incredibly, Reid got fifty-two Democratic senators (out of fifty-nine) to sign a letter promising to vote on the "fixes" proposed by the House. (Importantly, he agreed to vote *on*, not vote *for*, those "fixes.) But there was a poison pill in the letter's fine print: The fixes "will be approved by the Senate only after Obama signs the Senate bill into law."[32]

The Senate letter was e-mailed and photocopied, making its way into every office of the Democratic House majority. Pelosi worked the phones and approached members in the cloakroom. While her private appeals were bearing some fruit, she still didn't have the votes she needed. Pelosi-Care was poised to die.

On Thursday, January 28, Pelosi went public, announcing at a news conference that she was going to pass health care reform somehow. "We will go through the gate. If the gate is closed, we will go over the fence. If the fence is too high, we will pole-vault in. If that doesn't work, we will parachute in."[33]

To moderates and Republicans, Pelosi's determination sounded terrifying. To many Democrats in the House of Representatives, it sounded Churchillian. Pelosi would fight on the beaches, in the hedgerows, in the streets. She would never surrender.

Tellingly, the nation never heard anything like this from Obama.

During her January 28 press conference, Pelosi left no doubt that she meant what she said. She outlined a "possible path to approving health care legislation" in which the House Democrats would swallow their objections and vote to approve the Senate bill. Then the Senate would use a budget reconciliation process which, by Senate rules, Republicans could not filibuster.

It was a "politically fraught strategy," she admitted.[34] She knew her cherished reform was deeply unpopular with the public, with Republicans, and increasingly among House Democrats. But she was going to do it anyway. It was a gamble.

The lack of presidential leadership was starting to worry Democratic lawmakers.

In the first week of February 2010, senators met at the Newseum, a news industry museum a few blocks from the Capitol dome. They were angry. They had made what many thought was a career-risking vote—they, too, knew how deeply unpopular health care reform was at the moment—and now, they confided to reporters, "the House would not act on the Senate bill and the president would not lead."[35]

In an off-the-record discussion, the conversation turned hot. Former *Saturday Night Live* comedian Al Franken, now a U.S. senator from Minnesota, underscored the importance of presidential leadership. He told David Axelrod: "David, I'm doing a slow burn here—do you know what a slow burn is?"

Franken wanted to know how Obama was planning to push the Senate bill through the House.

Obama's chief strategist did not promise presidential action. Instead, he shifted the burden to Pelosi. "If you've got 218 votes in your pocket," Axelrod said, "we'll do that."[36]

The meaning was clear: Obama and his men had no plan. The president was not planning a heroic charge, a prime-time speech, or anything else. It was all up to Pelosi now.

Then the president threw Pelosi another curveball.

At a Democratic National Committee fund-raiser, Obama shocked Pelosi staffers when he announced a plan for a health care summit, which would include Republicans and moderate Democrats. The political benefits to Obama were obvious. He was distancing himself from legislation that was unpopular and seemed doomed. To Pelosi's people, it looked like betrayal.

Obama's speech sent conflicting signals, but also seemed designed to distance him from impending failure.

"I want to (host this meeting) . . . to go through systematically all the best ideas that are out there and move it forward," Obama said during the interview with Katie Couric in the White House Library.

Obama still had great faith in his abilities to use his eloquence to move aside entrenched interests. He was finally gambling, too, whether he realized it or not.

It didn't work. Republican congressmen came well informed and asked pointed, detailed questions. Obama, who didn't command the details, adopted an unattractive, lecturing tone. Public support for health care reform continued to fall.

If anything, the president's televised health care summit made Pelosi's job harder.

Health care reform was eventually passed on March 21, 2010, with few Republican votes, and President Obama signed it into law. A majority of the public loathed it and its unpopularity grew over the course of the year.

The Democrats lost their House majority in November 2010, having rejected Emanuel's advice, and Nancy Pelosi was no longer Speaker of the U.S. House of Representatives.

Leaders don't always win. Moses did not get to live in the Promised Land.

Obama might get the credit, from both critics and admirers of health care reform, but the participants see a different picture: a president whose biggest accomplishment isn't the sum of his decisions, and of a woman who risked it all and won, then lost her position.

As a measurement of Obama's leadership, health care reform is the study of a man ducking hard decisions and then taking credit for others' work, principally Pelosi's. If this is how Obama dealt with allies, how would he work with political enemies?

CHAPTER 3

NOTHING IS SURE
BUT DEBT AND TAXES

Everybody was prepared for the worst—and it got worse.

—Robert Gibbs, White House spokesman[1]

Watching the election returns on the night of November 2, 2010, in a small study in the White House residence, Barack Obama was shocked.

Outside the ornate window, a cold wind was sweeping across the Potomac and bending the bare branches of trees on the grounds of the executive mansion. Inside the White House, the mood was apprehensive, determined, fatalistic, grim, and sober.

Democrats were losing nearly every close election. By night's end some fifty-two Democratic Party incumbents had lost their places in Congress. Only two incumbent Republicans were defeated.

One was Joseph Cao, the son of Vietnamese immigrants who had won a special election in 2008 to represent a majority-black district in New Orleans. Few had expected him to prevail. Still, the Republican's loss was ominous for Democrats. He was the lone Republican in the House to support Obama's health care reforms. The other defeated Republican was

Charles Djou, who had catapulted into office in a low-turnout special election in May 2010 in Honolulu. He had been in office for less than seven months and the district tilted Democratic. The first congressional district of the Aloha State had been safely Democratic since Hawaii became a state in 1959. It would have been surprising if Djou had not lost. Neither victory brought Democrats much joy.

In the West Wing, the analyses were sharp and instant—much better than those of the television commentators, one participant said. On the TV screen, the red parts of the map kept growing and the blue parts shrinking. As with British lords watching their imperial possessions trade hands, humor kept resignation from sinking into fatalism.

Upstairs, in the presence of the president, it was quiet. The atmosphere was like the funeral of a beloved but distant aunt that makes her survivors introspective and cautious to speak.

It was how sharply the country's mood had shifted that startled the president. Voters didn't seem angry in general; they were angry at the Democratic Party and, incredibly, they were angry at *him*. As the night wore on, the only suspense was just how devastating the defeat would be in the U.S. House of Representatives and whether the Republicans would also capture the U.S. Senate.

By the next morning, the Republicans had won a net total of sixty-three seats (counting victories among incumbents and open seats), handing the GOP its largest House majority since the 1920s. All the gains the Democrats had made in 2006, when they regained control of Congress, and in 2008, when Obama's massive voter turnout efforts further engorged the Democratic majority, were gone. The hard-won victories earned during the Bush years were reversed in a single night. In addition, nine Democratic congressmen who had survived the 1994 Republican tidal wave were also washed out in 2010. To Democrats, it felt like Pearl Harbor. To Republicans, Waterloo.

Over in the U.S. Senate, the television screen held a little hope for Obama. The number of Republican senators grew from forty-one to forty-seven—narrowly preserving the Democrats' majority in that one-hundred-seat body. This was a massive loss, but it was slightly mitigated by the idea that the president would not have the entire legislative branch arrayed against him.

Rarely in American history had the fortunes of one party sunk so steeply, so suddenly. The liberal era was over, at least for the foreseeable future. The president's agenda—another stimulus program, more regulation for bankers and investors, greater power for union leaders—was now politically impossible.

Obama later confided that he was "humbled"[2] and "surprised by the depth of the loss," according to an outside advisor who met with him in the days after the historic defeat.[3]

Still, he had no one to blame but himself. Through his actions and inactions, he had called in air strikes on his own foxhole.

The president's defeat in the 2010 midterm elections was the result of two failures of leadership: vision and management.

Obama failed to act on the problems identified by the vast majority of Americans that year—growing joblessness, shrinking home values, mounting national debt, climbing gasoline prices—and failed to immediately address new problems that suddenly materialized (principally, the spreading oil slick in the Gulf of Mexico and the prospect of a multistory mosque near the edge of Manhattan's September 11 crater.)

Instead, Obama had spent much of the previous two years expending vast amounts of legislative energy and political capital to pass two measures that were increasingly unpopular: a $787 billion stimulus bill and health care reform. One bailed out business executives who had made poor business decisions; the other had simply been on the progressive wish list for a long time. Neither addressed the concerns of the large numbers of ordinary Americans who were primarily concerned about losing their jobs and homes.

The stimulus, which the White House liked to say "created or saved" 3 million jobs, had not restored all the jobs Americans held during the Bush years. The total U.S. workforce had shrunk by more than 2 million people between 2008 and 2010. Millions more were working in new jobs for less pay: construction workers washing dishes, software engineers joining Best Buy's Geek Squad. Meanwhile, joblessness continued its fitful, funereal march upward.

The stimulus didn't stimulate enough to earn political support beyond

the firms and state governments that received its largesse, while critics—
who called it "porkulus"—pointed to the politically connected who ben-
efitted. Overall, there was no political benefit in it.

The health care win may have been historic, but it hurt Obama more
than it helped him. David Corn, formerly Washington editor of *The Nation*
and now at *Mother Jones,* favored health care reform but saw its political
dangers: "The president had been left with a let-me-explain, hard-to-
understand win that had prompted rage on the Right and fired up the Tea
Party forces now threatening his party."[4] It had been a strategic mistake:
Obama's supporters were disappointed with his historic win (many still
wanted a "single-payer" system), while his foes were energized and their
constituents were alarmed.

The White House was now suffering a different feeling, exhaustion.
For the past two years, many staffers had been working fourteen-hour days.
Some longed to return to teaching positions as their sabbaticals came to an
end. Others sought less taxing, more remunerative jobs in the for-profit
world. And there was a dearth of new ideas. A senior administration official later confided to David Corn: "What else could we do? Crisis, war, the
BP spill, and health care had already sucked up all the oxygen."[5]

In the eyes of the public, Obama had done the things that he ought
not to have done and left undone the things he ought to have done.

Robert Gibbs, then the White House spokesman, put his finger on
the political problem that the president missed. "If people turned on the
television and saw stories and shouting about BP and the [Ground Zero]
mosque, they'd be right to ask, 'Is anybody paying attention to what's important in my life?"[6]

Instead of acting, Obama had been reacting. He had been driven by
the urgencies of cable news (which treated the Gulf oil slick as akin to the
September 11 attacks) and the imperatives of Congress (Pelosi's insistence
on making health care reform and stimulus spending the top priorities).
Despite the rhetoric and imaginations of his fiercest critics, Obama did
not actually set the agenda. He allowed others to establish his priorities—
and now he was paying the price.

He had made the biggest blunder a leader can make: He had surren-
dered the initiative.

• • • •

Obama had seen the crisis coming as early as March 2010, but he did little to avert it.

When he campaigned with Democrats, he was no longer Superman, but kryptonite. The president, who was still personally popular, couldn't transfer his popularity to Democrats running in swing districts. Indeed, he hurt their chances. Candidates began politely asking the president to stay away. Still, this did not lead Obama to change his strategy.

Part of the problem was a messaging strategy that consistently blamed Republicans in Congress, and former president George W. Bush, for America's woes. Obama's message came from Pelosi and her allies in the House, and from his message czar, David Axelrod.

Obama had blindly gone along. Consider his May 2010 remarks at a $15,000-per-plate Democratic Congressional Campaign Committee fund-raising dinner: "After they drove the car into the ditch, made it as difficult as possible for us to pull it back, now they want the keys back. No! You can't drive. We don't want to have to go back into the ditch. We just got the car out . . ."[7]

The crowd laughed loudly. Amid the applause, Rep. Chris Van Hollen (D-Maryland) gave a smiling thumbs-up sign to Pelosi. Van Hollen was then chairman of the Democratic Congressional Campaign Committee. He was pleased that Obama had adopted a line that the congressman had been using for months.

Pelosi nodded back, a gleam in her eye.

Obama was finally doing what Pelosi and Van Hollen had long recommended: savaging the Republicans.[8]

Axelrod and other White House advisors agreed with Pelosi's attack strategy. While Obama was doing what House Democratic leaders had wanted, the message wasn't moving independent voters, however. The president didn't seem to notice.

Instead, he continued to intone a losing melody. He was still trumpeting that theme by summer's end at an August fund-raiser in Atlanta. "They don't have a single idea that's different from George Bush's ideas— not one," he said.[9] He kept repeating this theme, despite polls that proved it wasn't working.

The message wasn't working because it was beside the point. Instead of addressing the record-high national debt that many voters linked to job losses and a slow economy, Obama was talking about "tax giveaways to the rich" and the Republicans' use of "secret donors." Thanks to a recent U.S. Supreme Court decision in the *Citizens United* case, unions and businesses could give large amounts, anonymously, to independent groups to buy television and radio advertisements. This enraged Democrats who thought the ruling would aid Republicans in competitive elections, but it left independents cold.

Still, Obama's message didn't change. "That left us with Republican ethics," a Democratic Congressional Campaign Committee official said. "And that led to us not having a dialogue with voters about what they cared about. There was no jobs message. The voters, rightly or not, saw debt as a contributing factor to the bad economy, and we were talking about who was spending what money in politics. We had an election driven by the enemy."[10]

An election driven by a strategy set by the House Speaker, not the president himself. Setting strategy is essential to leadership. But Obama had abdicated.

Obama's message was not chosen on a whim.

Throughout the spring of 2010, Pelosi and other House Democratic leaders had been campaigning for the president to become more partisan, to draw lines, to sharpen contrasts.

To their horror, Obama's initial impulse was to return to the moderate-sounding message that had vaulted him into office in 2008. They despaired when the president wanted a health care summit with Republicans and clucked their tongues when it failed. They believed the only way the Democratic House majority would survive in November was to paint the Republicans as dangerous extremists, benefit cutters, and friends of the powerful. They would have to override Obama's gut instinct somehow.

Pelosi found a fortunate ally in former Obama presidential campaign communications chief David Axelrod. Together, they changed the president's mind.

There are two kinds of political campaign leaders: technicians and true believers. While there are plenty of technicians with beliefs and true believers with strategies, campaign advisors generally lean one way or the other. Axelrod was always a true believer.

The son of a Manhattan psychologist and a journalist of the legendary left-wing daily *PM,* Axelrod started volunteering for political campaigns as a teenager. Right out of college, he covered city hall politics for the *Chicago Tribune,* but switched to running political campaigns in 1984—by joining the effort to elect Paul Simon to the U.S. Senate. Simon won and soon earned one of the most liberal voting records in the history of that body. Axelrod was his co-campaign manager.

On the back of that success, he opened Axelrod & Associates to advise other campaigns, which were invariably for left-of-center candidates. He helped elect Harold Washington, Chicago's first black mayor, in 1987. Washington became one of the most liberal mayors in the country in terms of taxes, spending, and regulation. Axelrod became known as the man who actually got progressives into power.

He met Obama at a voter registration drive in 1992 and, over the years, the two became close friends. Axelrod helped edit drafts of Obama's book *The Audacity of Hope* and, from 2002 onward, drafts of Obama's major speeches. He played pivotal roles in Obama's U.S. Senate and presidential campaigns. Indeed, he is usually credited with devising Obama's "hope and change" campaign mantra. (It was based on a theme Axelrod had used to elect Deval Patrick as Massachusetts's first black governor.)

This time, the message failed to resonate. For too many voters, a message complaining about Republicans—who had no power in any of the federal government's three branches—seemed irrelevant when joblessness and gas prices were rising along with the national debt. By Election Day 2010, the national debt, in dollar terms, was the highest ever in American history.

Axelrod, like Pelosi, was a partisan. He could expertly sail when the flood tide was with him, but he couldn't navigate when the tide ran out. He simply couldn't admit that the public mood had changed. He ignored poll results that challenged his beliefs and dismissed news that didn't square with his ideas.

Importantly, Obama didn't order Axelrod to change course despite the mounting evidence that a storm was approaching. He wasn't willing to defy the man who had helped him win the presidency or the Speaker of the House who had brought him his historic victory. While he might question or cavil, he couldn't decide.

After the historic defeat, Axelrod went on to teach a course called Campaign Strategy at Northwestern University in the Chicago suburbs.

The day after the election, many White House staffers described their mood as "depressed." The loss of the U.S. House of Representatives and only a skinny remaining majority in the U.S. Senate meant that passing new programs would be very difficult. Would the next two years be an endless and enervating siege?

Obama seemed strangely upbeat. The day after the midterm elections, the president convened a meeting with his senior staff.

While they saw clouds, he saw the sun through them. Democrats still ran both houses of Congress until January 3, 2011, when the new session convened. To the surprise of some staffers present, he enumerated an ambitious list of measures that he would like to see made law in the next sixty days: "a tax deal, extending unemployment benefits, ratification of New START treaty reducing nuclear arms, repeal of the Pentagon's Don't Ask/Don't Tell policy preventing gays and lesbians from openly serving in the military, passage of the DREAM Act (which would grant citizenship to undocumented young adults who met certain requirements), and a children's nutrition bill advocated by Michelle Obama."[11]

The list was unrealistic. It would have been a demanding agenda for Congress to accomplish over two years, let alone two months.

Besides, using a "lame duck" Congress to pass major legislation had enormous political risks. It would be seen as an end-run around voters who had just elected a new majority with a new agenda. When President Carter had used a "lame duck" Congress to pass major bills (including the costly "Superfund" program) following the November 1980 elections in which he lost his reelection bid and Republicans won control of the Senate for the first time since 1954, the public was outraged. The outrage would be much bigger this time: Since 1980, the Internet, talk radio, and the Fox News Channel had emerged as powerful forums for channeling outrage.

Even if Congress could actually adopt these controversial measures in a few short months, the political price of such a strategy would be high.

Still, Obama continued to back Axelrod's analysis, which held that "independent voters wanted a leader who would make all the squabbling schoolchildren in Washington do their assignments."[12] Who would do the "assigning"? The voters or the White House? Neither Obama nor Axelrod seemed to wonder. If the federal government would finally pass a liberal wish list, Axelrod and Obama contended, voters would be happy.

It was an unusual view. Independent voters in swing districts had actually voted down candidates who had supported the president's policies in the 2010 elections. Even in safely Democratic districts, independent voters had reduced their support of liberal lawmakers compared with 2008, exit polls showed.

Few staffers were persuaded that the president was right, although none dared to contradict him during that meeting.

Passing Obama's priorities during the Thanksgiving and Christmas holiday season had yet another obstacle. A massive White House staff reorganization was in progress. Rahm Emanuel had stepped down as chief of staff in October 2010 and many other staffers were returning to Chicago or to academia. Without staff, it would be harder to rally the already reluctant Congress to act.

Still, Obama was keen to proceed as planned. He was finally going to lead, but the timing and strategy were ill-considered.

"Obama didn't care about the criticism that he was too insular," a White House aide said. "He didn't give a shit."[13]

Obama's proposals were dutifully sent to Capitol Hill, but most were essentially dead on arrival. Congress was exhausted and didn't want to take any more political risks.

It soon became clear that the president would have to do something to address growing public fears about the national debt.

In the eyes of his critics, Obama's biggest monument is monumental public debt. At the end of the Bush administration, in 2008, the national debt was some $9 trillion. By 2010, the national debt had climbed to $13.5 trillion—nearing 100 percent of the nation's entire $15 trillion

economy, as measured by the gross domestic product. It was the largest
two-year increase in national debt in American history, even eclipsing the
record debts during World War II in nominal-dollar terms.

At first, Obama's advisors tried to minimize U.S. national debt levels
by comparing them to those of European nations. France's national debt
was some 80 percent of its gross domestic product while Germany's national
debt neared 87 percent.

Obama's team was trying to compare apples with oranges. Few investors were fooled.

European Union member states calculate their national debt by
combining all levels of government debt—muncipal, state, and federal
debt. And those nations count future pension obligations to public-sector
workers. If you calculated America's national debt that way, it would bal-
loon to 170 percent of gross domestic product. (Greece, which also calculates
using the European Union criteria, at the depth of its crisis, had a ratio of
debt to gross domestic product of 165 percent. America's debt was bigger.)
Properly understood, comparing America's national debt to those of European nations is frightening: By this calculation, it is more than double the
national debts of Germany and France. The Obama economic team quietly, and quickly, dropped this talking point.

The tea partiers and millions of ordinary Americans had put the issue
of the national debt on the agenda. Now the debate raged in the White
House: What to do about it?

During the first two years of Obama's term, the White House had all but
ignored the national debt. The strategy had been to delay discussing it.

In the final throes of the fight over health care reform, Obama announced the National Commission on Fiscal Responsibility and Reform[14]—
informally known as "Simpson-Bowles" after its two chairmen, former
senators Alan Simpson, a Republican, and Erskine Bowles, a Democrat.

The main political benefit of the Simpson-Bowles commission was
that it allowed Obama to "kick the can down the road," one participant
said. Throughout the 2010 election year and amid the surging tea party
protests, the commission gave Obama an excuse for inaction. He repeatedly said that he didn't want to preempt the commission and promised he

would act as soon as he had reviewed its final report. It allowed the president to say that he wasn't ignoring the public's concerns without forcing him to make any politically difficult decisions.

The commission was supposed to find ways to bring the federal budget into balance and to reduce the national debt. The "budget deficit" refers to the annual difference between what the federal government spends (roughly $3.2 trillion) and what it takes in (roughly $2.2 trillion). The "national debt" is the sum total of all borrowing, which financed previous years' deficits. Even if the federal budget deficit were reduced to zero, the national debt would continue to grow due to interest owed on the outstanding debt, a legacy of spending approved by both parties over the years. Cutting up your credit card doesn't erase past obligations. The commission was supposed to prescribe medication for both of these maladies.

But it was not medication the president wanted to take. The commission's cure was massive spending cuts and large tax hikes.

The Simpson-Bowles commission report landed on his desk shortly after the 2010 elections. The timing couldn't have been worse for Obama.

The election underscored the public's demand for federal debt reduction. The incoming Republican leadership had repeatedly vowed to slash "wasteful spending." The commission's report added to the roar.

Touring Asia when the preliminary recommendations came in, Obama addressed the commission's findings at a press conference in Seoul, South Korea.

His remarks were tepid by design. Commission chairmen Alan Simpson and Erskine Bowles had asked the president to avoid saying anything that would increase political divisions back in Washington.[15] The commissioners still hoped that their proposals could be debated calmly in advance of a scheduled December vote in Congress.

Obama played along. "The only way to make those tough choices historically has been if both parties are willing to move forward together," he said. "And so before anybody starts shooting down proposals, I think we need to listen, we need to gather up all the facts. I think we have to be straight with the American people."

But behind the scenes, Obama's team was desperate to stop any spending cuts.

• • •

White House staffers invited progressive activists and liberal lobbyists over for a working meeting to devise a way to snake around Simpson-Bowles. As if to mirror their reluctance to put the nation on a spending diet, they ate chocolate chip cookies and drank Diet Coke.

Progressives were adamant that raising taxes on all Americans earning more than $250,000 had to be the center of any budget-cutting plan. Axelrod tried to calm them down, denying any White House softening on the plan to raise taxes on "the rich."

No one heeded Obama's advice to avoid "shouting down proposals" prematurely. When the Senate took up the Simpson-Bowles proposal, it failed its test vote on December 3, 2010. Both parties found reasons to object.

Some progressives had taken to calling Simpson-Bowles the latest "cat food commission" because the Social Security cuts it recommended meant indigent seniors would only be able to afford cat food to eat. In fact, the commission only considered reducing the rate of increase in payments to senior citizens, not cutting the payments themselves.

And conservatives in Congress were united in their opposition to the tax hikes buried in the Simpson-Bowles plan. They believed tax increases would deepen the nation's economic woes.

Somehow the commission's plan lived on for months, as its members continued to meet with senators in hopes of forging a compromise. Nearly every lawmaker believed something had to be done about the deficit and debt. They simply couldn't agree on what that something was.

Eventually a "gang of six" emerged: Commission members and senators Dick Durbin (D-Illinois), Kent Conrad (D-North Dakota), Mike Crapo (R-Idaho), and Tom Coburn (R-Oklahoma), along with senators Mark Warner (D-Virginia) and Saxby Chambliss (R-Georgia).[16] They met informally outside the halls of the Senate, over chicken dinners at the homes of various lawmakers, often inviting others to voice their concerns and opinions.[17] Hopes for a deficit-cutting compromise ran high.

Obama was heading in the opposite direction. He called for dramatic spending increases, which he called "investments," in his January 25, 2011, State of the Union address to Congress. Calling this America's "Sputnik moment," he imagined new spending levels not seen since the 1960s "space race." While the president gave a rhetorical nod to a "freeze on annual domestic spending for the next five years," he announced plans to spend billions on solar energy and light rail.[18] It seemed that the president had just arrived from a distant planet.

The pattern continued. Obama released his much-unloved 2012 budget proposal on Valentine's Day. That budget included massive new spending programs for alternative energy and many other spending increases.

Republicans were incredulous. Senate Minority Leader Mitch Mc-Connell said: "I would best sum it up as a sort of lack of seriousness."

Echoing McConnell, Sen. Jeff Sessions (R-Alabama), ranking minority member of the Senate Budget Committee, said: "It was a very unserious response to a very serious situation."[19] The Republicans couldn't believe the president would propose billions in new spending when the deficit and the debt were hitting new highs.

The response on the left was equally negative. *The Washington Post*'s reliably liberal Dana Milbank wrote, "Obama's budget proposal is a remarkably weak and timid document."[20] Even *The New York Times* editorial page, while praising Obama's budget as "responsible," conceded it was, in fact, the opposite: "What Mr. Obama's budget is most definitely not is a blueprint for dealing with the real long-term problems that feed the budget deficit."[21]

Obama had a rare opportunity for an historic reform of entitlements, which account for the lion's share of the federal budget. He either didn't sense the opportunity or chose not to take it. Either way, it was a failure of leadership.

Next, Obama switched to attacking any plans to cut spending. When the Republicans had released their budget, he said, "Their vision is less about reducing the deficit than it is about changing the basic social compact in America."

He continued to rely on the negative message that had failed to woo majority support in the 2010 midterm elections: "There's nothing serious about a plan that claims to reduce the deficit by spending a trillion dollars on tax cuts for millionaires and billionaires. And I don't think there's anything courageous about asking for sacrifice from those who can least afford it and don't have any clout on Capitol Hill."[22]

By spring 2011, Obama had doubled down on his 2010 attack message, a tactic that gained him very little traction. William A. Galston, a prominent Democratic strategist and former domestic policy advisor to President Clinton, told *Bloomberg News,* "What did it get him? If your objective is to be a president who achieves transformational change, then I'm not sure waiting from December to mid-April is wise."[23]

Instead of "fundamentally transforming the United States of America," as the president promised five days before his 2008 election, he was trying to run out the clock.

House Republicans continued pushing forward. The "Path to Prosperity," a budget devised by Rep. Paul Ryan (R-Wisconsin), was brought to the floor of the House of Representatives. Speaker John Boehner hailed it as "a serious step in the right direction."[24] It passed overwhelmingly, though it attracted few Democratic votes.

In the Senate, Majority Leader Harry Reid insisted on getting Republicans on the record on major spending cuts and announced he was bringing the Ryan budget up for a vote. "There will be an opportunity in the Senate to vote on the Ryan budget to see if Republican senators like the Ryan budget as much as the House did."[25]

When the Ryan budget was finally brought forward in late May, it was voted down on partisan lines. Few wanted to take the risk of supporting spending cuts that the president would likely veto.

Meanwhile, Obama's budget was seen as "dead on arrival." It failed miserably in a Democratic-run Senate. Indeed, ninety-seven of one hundred senators voted against Obama's budget that May. The other three senators were not present in the chamber when it came time to vote.[26]

It was the most devastating budget defeat for a sitting president in American history. This is the price for not seeming "serious."

The result? Stalemate. For the next two years, the U.S. government would operate without a budget passed by Congress. Instead, it was legally funded through a string of stopgap bills known as "supplementals" and "continuing resolutions."

And the worst was yet to come. The president continued to criticize, rather than decide or negotiate. Like everyone else, he saw the crisis coming. Unlike everyone else, he was in a position to do something about it.

By May 2011, a new specter was haunting Washington, the threat of a government shutdown. One had been narrowly averted in April when the White House agreed to some spending cuts in exchange for closing some tax loopholes. But it only pushed off the day of reckoning to August, when a far bigger compromise would be needed to stave off a government shutdown—and a possible default on national debt payments.

Without an agreement from the Republicans who now ran the House of Representatives, the federal government would lack the legal right to keep spending money. Yet finding agreement would be hard.

The Republicans did not have much room to manuever. The Republican majority was elected on a surge of conservative support. Some 40 million American "tea partiers" were outraged by the historic levels of spending and the record national debt. Many were new to political activism and only provisionally gave their support to Republicans. If the GOP failed, they would back a third party or stay home—perhaps even returning the Democrats to power.

The tea party was collectively mesmerized by a national debt that had climbed some 50 percent since Obama's 2009 swearing-in, from less than $9 trillion to more than $13.5 trillion. And it was set to grow to $15 trillion by 2012—the size of the entire American economy. Tea partiers didn't want Congress to agree to any increase in the debt ceiling or in taxes. Instead they wanted the federal government to do what they had reluctantly done in their private lives—reduce spending. (Indeed, 2009 was the first year since 1948 that total consumer debt actually fell.)

The Democrats, who ran the U.S. Senate and the White House, did not want to cut spending. Since the 1930s, the federal government had grown to have a department or agency for every major element of the Democratic Party coalition. The Labor and Education Departments provided grants and consulting contracts for unions. The Department of Health and Human Services and the Agriculture Department's food-stamp program funded various welfare programs, plus Medicare and Medicaid. The Interior Department and the Environmental Protection

Agency looked after the concerns of environmentalists. The Agriculture Department delivered farm subsidies in an array of forms. The Commerce Department watched over big, unionized companies and (through its National Oceanic and Atmospheric Agency) paid for global-warming research. The Urban Mass Transit agency funded buses and trains in big cities run by Democrats. And so on. Nearly every tentacle of the federal government was a lifeline for another Democratic Party interest group. Slashing spending meant starving the very groups Democrats would need for the next election. So their opposition to spending cuts was not simply ideological. It was practical.

At the same time, the general public—outside of Democratic precincts—was demanding debt and deficit reductions. Tax increases, though politically risky, were the only solution the Democrats favored or could favor.

That was no solution to Republicans, who feared tax hikes would draw money out of the private economy and rob it of investment capital needed to create jobs, design new products, and grow the economy. Any tax increases on "the rich" would inevitably skewer middle-class voters, the Republicans' main supporters. Equally important, most Republicans in Congress had signed on to a pledge never to vote for any income tax hike. Many would lose their reelections if they broke faith with voters on taxes. When President George H. W. Bush broke his promise not to raise taxes, he lost his reelection in 1992.

The result? Impasse. Neither party was willing to wound itself to heal the nation.

The only way out required presidential leadership. The traditional Washington solution was to persuade both parties to feel some pain—to accept a mix of spending cuts and revenue increases—in order to avoid a government shutdown. In other words, a "grand bargain" along the lines suggested by Simpson-Bowles. That is exactly what the liberal congressional solons did in 1982, persuading President Reagan to double the federal gasoline tax to nine cents per gallon in exchange for massive spending cuts that never became law. The Democrats promised to cut two dollars of spending for every dollar of new revenue in that deal. Instead, spending climbed every year thereafter. Fully aware of this history, tea partiers weren't wild about the idea, but Speaker Boehner's team was prepared to try it.

Obama wasn't interested. Instead, he wanted to gamble.

He believed fear of an unprecedented downgrading in America's creditworthiness would shock Republicans into accepting tax hikes, or at least raising the national debt limit. He was betting that they would blink.

For most of the warm months of 2011, the president and his administration kept raising Washington's fever.

Secretary of the Treasury Timothy Geithner kept telegraphing August 2 as the deadline for raising the limit. He warned that failing to address the issue by that time would have huge ramifications. It would cause federal payments to stop instantly and "would likely push us into a double dip recession."

Geithner was right to worry the nation's leaders. America's national government had not faced a possible credit downgrade since the years of Franklin Delano Roosevelt, when the already large reach of the federal government into the lives of its citizens was far smaller than today. In those days, Medicare and Medicaid did not yet exist, Social Security applied to a far smaller percentage of citizens, federal workers were fewer in number and not yet unionized, and federal pensions and debt interest payments were minor liabilities. Today, these line items account for more than two-thirds of the federal budget. No one knew how credit ratings agencies would react when they took a hard look at America's balance sheet—or how high the future cost of federal borrowing might climb.

As for default, that would be unthinkable. The American government had successfully avoided defaulting on its debts since the presidency of George Washington, the longest unbroken series of interest payments of any nation on earth. If it defaulted—if it missed scheduled interest payments—the soundness of America's promises would be forever questioned. And questionable debts demand higher interest fees.

Nevertheless, the Obama administration kept inflating the fears of investors. In a May 12 letter to Congress, which was actually intended for public distribution, Geithner wrote, "A default on Treasury debt could lead to concerns about the solvency of the investment funds and financial institutions that hold Treasury securities in their portfolios, which could cause a run on money market mutual funds and the broader financial system—similar to what happened in the wake of the collapse of Lehman Brothers. As the recent financial crisis demonstrated, a severe and sudden blow to confidence in the financial markets can spark a panic that threatens the health of our entire global economy and the jobs of millions of Americans."[27]

To House Republicans, this sounded like "give us what we want or the world ends." Indeed, that was the White House strategy.

Obama might have settled on a different strategy if he had a better idea of how the world looked through eyes of his Republican counterparts.

House Speaker John Boehner was facing his own version of the battle between the immovable object and the irresistible force.

Boehner knew the investors were adamant that the federal government could not default on its debt obligations, while the tea party had given him a congressional majority on the promise to shrink the national debt and budget deficit. To make matters harder, Republicans had campaigned on a pledge to trim federal spending by $100 billion in the first two years of a GOP-led House.

And for many freshman congressman, that $100 billion cut was "a floor, not a ceiling." They repeatedly used this line on the floor of the House. There was no doubt about their passionate position. They wanted deeper cuts, in the hundreds of billions of dollars. Many wanted to eliminate entire federal government departments, laying off hundreds of thousands of public-sector workers.

Others wanted to sell federal assets, everything from unused public land to electromagnetic spectrum used for cell phones. One out of every three acres in the United States is owned by the federal government. Europeans have raised hundreds of millions selling mobile phone frequencies. They wanted all of the money raised to go to paying down debt, not current spending.

Obama opposed selling assets at all.

Recent history only hardened the opposition of Boehner's caucus to any accommodation with Obama. In April, the Speaker had cut a deal with the president to increase the debt limit for a few months' worth of debt-based spending, in exchange for cuts larger than the size of the new debt. Or so it seemed, on paper. When the freshmen Republicans read the fine print, they were angry. Most of the savings came from repurposing money that the federal government had budgeted but not yet spent. The billions in "cuts" boiled down to some $300 million of real reductions. They felt betrayed. There were shouting matches between some freshmen congressmen and members of Boehner's staff. In a closed-door meeting of all House Republicans, several members of Congress attacked Boehner personally. He took the podium to defend himself. Pandemonium briefly followed. It was an experience no one wanted to repeat.

So the Speaker was backed into a position in which he would only agree to increase the federal debt limit if the compensating cuts were larger than the increase in new debt—in other words, if the result was a net decrease in federal liabilities. He made his position plain at the Economic Club of New York: "Without significant spending cuts and changes to the way we spend the American people's money, there will be no debt limit increase. And cuts should be greater than the accompanying increase in debt authority the president is given."[28]

Boehner badly wanted to make a deal. But his room to negotiate was small and shrinking.

Incredibly, Obama took this moment to cram Boehner into an even smaller space. The president said he wanted to see revenue increases and insisted on repealing the Bush-era tax cuts on every American earning more than $250,000 per year.[29] This was in line with the promises he had been making to progressive interest groups since the spring of 2011, but it clashed with political and economic realities.

Ending the Bush-era tax cuts for Americans earning more than $250,000 per year would raise, at most, $700 billion, according to White House budget projections. (And those projections were rosy. The wealthy have easy means to avoid the tax bite, by deferring income from the sales of stock, property, or family firms from one tax year to another or by staggering the payments. They could also reduce their incomes by buying new tax-deductible equipment or land for their enterprises. The perfectly legal tax dodges were many. So the $700 billion in promised new revenue was largely an illusion.)

More importantly, the budget deficit was projected to be more than $1.1 trillion that year and the debt was nearly $15 trillion—$700 billion was taking a teaspoon of water from a boiling kettle: It wouldn't silence the whistle.

And everyone, on both sides of the aisle and on both ends of Pennsylvania Avenue, knew that ending upper-income tax cuts wouldn't relieve the debt crisis. What few could puzzle out was why Obama was doing it. It wouldn't solve the problem and it just made people on both sides of the aisle angry. It was divisive and distracting.

Yet the president and the president's men continued to insist on tax hikes—rather than spending cuts—while still ignoring most of the underlying problem. For Republicans, this was all political risk with no compensating reward. There was nothing in it for them. It would have been easier to get Boehner to take a swan dive into an empty concrete pool, said one person involved in the negotiations. So why did Obama repeatedly offer an alternative that he knew would never be accepted?

Once again, Obama was blaming, not leading.

Nevertheless, negotiations had to begin if the president was going to avoid being blamed for a government shutdown. Obama asked Vice President Joe Biden to confer with budget leaders in Congress to see if a deal could be struck. Biden, a former long-term senator himself, had extensive experience with budget talks and strong relationships with many of the decision makers. Still, it was a daunting task.

In a May 2011 kickoff meeting held in the New Executive Office Building across Sixteenth Street from the White House, Geithner joined Biden in meeting with House Majority Leader Eric Cantor, and Democrats Chris Van Hollen, the combative former campaign chief, and James Clyburn, the House Minority Whip. From the Senate, they were joined by Senate Appropriations Committee Chairman Daniel Inouye and Senate Finance Committee Chairman Max Baucus, both Democrats, and Sen. Jon Kyl, the Finance Committee's ranking Republican.[30]

Both sides started out with some optimism. "We have to make some real progress," Biden said, "to try and deal with the hard business of what's at hand here." Everyone knew he was right.

Cantor echoed Biden's focus on trying to solve the problem: "There is a fairly clear sense of where we need to head, and that is to find some common ground. We are trying to find ways to produce a result."

The group hoped to have a compromise in place by June.[31] A banking lobbyist who was a longtime friend and golf partner of Boehner's was briefed on the first meeting. He recalled Boehner's reaction: "He was relieved. The adults were in the room."

The public would likely support a compromise. Opposition to increasing the national debt had soared to a record high. In the middle of May, Gallup released its latest poll numbers on the debt ceiling. More than half of Americans surveyed opposed taking on more federal debt. When asked how they wanted their member of Congress to vote on the pending debt ceiling incease, 47 percent favored a "no" vote; 34 percent were undecided; and only 19 percent supported a vote approving more debt.

But opposition to increasing federal debt levels varied by party identification. Seventy percent of Republicans and 46 percent of independents were against increasing the debt ceiling. Democrats weren't so sure. A plurality, 40 percent, said they didn't know enough about the issue to say one way or the other. Twenty-six percent definitely opposed letting the U.S. Treasury go deeper into debt, while 33 percent approved of the idea.[32]

Obama held the minority view—not just among the public, but among Democrats. He wanted to take on more debt.

Bolstered by American public opinion, Boehner scheduled a House floor vote to test Obama's request to raise the debt limit without any compensating spending cuts. This was the dream position of House liberals, but everyone knew the measure could not pass. Putting the idea up for a vote at all was considered a political stunt: Democrats would be forced to either support the president's unpopular position of raising the debt limit without reforms or vote against the White House.

House Democrats immediately abandoned Obama. Democrat

Minority Whip Steny Hoyer said, "I'm going to advise my members that they not subject themselves to the demagoguery that is sure to follow."[33] The measure to increase the debt, now totaling $14.3 trillion, failed 318–97. Even Democrats who, in principle, supported increasing the debt limit, voted against it.[34] They knew it was politically toxic.

Now it was Obama's strategic options that were narrowing fast.

The next day, in a closed meeting at the White House's East Room, Republicans tried appealing to reason. Let's stop attacking each other, they pleaded, and make a deal.

Boehner's opening remarks were a direct challenge to the president: "We put a plan on the table. Where is your plan?"[35]

While the Republican plan had been put in legislative language and passed by a strong majority in the House, the White House had no written plan. And Republicans were annoyed by constant criticisms from Obama administration surrogates—and by Obama himself—on cable television.

House Budget Committee Chairman Paul Ryan, microphone in hand, plaintively pointed out, "Mr. President, the demagoguery only stops if the leaders stop it."[36]

Obama looked on impassively.

Rep. Virginia Foxx, a Republican, tweeted that Ryan "received [a] standing ovation"[37] from the Republicans present.

When the applause died down, Ryan continued. He asked the president not to "mis-describe" and "mis-characterize" Republican proposals.[38] It wouldn't help the parties make a deal.

It wasn't a friendly session. "Frosty is the word," said Rep. Phil Gingrey, a Republican.[39]

Obama's reponse was defensive, saying he knew a thing or two about misrepresentations, having been subjected to epithets such as the "job killing, death panel, probably-wasn't-born-here president."[40] Of course, those remarks were from the previous year, not the previous month.

The Republicans didn't back down and continued to press Obama.

Cantor said the Obama team's "Medi-scare" comments were hurting their chances of cooperation from the GOP.[41] He asked the president to "keep out of the discussions surrounding the debt limit, and in the Biden talks, any notion that we're going to increase taxes."

He got no meaningful answer. Obama was not interested in any confidence-building compromises.

Mindful of the Obama administration's history of keeping proposals vague, Rep. Kevin McCarthy (R-California) insisted that all proposals and plans be specific enough that the Congressional Budget Office could score them. He insisted that the cuts were "phony cuts."

The president appeared to concur. Whatever they agree to would have to be scoreable, he said. He told aides to "look into it" and to "have a serious conversation about it."[42] He even agreed to put entitlement reform on the table.[43]

Attention then shifted to the ongoing "Biden talks." But for all the talk of cooperation, even that initiative floundered within two and a half weeks. House Majority Leader Eric Cantor and Vice President Joe Biden had identified close to $2 trillion in cuts to take place over ten years.[44] Obama refused to agree with his own vice president.

The big sticking point remained: taxes. Obama still seemed to favor ending the Bush-era tax cuts for Americans earning more than $250,000 per year, and some Republicans believed that Biden had secret orders to make sure that a tax increase was part of any final deal. This made an agreement with Republicans all but impossible.

On June 23, 2011, Cantor released a statement:

Since early May, Vice President Biden has led meetings surrounding the debt limit. The Vice President deserves a great deal of credit for his leadership in bringing us this far. We have worked to find areas of commonality to meet the goal of identifying spending cuts commensurate with or exceeding the amount of the Obama administration's request for a debt limit increase. I believe that we have identified trillions in spending cuts, and to date, we have established a blueprint that could institute the fiscal reforms needed to start getting our fiscal house in order. That said, each side came into these talks with certain orders, and as it stands the Democrats continue to insist that any deal must include tax increases. There is not support in the House for a tax increase, and I don't believe now is the time to raise taxes in light of our current economic situation. Regardless of the progress that has been made, the tax issue must be resolved before discussions can continue. Given this impasse, I will not be participating in today's meeting and I believe it is time for the President to speak clearly and resolve the tax issue. Once resolved, we have a blueprint to move forward to trillions of spending cuts and binding mechanisms to change the way things are done around here.[45]

At the June 1 East Room meeting between the president and Republicans in Congress, Cantor complained to Obama that his administration was misrepresenting Republican proposals as denying medicine to grandmothers so that the rich could get richer.[46] Yet right after Cantor withdrew from Biden's talks and issued his statement, Obama went right back to the hurting-grandma script.

Biden himself soon joined in. Making seniors on Medicare pay more while big companies and the wealthy get tax breaks "not only is unfair," said Biden, "but I think it borders on being immoral."

Appearing on Bloomberg Television on June 24, Rep. Kevin McCarthy, the third most senior Republican in the House, complained of Obama's detachment and lack of leadership. "He's got to get off the golf course, and he's got to get engaged."[47] It was a view widely shared among House Republican leaders and staff. The president was fiddling while Rome burned.

The next day, the Obama administration reiterated its line of attack. Biden told donors at a dinner for Ohio Democrats: "We're never going to solve our debt problem if we ask only those who are struggling in this economy to bear the burden and let the most fortunate among us off the hook."[48] It was more of the blame game, which Republicans saw as a tactic of delay and distraction. Importantly, the Republicans were not out blaming Obama or the Democrats for bankrupting the nation. Their only public negative remarks—Representative McCarthy's, for instance—expressed frustration and urged Obama to sit down and negotiate.

But the attacks from the Obama administration continued. On June 29, Obama went before the cameras in the White House press room and told Republicans to "eat your peas" and come up with a deal he could accept. The "peas" line had come from Axelrod.

The attack strategy was continuing, even while the parties were trying to compromise.

Off the political stage, President Obama and Speaker Boehner were quietly talking.

It began with a public round of golf at Andrews Air Force Base outside Washington. Both leaders had an incentive to seem to be getting along. Boehner asked Obama if they could talk away from the cameras. The president agreed.

Around an outdoor table near the Rose Garden, the men began seriously discussing a bargain.[49] At this stage, Republican House leadership staff believed there would ultimately be a deal with the president—maybe not a pretty deal, but a compromise that Congress could pass and Obama could sign. They thought some kind of bargain was inevitable. Boehner's secret talks supported their view that ultimately Obama wanted one, too.

The two men developed a rough rapport—Boehner, the consummate politician, explained his political reality and vision with expansive gestures in the relaxed setting of the White House terrace, while the president listened and then explained his own vision and constraints. As the two worked to strike a deal, Boehner aides were under strict orders to "protect Boehner," lest tea-party-aligned House freshmen get wind of the secret talks and misconstrue them as Boehner caving in to Obama. Only doubt hung in the minds of the president and the Speaker: Could Boehner deliver the votes?

Obama surprised Boehner and his Democratic allies, when he said he was willing to talk about "reducing cost-of-living adjustments to Social Security" in exchange for tax increases. It was the first glimmer of daylight that a deal might be possible.

By July 5, Obama was ready to go public with the talk of doing "something big." Strangely, Obama asked for $4 trillion more in deficit reductions over the next decade, but he said he was willing to reduce the growth rates of cost increases in Medicare and Medicaid and end a range of business tax exemptions for top income earners.[50]

On Thursday, July 7, a group of Republican negotiators met with the Obama team, in a ninety-minute session that Obama called "very constructive" and Boehner called "productive."[51]

The quiet negotiations between the Speaker and the president were difficult to extend beyond the two men. Though they had established an understanding of sorts, those around them would not necessarily see this as productive.

On the Republican side, Cantor caught wind of the Obama-Boehner talks from an offhand comment made by Biden, who is not known for his tight-lipped reticence. Cantor was astonished that Boehner had excluded him and dismayed that he was talking about revenue—Washington-speak for tax hikes.

He sought out Boehner. If the Speaker was thinking about trading new taxes for spending cuts that might never come, Cantor said, he should think again. Such a deal would never pass the House.

After a tense talk, Boehner conceded that Cantor was right. The Republican majority had been elected to cut spending and hold down debt, not to deliver new money for Democratic constituencies.

Boehner phoned Obama the next day, July 9, while the president was enjoying a weekend at Camp David. A "grand bargain" would probably not be possible, he said. An incremental debt increase and a new round of spending caps would be all the House could do. Obama was noncommittal.

After making that call, Boehner issued a statement calling for a small, stopgap solution as the most reasonable and workable path forward.[52]

Obama didn't want another debt-limit fight before the 2012 election. Having to go back to Congress again, closer to Election Day, would make him unpopular with voters and imperil his reelection chances.

While Cantor and Obama had a fraught relationship before this attempt at detente, the hostility surged when Boehner mentioned a short-term solution. It sounded like a Cantor idea. Obama was angry.

And when Cantor and the rest of the Republican negotiating team arrived at the White House for scheduled talks on Wednesday, July 13, the animosity between Obama and Cantor came to a boil.

The spark that ignited the blaze was Cantor's suggestion to move the August 2 deadline on the national debt ceiling increase. He also suggested an interim debt-limit increase with smaller spending cuts to keep the talks going.

That is when Obama became animated and, according to Cantor, started to lecture him.[53]

A Democratic aide who was in the room said, "Cantor rudely interrupted the president three times to advocate for short-term debt ceiling increases while the president was wrapping up the meeting. This is just more juvenile behavior from him and Boehner needs to rein him in, and let the grown-ups get to work."[54]

Cantor presented a different version of events. He said he was "deferential" while trying to get permission to speak, but the president was simply unwilling to have a give-and-take conversation. Instead, Cantor recalled, Obama insisted on doing all the talking. Cantor said he was trying to explain that without more cuts no deal could pass the House. The president, he said, was unwilling to consider a smaller interim deal because he needed at least $2.5 trillion to get through the 2012 elections. Cantor believed that consideration—not the risk of government shutdown or U.S. default—was driving the Obama's negotiating position.

Obama simply refused to consider any incremental increases to the debt limit and even threatened to veto any such bill. As soon as Cantor suggested a temporary debt increase to buy time for negotiation, according to Cantor, "(t)hat's when he got very agitated."[55]

It also seemed that Obama was offended at having to personally negotiate this deal. "I have reached the point where I say 'enough.' Would Ronald Reagan be sitting here? I've reached my limit. This may bring my presidency down, but I will not yield on this."[56]

Actually, President Reagan negotiated spending deals with House Speaker Tip O'Neill several times.

Cantor was direct. "I'm trying to represent where the votes are in the House. And we've always said the votes in the House are consistent with the principles that the Speaker's laid out that we've been operating on." He went on to explain that Obama kept insisting Republicans would have to give in on tax increases or surrender the goal of a dollar-for-dollar match of cuts to the debt hike,[57] one that would allow the total national debt to remain unchanged.

Giving up either principle was unthinkable for Cantor, and for most House Republicans. "I understand why he's frustrated. But again, we're trying to get this thing done, and that's why I was a little taken aback."[58]

Obama responded by giving Cantor a warning—"Eric, don't call my bluff," he said—and promising he would tell his side "to the American people."

Obama had misread the political situation. He thought it was a replay of President Clinton's 1996 showdown with House Republicans, when the public was less alarmed about the national debt, the economy was growing, and the tea party didn't yet exist. His threat was hollow.

With anger, frustration, or forcefulness, depending on whom you listen to, Obama pushed away from the table, stood up and told Cantor and everyone else, "I'll see you tomorrow."[59]

Leaving a meeting petulantly had become a trademark Obama move. But his timing couldn't have been worse.

That same day, the credit rating agency Moody's Investors Service announced it was reviewing the United States' AAA rating. A downgrade of U.S. debt would likely increase borrowing costs and eliminate some credit sources.[60] It would also be a national embarrassment.

Moody's cited the "rising possibility that the statutory debt limit will not be raised on a timely basis, leading to a default on U.S. Treasury debt obligations." Moody's was concerned that without a new debt limit increase, the U.S. government could miss payments on principal, interest, or both.

Any potential downgrade would apply, according to a spokesman for Moody's, to "financial institutions directly linked to the U.S. government: Fannie Mae, Freddie Mac, the Federal Home Loan Banks, and the Federal Farm Credit Banks." So every element of the federal government, even its galaxy of quasi-governmental institutions, could find it harder and costlier to borrow money.

The stakes had been raised while Obama fumed.

•   •   •

In the face of this news, Boehner didn't hesitate to keep the pressure on the president to keep talking. Citing Moody's, Boehner issued a short statement that read, in full: "This report underscores the warning I outlined months ago. If the White House does not take action soon to address our nation's debt crisis by reining in spending, the markets may do it for us."[61]

But Obama didn't have full rein to negotiate. Boehner complained that Jack Lew, then the director of Obama's Office of Management and Budget, didn't seem willing to make compromises. Whatever Boehner proposed, Lew would spurn in favor of his own, usually more complicated ideas. And Lew returned again and again to proposals Boehner had unambiguously refused. Lew had lost the trust of the House Republicans. Reluctantly, Boehner phoned Obama and asked for someone else to deal with.[62]

To complicate matters further, Senate Democrats may not have wanted a deal at all if it didn't include tax increases. They faulted the president for failing to identify new tax dollars for Democratic voters. Democratic senator Carl Levin wanted Obama to take a harder line: "I just don't think the president has been willing to really fight hard for revenues."[63]

Levin was not alone. Liberal journalist Eric Alterman summed up liberals' frustration: "Clearly Obama and his advisers believe he benefits from refusing to take a side between battling House Republicans and Senate Democrats and appearing to hover above the bloody battlefield. What is most infuriating to liberals, however, is this time—unlike the government shutdown fracas or the extension of the Bush tax cuts—he is holding all the cards." Alterman ended with some unsolicited advice, telling Obama, "It's long past time for this president to get off the ropes and come out punching."[64]

This was the consensus view among Democrats and pundits on the White House's daily talking-points list: There was no need to compromise, only to compel the Republicans to capitulate.

With the pressure mounting, Obama and Boehner met again on Friday, July 15, this time with some changes in the team and location.

Boehner brought Cantor in. Once the majority leader knew about the talks, there was no point in excluding him. Besides, any deal hammered out between Obama and Boehner would need Cantor's help in drumming up votes.

Instead of Jack Lew, Obama put chief of staff Bill Daley and Treasury secretary Timothy Geithner in charge.

Instead of the White House, they met on Capitol Hill.

The quartet and their aides structured a deal that skirted some of the timing problems that had stood in the way of previous deal proposals. Boehner had always wanted spending cuts first, tax reform second. Obama worried that the work of closing tax loopholes would never happen. Now the team was debating a framework with target numbers for cutting spending and reforming taxes that Congress could approve at the same time.[65]

After church on Sunday, July 17, Boehner and Cantor slipped into the White House to work out more of the details. While a final deal was not yet in place, both sides were close. An historic deal seemed to be waiting in the wings.

After a long day of negotiations in Daley's West Wing office, both sides were exhausted. Large parts of the deal to fund the $2.5 trillion debt ceiling increase were in place, including $1.2 trillion in cuts over ten years. The retirement age for Medicare would be raised and the premium structure changed. Social Security reforms were discussed that would keep the program solvent for an additional seventy-five years.[66] Total spending cuts would equal some $1.7 trillion in the next ten years with $800 billion in revenue generated through changes in the tax law,[67] mostly by closing loopholes and ending exemptions.

Both sides were uneasy. Obama's team had not wanted Social Security included in the deal since they considered that program technically separate from federal debt. Their argument was that Social Security was paid for by a separate payroll tax; therefore it was off budget and should not be factored in.[68]

Republicans countered that the national debt included all federal obligations, including Social Security. The payroll tax was not going into a so-called "lockbox" funding Social Security payments, but rather went into general funds, masking the debt—until 2011, that is, when President Obama's Social Security payroll tax cut plunged the program tens of billions into the red for the first time in its seventy-five-year history.

Cantor and Boehner knew they faced huge challenges in getting the package through Congress.[69] Still, they trudged forward and, while there were some details still to work out that Sunday, they were getting close.

Cantor and Boehner chatted with Obama in the Oval Office before leaving for the day. It did nothing to dampen their optimism. When the trio emerged and returned to the roomful of aides, Obama appeared upbeat. "I want a deal," he said.

Secrecy would be essential as the details came together, the president said. He spoke openly with Boehner about how the two sides might sell the emerging plan to their respective parties, an imposing task for either one of them.

"How soon can we get this drafted?" the president asked, according to notes taken during the meeting by a top Republican staff member.

When Obama left, staffers on both sides were now energized by the prospect of a deal. After months of meetings and false starts, they were about to make history. But two last-minute offhand comments planted the seeds of its demise.

As they were finishing, Boehner mentioned that economic growth had to be included in the calculations. As the economy grows, tax revenues grow in tandem. So a tax rate of 35 percent raises more tax money in a $17 trillion economy than in a $15 trillion economy. Boehner wanted something known as "dynamic scoring," which anticipates that higher economic growth rates will produce more tax revenue. Democrats, on the other hand, wanted to be more cautious: What if the growth did not come as projected? And Geithner tended to think of revenue growth in terms of a higher percentage of the take, not the same tax rate in a larger economy. Still, Boehner's aides thought Geithner was amenable and heard him say, "Yes, we accept that."

Obama officials later denied that they ever agreed to "dynamic scoring," which has been a battleground for liberals and conservatives since the 1980s. These officials added that they would never have agreed to it.[70] It would have been political heresy if they had. The negotiators parted.

Boehner's aides went back to the Hill to work on some details. Brett Loper, a Boehner aide, sent an e-mail to Obama negotiator Rob Nabors just before 7:00 P.M. that night about these final details. Nabors wrote back that they would be working on them.[71]

It was as close to a deal as the negotiators would ever come.

Reenter the almost forgotten Gang of Six.

Unaware that Boehner and Obama had been negotiating a "grand bargain," these six senators had been working intensely on their own spending reduction package. Sen. Tom Coburn, who had left the group in frustration, was now back. The group saw the looming deadline to raise the national debt limit and believed it was time to get their proposals out to their fellow senators. They set an 8:30 A.M. morning briefing for Tuesday, July 19. The Obama-Boehner negotiators were so immersed in their own work that they hardly noticed.[72]

The Senate, however, was paying full attention. The prior week's Moody's downgrade threat had electrified senators. Constituents were lighting up the phones. People were truly worried about another government shutdown or a default on the nation's debt. So the Senate's conference room was packed.[73]

"It's back!" the group's former top cynic, Senator Coburn crowed. Sen. Joe Lieberman said, "Sign me up." Sen. Mike Johanns called the plan "thoughtful, serious," and said, "I'm excited." Sen. Susan Collins was "very encouraged" and said there was a "sense of relief" among everyone in the room.[74]

Though the briefing had been closed to the press, the level of enthusiasm and the big numbers—$3.75 trillion in spending cuts—made it major news. The headlines were upbeat. Reuters led with "New plan offers hope for debt talk progress."[75]

With words like "momentum"[76] and "hope"[77] in the headlines, the Gang of Six plan could hardly be ignored.

But Obama's reaction to this development shocked and surprised House leaders, instantly dooming months of work.

That same afternoon, Obama gave a press conference lauding the Gang of Six plan and drove a stake through the heart of his deal with Boehner.

Days before, he had said of the Boehner negotiations, "I want a deal."[78] But in this press conference he told a different story. The Boehner approach, he said, was "not an approach that could pass both chambers, it's not an approach that I would sign and it's not balanced."

Obama lavished praise on the work of the Gang of Six as "broadly consistent with the approach that I've urged." He implored lawmakers to "start talking turkey and actually getting down to the hard business of crafting a plan."[79]

Boehner and Cantor were stunned. Months of hard work had disappeared in seconds.

The surprises kept coming.

As the two House leaders were discussing what the day's turnabout meant, the phone rang. It was a White House staffer with whom they had been working for weeks. As far as that official knew, the White House still wanted to cut a deal.[80]

Only the terms had changed. Drastically.

As President Obama stood praising the Gang of Six proposal, just two days after taking Boehner and Cantor into his confidence, the president's aides began to feel uneasy. In his rush to link himself with the hope and positive energy of the senators' proposals, Obama unwittingly painted himself in a corner. He had not been scheduled to speak to the media that day, and aides were surprised when he ducked into the press room to take the mic.

Daley was concerned. "The Democratic leaders already thought we were idiot negotiators," he said. "So I called [Boehner chief of staff] Barry [Jackson] and said, 'What are we going to do here? How are we going to sell Democrats to take $800 billion [in increased revenue] when Republican senators have signed on to nearly $2 trillion?' "[81]

Obama's negotiators had dropped a bomb on Boehner and Cantor. They needed $400 billion in new tax revenue so that Obama could save face with his party and his base.[82]

In a meeting with the president later that day, Boehner opened by expressing continued support for striking "a big deal." But he told Obama that Republicans could not sign off on $1.2 trillion in new taxes. "I cannot go there," he said. Nor could he even sell $800 billion in tax increases—the Gang of Six's cornerstone—without cuts in federal health entitlements.

Sure enough, on the morning of July 20, congressional Democrats began to grumble. If three GOP senators—four, actually, as Lamar Alexander, the Senate's No. 3 Republican, had since signed on—could embrace the Gang of Six plan, why couldn't Obama get Boehner to do the same?

It was an unrealistic complaint. The dynamics of the House and Senate are very different and the whole House had just been through a tough election whose top issue was the national debt. Only one-third of the Senate was up for election in 2010 and many Democrats had lost.

Nor were Democratic interest groups eager for compromise. "Seeing a Democratic president take taxing the rich off the table and instead push a deal that will lead to Social Security, Medicare, and Medicaid benefit cuts is like entering a bizarre parallel universe," said Stephanie Taylor, cofounder of the Progressive Change Campaign Committee, a Washington-based Democratic group.

White House budget director Jack Lew met with congressional staff at the White House to discuss some of the technical details. The bill would have to be split in two because of time constraints.

The next morning, July 21, aides to Boehner and Cantor gathered again at the White House. During a two-hour meeting, the two sides discussed the details of a deal, never actually turning down the president's request for more tax revenue.

Boehner met with Obama to save the "grand compromise." Responding to pressure from Democrats who thought he was giving away too much, the president pushed back, insisting on another $400 billion in new revenue.

But his position made it even harder for Boehner, whose new majority didn't want any new taxes. The meeting ended soon after it had begun. Both leaders had big decisions to make.

Obama phoned Boehner at 4 P.M. on July 21. Boehner did not return the call until 5:30 P.M. the next day, when he reluctantly said he needed more time.

Then Obama fired a final torpedo. At a hastily called press briefing on Friday night, Obama said Boehner had called him half an hour earlier and "indicated he was going to be walking away" from the compromise the two of them had been privately working on. Obama said angrily that he had been "left at the altar."

In reality, it was Obama who was walking away. Boehner had said he needed more time to square the deal with the circle of conservative opposition. It was going to be a tough sell, but perhaps doable.

There is evidence that Boehner was right. In the interim period before Boehner returned Obama's call, the House debated the Boehner plan but postponed the final vote because of lack of support within the House GOP conference. In a "Dear Colleague" letter released later that night, after Obama's press conference, Boehner accused the White House of having "moved the goal posts" duing their negotiations. "The president demanded $400 billion more" in revenues when the two of them met Thursday, Boehner said, which was politically impossible—and Obama likely knew that.

Also that same Friday, the Senate voted down the House's "Cut, Cap and Balance" bill, the measure favored by Republicans that would reduce spending, limit the federal debt to a single increase, and move to a balanced budget over a few years.

The next day, President Obama asked congressional leaders to join him at the White House for what turned out to be another round of fruitless talks. Everyone sensed that time was running out. By Wednesday, July 27, fifty-three members of the Senate—Democrats and independents who caucused with them—announced their opposition to the Boehner plan.

On Friday, July 29, the Speaker, who rarely addresses the body over which he presides, came to the floor of the House of Represenatives. He reminded the members about the looming credit downgrade and the threat of a government shutdown. He begged them to pass an updated version of the compromise that he had negotiated earlier with the president. Obama had already walked away from that deal when he demanded $400 billion more in revenues. The updated Boehner plan passed in the House, 218–210.

It was an incredible strategic victory. Most of the Republicans who voted for it didn't like it.

Boehner's plan was immediately sent to the Senate, where Democratic leaders put it on the back burner: It too closely resembled a bill that they had voted down only days before. The next day, Saturday, July 30, the Senate took up a plan from Senate Majority Leader Harry Reid, but delayed a final vote.

Boehner played his last card. The House preemptively voted down the Reid plan before the Senate could weigh in. This meant that the White House would have to negotiate either with Boehner, or with Senate Minority Leader Mitch McConnell.

Despite his months working with Boehner, Obama went to McConnell.

On the last day of July, President Obama entered the East Room, the same room where back in June, Republicans had scolded him about demoguery.

Now he faced a crowd of reporters. He gazed into his teleprompter and began to repeat what by now was an all too familiar mantra. The only reason he couldn't complete a grand bargain, Obama said, was "because a significant number of Republicans in Congress are insisting on a different approach—a cuts-only approach—an approach that doesn't ask the wealthiest Americans or biggest corporations to contribute anything at all."[83]

It was a revealing leadership choice. Obama preferred to attack a compromise.

While a bold move, it meant that he would be held responsible if the nation's creditworthiness were downgraded or the government defaulted on its debt payments.

On Monday, August 1, the House of Representatives passed a debt plan. Boehner called it a win of sorts because it was "all spending cuts. The White House bid to raise taxes has been shut down."[84]

The next day, the Senate passed its version of the bill and entered into a quick reconciliation conference with House, and both houses passed the final version. It was raced down Pennsylvania Avenue for a presidential signature, just hours before the debt deadline.[85]

In the end, the president did not get the new revenues he sought. Instead, a mechanism was put in place to automatically make massive cuts in defense and discretionary spending—unless Congress approved new spending cuts by January 1, 2013. The can was kicked one more block down the road.

Standard and Poor's downgraded America's credit on Friday, August 5. Moody's made a similar move. In the following weeks, Obama's public approval rating dipped to 39 percent, the lowest of his administration.[86]

Congress was not happy with Obama, either. A Senate Democrat anonymously told *The New York Times,* "We are watching him turn into Jimmy Carter right before our eyes."[87]

If the United States were a parliamentary democracy, Obama would have been removed by a "no confidence" vote in the late summer of 2011.

The test of any leader, especially any American president, is his ability to draw others to his position—to persuade and to pull. To do this, leaders must be trusted by their rivals and adversaries to bargain in good faith and to give something in return.

Instead, Obama delayed negotiations while warning of default and attacking his political rivals. When that pressure failed, he bargained between bouts of emotional outbursts. On the verge of an historic deal, he surprised his staff by speaking to the press in a way that upended months of deliberations. In the end, his political rivals in the House would never trust him again and his political allies in the Senate would be forever wary of him.

The test of any president is working with leaders of the other party, even if their political philosophies are miles apart. President Reagan worked with House Speaker Tip O'Neill. President Clinton worked with House Speaker Newt Gingrich. President George W. Bush worked with House Speaker Nancy Pelosi. Obama simply wasn't able to constructively work with leaders with whom he had sharp disagreements.

Worse still, he had failed to avert the crisis that he had been warning about for months: a downgrade in America's creditworthiness.

CHAPTER 4

KILLING BIN LADEN LOUDLY

Many of Obama's critics still view a President who rid the world of Osama bin Laden (something that George Bush failed to do) and helped bring down Muammar Qaddafi (something that Ronald Reagan failed to do) as supinely selling out American power.

—David Remnick, *The New Yorker,* September 5, 2011[1]

Obama's critics overlook his "real accomplishments, achieved despite a brutally divided government. Lost in the shouting is the fact that Obama . . . authorized the risky mission that got Osama bin Laden."

—Bill Keller, *The New York Times,* September 18, 2011[2]

President Obama's greatest achievement, in the minds of independent voters as well as large pluralities of both liberals and conservatives, is killing Osama bin Laden. It was swift, decisive, and bold.

Ordering the bin Laden mission is easily Obama's most popular decision and the one that seems to showcase his best qualities as a leader. The Obama campaign presents his decision as bold, gutsy, and decisive. More than ten years after the September 11 atrocities, bin Laden had eluded capture, judgment, and justice. Then, in one masterstroke, Obama did what Presidents Bush and Clinton had failed to do. The bin Laden raid is portrayed as a defining act of leadership. A champion's knockout blow.

Image is one thing, reality another.

In reality, the president canceled the mission three times in 2011 alone and delayed it throughout 2010 and, according to officials directly involved, Obama stunned his staff with a string of dangerous delays and paralyzing indecision that threatened the mission's timing and nearly compromised its success. Far from being a decisive break with President George W. Bush, senior CIA officials say, the bin Laden mission was built on evidence and sources accumulated in the Bush years—practices and policies that Obama ended on his second day in office. While Obama never publicly gave Bush any credit, many intelligence and military officers involved in the hunt for bin Laden do.

Indeed, the very policies that Obama had criticized as a candidate—the Iraq War, the CIA's secret prisons, seemingly harsh interrogation techniques, and indefinite detention without access to defense attorneys—were instrumental in locating bin Laden. Obama ended many of those Bush practices within days of being sworn in as president.

A closer look at the tangled history of the Obama administration's bin Laden operation and the role of the president and his senior staff, paints a starkly different portrait of Obama's leadership style—paralyzing indecision, political calculation, and a squandering of intelligence secrets.

Finally, the Obama administration's account of Pakistan's role is misleading and incomplete. A colonel in Pakistan's feared intelligence service, the Inter-Services Institute or ISI, provided vital help in locating bin Laden when he walked into the CIA's Islamabad station in August 2010. And Pakistan's Army chief of staff may have been briefed in December 2010, five months before the nighttime raid on bin Laden's concrete castle. Far from taking a risk, there are indications that a cover story had been developed with the Pakistani military and that Obama had their tacit consent for the mission.

• • •

Bin Laden had ordered attacks on Americans on three continents for more than two decades, killing or maiming some six thousand people worldwide. On 9/11, his attacks on Americans at home stole their casual sense of safety, replacing it with a reservoir of anxiety that would surface suddenly whenever a plane flew low over a skyline or a passenger acted strangely. He made Americans feel afraid and that fear made them angry.

Key clues to bin Laden's hideout, especially the identity of the courier who was his main link to the outside world, were first uncovered in the Bush years. Thanks to that patient and painstaking work by career interrogators and intelligence officers, the CIA found bin Laden's hideout in the first few months of the Obama administration. Yet it took the president almost two years to make a decision to act on this valuable intelligence as he deliberated and delayed. Meanwhile, he allowed his aides and cabinet secretaries to war, to conspire, and to jockey for position.

Absorbed by feuding among Obama's inner circle, the cabinet members and officials charged with national security sometimes kept White House senior staff, and the president himself, in the dark as vital decisions loomed because, incredibly, they needed to keep the president's most-trusted advisor, Jarrett, from killing the bin Laden mission in its cradle. Indeed, the operation was repeatedly called off, reduced in scope, or otherwise delayed, often by the president himself.

Obama demanded complete certainty about every aspect of the intelligence on bin Laden and the competing plans to eliminate the arch-terrorist—something veteran intelligence and military officials repeatedly cautioned him was "impossible." Without perfect certainty, Obama often refused to make decisions. To some aides, he was simply being prudent and careful; to others, he risked losing bin Laden just as Presidents Clinton and Bush had. If the intelligence about bin Laden's whereabouts was correct, it would be the first time the federal government knew precisely where the al-Qaeda leader was since August 20, 1998, when President Clinton tried to kill him with a cruise-missile strike. Some aides feared that if they missed this chance, it might be another twelve years before they got a similar opportunity.

Throughout the nearly eighteen months of planning the bin Laden operation—eventually code-named Neptune's Spear—the president's closest advisor, Valerie Jarrett, played a pivotal role. Once again, she exercised her Rasputin-like magic over Obama, provoking bitter fights with the CIA director and secretaries of state and defense. Jarrett, who saw herself as the president's protector, repeatedly warned that Obama could be blamed if the operation went awry.

When the president consulted with the CIA director or the secretary of defense, he often seemed to be "playing for time," canceling meetings with senior officials that would require him to make decisions or abruptly walking out midway through conferences with his senior advisors, cabinet secretaries, and military officers.

When Obama walked out, he would wander the White House in search of Jarrett. If she had been in the meeting with him, he would signal for her to join him. Her advice and reassurance was critical, as always.

As a result, Obama was often disengaged as the bin Laden operation took shape; he left critical decisions to the then–CIA director Leon Panetta, then–secretary of defense Robert Gates, and Secretary of State Hillary Clinton. Obama feared taking responsibility for a risky raid that might go tragically wrong.

On the handful of occasions when Obama did get involved in shaping the covert operation, it was to cause delays, to change, or to cancel parts of the plan that had been previously agreed on. Obama canceled the mission three times at the urging of Valerie Jarrett, according to an official affiliated with the Joint Special Forces Command, who had knowledge of the operation and who requested anonymity. Obama canceled the mission in January, again in February, and a third time in March 2011.

Contrary to the later suggestions of some officials, the president did not give this consequential operation his undivided attention. During the few days before the assault on the bin Laden compound, Obama insisted on traveling to Alabama to console hurricane victims, giving a commencement address at Miami Dade College, and touring the NASA facilities at Cape Canaveral. When a space shuttle launch was canceled, he visited anyway. On Saturday night, just hours before the operation was due to begin, he joked with Donald Trump at the White House Correspondents' Association annual dinner. Sunday, on the day of the raid, he played golf and complained loudly of having to return to the White House after only nine holes—just as the Navy SEALs' helicopters lifted off in pursuit of their elusive target.[3]

But once bin Laden's body had been dumped at sea, the president sprang into action and scrambled to seize credit—presenting a muddled and inaccurate narrative that undermined the media's confidence in the White House's knowledge of operational details. Most appallingly, the president's headline-grabbing address ultimately endangered Americans by denying Special Forces the secrecy needed to launch surprise attacks based on intelligence gathered in bin Laden's compound.

The official story of the bin Laden mission was so inaccurate and incomplete that the full account has never been told. New evidence about the hunt for bin Laden, the raid itself, and its aftermath shows us something important about Obama's leadership style. It also diminishes his greatest success.

The CIA and U.S. Special Forces had been searching for bin Laden for nearly ten years. During the battle of Tora Bora in the White Mountains of Afghanistan, in December 2001, a CIA team intercepted a brief string of radio commands from bin Laden. The team tried triangulating. Perhaps they were within a mile of the archterrorist, lurking somewhere in the crags above.

Then, nothing. Static. Silence.

A few days later, bin Laden's driver and bodyguard, Ibrahim al-Qosi, was captured carrying his master's satellite phone. He later admitted to interrogators that bin Laden himself gave him the phone, instructed him to leave it switched on, and told him to walk west—away from Pakistan's frontier. He did. Bin Laden went east. The ruse worked. The decoy radio signals lured American special forces and the CIA's paramilitary team into tracking the wrong man—giving bin Laden time to escape to Pakistan.

Despite weeks of intensive interrogation, the uncomplicated truth was that al-Qosi simply didn't know where bin Laden was.

And neither did anyone in the U.S. government.

Gen. Richard Myers, then-chairman of the Joint Chiefs of Staff, told me he wasn't even confident that bin Laden was in Tora Bora. "Our intelligence thought he [bin Laden] *might* be there. There was a high like-lihood," he said, "but no certainty."

Most important, the U.S. military had no set of map coordinates where they believed bin Laden might be. So there was no precise target where a laser could guide a bomb to destroy or a particular cave that a commander could order his irregular forces to assault. "If we had known what cave bin Laden was in," Myers said, "Tommy Franks would have drug him out himself."

General Myers recalled a conversation with Gen. Tommy Franks, who was in command of military operations in the Afghan theater. In December 2001, the CIA and the military had relatively few people on the ground: a few two- and four-man teams of forward air controllers and CIA paramilitary forces. Winter winds kept the earlier versions of the Predator drones from flying and much of America's panoply of air assets— everything from sophisticated surveillance planes to B-52 bombers—had yet to reach the region. The thousands of Afghan irregulars drawn from the Northern Alliance forces "didn't know the South well," Myers said, and often didn't speak the local languages or have local human-intelligence sources. A bigger question: "We had no idea of the [northern] Afghans' willingness to fight."

But General Franks wanted the prize: Osama bin Laden, dead or alive. They decided to try. The enemy was impressed with the sustained fire, disciplined troop movements, and precise air attacks that came from un-seen and unheard aircraft, at more than twenty thousand feet overhead, which seemed to come out of nowhere. Myers remembers the enemy radio intercepts. "They thought that God was on our side. And we wanted them to think that."

If he was ever there, bin Laden slipped away in the darkness and con-fusion of battle.

Officials would spend years chasing false leads. Reports put bin Laden in Lake Tharthar, northwest of Baghdad, at a Quetta café in west-ern Pakistan, in a bolthole in Iran, a mountain hideout in Yemen, a ship yard in Manila. Not one of these tips checked out.

In a never-before reported detail, the CIA believed it was close to get-ting bin Laden twice in the years between 2001 and 2005, according to

Myers. "This lady had been working at the CIA for six to eight years and she and her team came down to the Pentagon for a briefing." She had been involved in the hunt for bin Laden since 1998. The agency needed Defense department personnel and equipment to attempt the capture-or-kill raid and therefore needed the defense secretary's approval. The hard part, he explained, wasn't finding out where bin Laden had been, but where he would likely be. This time, the CIA had "high confidence" that there would be a meeting of high-level al-Qaeda officers "and that bin Laden will be there."

Secretary of Defense Donald Rumsfeld and Myers had to weigh risks and rewards. The al-Qaeda meeting would be in Pakistan, where a raid would send political shockwaves that might bring down America's ally. At the time, "Pakistan cooperation was very good. Musharraf was a good partner," Myers said. Nevertheless, Pakistan was only told about American military operations after they had occurred. Operational security was the stated reason and Pakistan seemed to accept that reality. It wasn't a "group hug," Myers said. Lives were on the line.

And the evidence wasn't overwhelming. "The Secretary and I felt that the information wasn't that compelling." The CIA's request was denied.

Later, the Pakistanis conducted a raid of their own at the location that won the CIA's attention. Bin Laden had never been there, Pakistan's intelligence liaison officer said.

The CIA had been hunting bin Laden ever since the August 7, 1998, bombings of two U.S. embassies in East Africa that killed 224 people, including 12 American diplomats. "That certainly got our attention," Myers said.

President Clinton responded with a cruise missile strike that famously missed bin Laden. The archterrorist gave a press conference the following day, taunting the United States. The attack "was perceived by the adversary as a weak response. It was their technology that came after us. They didn't put their people at risk," Myers said. "It emboldened them."

By 2000, when he was vice chairman of the Joint Chiefs of Staff, Myers remembers President Clinton's national security advisor, Sandy Berger, pressing the CIA and the military to develop options and intelligence assets. "There were no tight or light options," he said. Afghanistan is a landlocked country some seven thousand miles from the American mainland.

America had no real allies in the late 1990s that neighbored Afghanistan. Iran, which the U.S. State Department had repeatedly branded as the world's largest state sponsor of terrorism, was an avowed enemy. The post-Soviet states to the north had no meaningful relationship with America's military or intelligence services. The Pressler amendment, passed by South Dakota Republican senator Larry Pressler, had cut off military-to-military contacts between U.S. and Pakistani forces. Intelligence and diplomatic contacts were frequent, but not deep. "There was no sense of urgency."

The hunt for bin Laden accelerated before the September 11 attacks. The CIA had developed a "pretty good read" on bin Laden's "signature," based on the number of vehicles, number of people, and other factors, Myers said. In the first few months, planning to strike bin Laden shifted to high gear. The internal debate was not whether to hit bin Laden, but when. By March 2001, when Myers became involved in the meetings of the deputy national security advisor and his counterparts in the intelligence and military agencies, a sense of urgency had emerged. The debate was "do we go for it in late summer or wait for early fall to go for it?" he said.

Weather and available aircraft were the technical considerations driving the debate. No one in the American government realized that they were in a race against time.

After the September 11 attacks, the intelligence community was not starting from scratch. It had more than three years of effort. The war helped the agency clear away bureaucratic hurdles. And the effort massively expanded—all of which laid the groundwork for Obama's opportunity to order the bin Laden raid.

All sixteen intelligence agencies of the U.S. government went to work sifting the world for clues. New units of mixed special forces, such as Team 181, were formed and disbanded. Bin Laden's video and audiotapes, delivered to Al Jazeera via a series of couriers who didn't know each other, were scrutinized by the technical divisions of the CIA and National Security Agency. All attempts to trace the couriers failed. Powerful spy satellites, run by the National Reconnaissance Office, intercepted phone calls, texts, e-mails, and other electronic data from sources all over the globe. In the National Security Agency's "puzzle palace," teams translated a torrent of satellite-intercepted transmissions and hunted for leads. While a growing number of al-Qaeda operatives were identified, tracked, and captured, bin Laden himself remained remote and invisible.

Congress repeatedly raised the reward for information on bin Laden's whereabouts: first $5 million, then $25 million, and later $50 million. It was the largest reward ever offered by the U.S. government for a fugitive. Thousands of matchbooks with the bin Laden reward above the striking strip were distributed throughout Pakistan and Afghanistan. "Wanted" posters in local languages were tacked up all over Pakistan's Northwest Frontier Province and Federally-Administered Tribal Areas. The region was blanketed with radio ads in six languages. The few leads the campaign generated proved useless.

FBI "legat officers," who work inside U.S. embassies around the world as liaisons between the bureau and foreign intelligence and law enforcement agencies, worked overtime to develop information on bin Laden and other high-value targets. Working along parallel lines, CIA officers in stations around the world pushed their foreign counterparts for clues. This double-teaming effort of foreign intelligence services had several advantages. It allowed foreign services to communicate vital information to the U.S. government, even if a personality conflict with a CIA officer or FBI special agent might have otherwise prevented such contacts (which happened in Khartoum and Amman in the early Bush years). It also vastly increased the points of contact between allied services and their counterparts in America.

Arab intelligence services, in particular, had long kept an eye on extremist groups, both within their borders and across the region. They had a depth of knowledge about bin Laden and the al-Qaeda network that was initially lacking in America's intelligence services, especially in the immediate aftermath of the September 11 attacks. And Arab services had other means of collecting information—warrantless wiretaps of their own citizens and others, and interrogation methods that would never even be considered by Western governments—which provided some useful nuggets. Virtually all of the "human intelligence" collected by the CIA was, in reality, generated by foreign intelligence services, due to a series of legal restrictions on the agency imposed in the 1970s and 1990s. These liaison relationships with Arab intelligence services produced important pieces of the puzzle, but as one intelligence official said, "no smoking gun" about bin Laden's whereabouts.

European intelligence services also made valuable contributions. Britain's MI-5 and MI-6 provided phone intercepts, arrest reports, and facts from their well-stocked storehouses of information on radical Islamic groups. The French intelligence community, collectively known as *La Piscine*—"the swimming pool"—presented a wealth of information on the movements of terror suspects and, along with Belgium and Luxembourg, helped track and halt the movement of al-Qaeda's money.

Swiss intelligence, through the mobile telecom provider Swisscom, helped track cell phones of al-Qaeda operatives who used Swisscom SIM cards and phone cards, which in 2002 and 2003 meant most of al-Qaeda's senior leadership. Germany's *Bundeskriminalamt*, that nation's version of the FBI, developed new leads on al-Qaeda recruiters and the pre-attack movements of the September 11 bombers, and intercepted phone calls from Khalid Shaikh Mohammed, then-al-Qaeda's No. 3, to sleeper agents across Europe and North Africa. Denmark, Sweden, Poland, Italy, and the states of the former Yugoslavia, all added bits of new information on bin Laden or al-Qaeda.

Meanwhile, the U.S. Army maintained an interrogation facility near Bagram Air Base in Kabul, Afghanistan, where uniformed interrogators questioned al-Qaeda and Taliban prisoners and examined captured documents. They, too, were always on the lookout for information about bin Laden and contributed many, many valuable shards.

The CIA's so-called "bin Laden station," a series of worn cubicles at its sprawling tree-shrouded Langley, Virginia, campus perched above the Potomac River, coordinated and collated the cascade of foreign intelligence reports. Drinking hot coffee and cold Diet Coke, the CIA team reviewed reams of old and new reports on bin Laden, hunting for clues. Working long days, many CIA officers did not see the sun unless they stepped outside for a smoke.

Even the U.S. Library of Congress, one of the world's largest collections of books and official documents, played its part in the hunt for the archterrorist. Raymond Ibrahim, a diligent researcher in the library's Arabic-language collection, discovered a trove of obscure Arabic texts in

2005. They had been published years before the September 11 attacks and were written by Osama bin Laden and his deputy Ayman al-Zawahiri. Ibrahim painstakingly compiled, translated, and annotated those works and ultimately shared his research with the CIA. In 2007, he published *The Al Qaeda Reader,* a compendium of his findings.

Every resource of the world's most powerful government was brought to bear in the search for the world's most wanted man. Yet despite oceans of money, fleets of intelligence officers, and floods of high-technology advances (satellites, stealth planes, supercomputers, ships, and search programs), bin Laden remained invisible.

All these worldwide efforts, involving hundreds of thousands of man-hours, were part of what intelligence professionals refer to as a "mosaic effort." A "mosaic" is a picture formed by many tiny tiles of different shapes and colors. The aim was to assemble enough data points, through immense human efforts and the crunching of computerized databases, to paint a pointillist portrait of bin Laden.

Assembling the mosaic was an arduous effort. One intelligence professional involved explained it this way: "Imagine someone has dumped some of the pieces for a hundred different puzzles on your desk. Many of the pieces are upside down and cannot be turned over. And you don't have the picture on the box cover to show you what the puzzle is supposed to look like."[4]

The hunt for bin Laden was made immeasurably difficult because the terror leader was wily and disciplined. Bin Laden seldom, if ever, used his satellite or cell phones after 2001. He largely avoided electronic data systems, such as e-mail and text messages. He rarely moved in daylight hours and, after 2005, he barely moved at all.

Bin Laden communicated only with a small cadre of al-Qaeda leaders and used only trusted couriers. The couriers themselves did not carry the messages directly to or from bin Laden, but used a "dead drop" for yet another courier to retrieve the message. A "dead drop" is a specified place where a message can be hidden to be picked up by another party. They can be bottoms of trash cans in public parks or masonry cracks in public parking garages—any place where someone could routinely and lawfully visit anytime, day or night. And the couriers usually did not know each other;

if one were captured, he could not reveal the identity or the location of the next courier in the chain.

Finding and capturing couriers became a cottage industry among spies and special forces. It was very hard work and required a bit of luck. The chase usually began with an electronic intercept (phone, text, or e-mail) that led to a "person of interest" who would be tracked by air or ground. Over many patient weeks of watching, the intelligence team would decide if the person was a part of al-Qaeda or simply a friend or family member of someone in the terror network. This was essentially a budgeting decision, allocating money and manpower to the most promising leads. Sometimes U.S. intelligence operatives would suspend surveillance and "circle back" later. More often, once a surveillance target was dropped, he stayed off America's radar. Occasionally, one was identified as a courier and was marked for capture.

Capturing a courier usually required a special team to move covertly in hostile territory, seize the target without mortally wounding or killing him, and safely move him to a waiting American aircraft or submarine. This was always difficult and dangerous.

In the later years of the Bush administration, captured computers, cell phones, and commanders provided more detailed information on targets. It made the job of locating possible suspects to track much easier and vastly improved America's ability to assess potential targets. But it didn't reduce the perils of such "snatch and grab" missions.

While capturing couriers often generated excitement in the intelligence community, it rarely provided war-winning information. Consider the case of the courier who carried messages between bin Laden and Mullah Omar, the head of the Taliban. When he was seized in Pakistan in 2004, CIA officers initially had high hopes that he could lead them to either bin Laden or Mullah Omar. Despite extensive debriefings by experienced military and CIA interrogators, he had no useful information. As with al-Qosi, he simply did not know. Al-Qaeda's strategy of compartmentalizing information worked.

But captured commanders sometimes knew what couriers did not.

The U.S. Navy's detention facility at Guantánamo Bay—already the center of global controversy over allegedly harsh interrogation tactics—

and CIA "black sites"—secret prisons—were ground zero in the effort to find bin Laden. The Obama administration "would never have had the opportunity to do the right thing had it not been for some extraordinary work during the George W. Bush administration," former head of the CIA's National Clandestine Service Jose A. Rodriguez wrote. "No single tactic, technique or approach led to the successful operation against bin Laden. But those who suggest that it was all a result of a fresh approach taken after Jan. 20, 2009 [when Obama was sworn in], are mistaken."[5] Without the work of counterterrorism professionals in the Bush years, bin Laden never would have been found.

Yet Obama never publicly credited his predecessor and only vaguely thanked the intelligence community as a whole.

The path to bin Laden's lair began in 2004, when an al-Qaeda operative was captured in Iraq. Obama had opposed the war that enabled the U.S. military to track and capture the terror leader less than a fifteen-minute helicopter trip from Baghdad. He was trying to arrange a meeting with Abu Musab al-Zarqawi, the Jordanian leader of the insurgent group that called itself "Al-Qaeda in Iraq."

After a brief battlefield interrogation, uniformed soldiers turned the captured terrorist over to the CIA, which transported him to a secret "black site." While the prisoner was not "waterboarded," he was made to cooperate after receiving several of the agency's eleven "enhanced interrogation techniques." Obama faulted these techniques while he was campaigning for president.

The techniques—which include a single belly slap with spread fingers to throwing the detainee against a false wall that is designed to collapse while making a loud bang (known as "walling")—worked. As per regulations, a doctor and translator were present throughout the interrogation. He told CIA officials a number of valuable things, including that bin Laden had ceased communicating by electronic means and that he communicated solely through a courier named "Abu Ahmed al-Kuwaiti," Brother Ahmed from Kuwait.

As head of the CIA's counterterrorism center, Rodriguez drew two conclusions. Bin Laden no longer had direct control over his terror organization and that "capturing him would be much harder than we had thought."

After his September 2006 transfer from a CIA "black site" to Guantánamo Bay, Khalid Shaikh Mohammed (KSM), the operational planner of the September 11 attacks, was interviewed by a U.S. Navy officer. The interviewer was friendly and brought food. Food was important to KSM. Al-Qaeda's former No. 3 had requested double rations shortly after his arrival in Cuba. This request was quickly granted and meant that the five-foot four-inch tall terror master was eating almost six thousand calories per day of halal food, carefully certified by an Islamic authority.

One navy officer familiar with the interrogation experience of KSM said he liked the attention as much as the food. He had grown used to the routine and was usually cooperative, especially if the food bribe had been paid.

But not today. When a naval officer asked KSM about a character known mostly by the name al-Kuwaiti, he responded in an uncharacteristically gruff tone of voice: "He is nobody." He said that he had never heard of the man. But the look on his face gave him away. There was "horror when he heard the name," Rodriguez wrote.[6]

KSM's strangely sharp response intrigued the intelligence officer. Maybe they had something here, he wondered.

Later, a handwritten message from KSM was intercepted. The planner of the September 11 attacks wrote: "Tell them nothing about the courier!"

Interrogations of another detainee, Abu Faraj al-Libi, who had replaced KSM as al-Qaeda's No. 3 and had been seized in Pakistan in 2005, yielded more. Al-Libi had lived in Abbottabad for a year before his capture.[7] He provided more information about this mysterious figure, who, it so happened, was bin Laden's key surviving courier. By ping-ponging among KSM, al-Libi, and other high-value detainees, a composite portrait of bin Laden's courier slowly emerged in 2006 and 2007. At this point, no one knew that this courier would actually lead them to bin Laden. It was simply another courier hunt. No need to get excited.

But by 2008, the excitement grew. U.S. intelligence now knew two valuable things about him: Sheikh Abu Ahmed al-Kuwaiti was a *nom de guerre,* and the alias belonged to the man who was bin Laden's link to the outside world. Known variously as Shaikh Abu Ahmed, Arshad Khan, and Mohammed Arshad (different Guantánamo detainees knew him by different names), this Kuwait-born Pakistani most likely saw bin Laden on a daily basis. If they could find that man, they could follow him to bin Laden.[8]

Still, finding bin Laden's most trusted man was many times harder than finding a needle in a haystack. By 2008, the CIA had a name, several aliases, and a sketch of his face based on the recollections of a number of detainees held at Guantánamo. He could be anywhere in the world, using an unknown alias. He may have changed his appearance. He could even be dead.

No matter. The hunt continued. The agency focused on Pakistan because more high-value al-Qaeda operatives had been captured there than anywhere else on earth—more than in Afghanistan and Iraq combined. Additionally, KSM and al-Libi had last seen the courier in Pakistan. As a matter of pure probability, it made sense to put Pakistan at the center of the search grid.

It was the waning days of the Bush administration. America, after more than seven years of patient and persistent intelligence work, was closer than ever to finding bin Laden. "No one thought about the election," one intelligence officer involved in the operation said. "We were just doing our jobs."

Is it fair to say the foundation for finding bin Laden was laid in the Bush years and that Bush-era interrogation efforts played a vital part? "Absolutely," he said. "Without question."

Back in Washington, President Obama would soon move into the White House and new faces began appearing atop the national security organizational chart. But for most intelligence officers, nothing changed. The mission was the same.

Heading up the mission was Leon Panetta, sworn in as CIA director on February 19, 2009.[9]

In the intelligence community, Panetta was a surprising choice as Director of Central Intelligence. Born in 1938 to Italian immigrants who ran a restaurant in Monterey, California, he learned to relate to a wide variety of people by working in the family business.

Taking an early interest in politics, he was elected student body president at Monterey High School.[10] After he majored in political science in college and earned a law degree from Santa Clara University, graduating magna cum laude, he began thinking about a career in politics. He had also acquired some intelligence experience at an early age: During the Vietnam War, Panetta served as a military intelligence officer for the U.S. Army until his discharge in 1966.

He entered politics as a liberal Republican and worked variously as a legislative assistant to Sen. Thomas Kuchel (R-California), as an assistant to Robert H. Finch, Richard Nixon's secretary of health, education, and welfare, and as executive assistant to John Lindsay, perhaps the most liberal Republican ever to be mayor of New York City.

But the New York experience was traumatic. Lindsay's costly concessions to public-sector unions and his policies expanding the city's social safety net drove many working and middle-class voters to move to lower-tax and lower-crime neighborhoods outside of the city—shrinking tax collections while expenses climbed. New York City suffered a series of financial crises and nearly declared bankruptcy.

After a period of reflection, Panetta decided to switch parties and, in 1976, won a seat in Congress. He served first as a member and later as chairman of the powerful House Budget Committee until 1993. There the new Democrat won a reputation as a liberal on social and economic issues, a skeptic on foreign interventions, and an honest broker on budgetary matters. He won the trust of lawmakers in both parties, an unusual feat in an increasingly combative Congress.

President Clinton tapped him to run the Office of Management and Budget at the White House, where he worked to develop a tough plan that put the federal budget on a glide path toward balance in 1998.

During countless budget meetings, Panetta became close to both Bill and Hillary Clinton. They shared a kind of liberal realism. While they had goals for reshaping society, they understood that public institutions moved incrementally and that Congress and the media had to be won over.

With the departure of Clinton's longtime Arkansas friend and White House chief of staff Mack McLarty, the president's choice of a successor seemed obvious. Panetta became chief of staff in 1994 and his bond with the Clintons deepened.

Panetta returned to public life with a phone call from President-Elect Obama. The first black president wanted the longtime liberal critic of the CIA to run the agency. It was a storyline that would have seemed too improbable even for the television series *The West Wing.*"[11]

Still, there was no substantial opposition in the U.S. Senate to confirming Panetta. Though some Senate staffers pointed to his limited experience in intelligence, others saw an opportunity for a fresh approach, free from the habits and biases of career experts. Among the senators themselves there was even less doubt. Stalwarts from both parties had known Panetta for years; they liked and trusted him. He was confirmed on February 12, 2009, and sworn in as director of central intelligence by Vice President Joe Biden a few days later.[12]

Once in the post, Panetta surprised both agency staff and his handful of critics on Capitol Hill. He strongly supported bringing the fight to the enemy and made targeting al-Qaeda leaders with drone attacks a key initiative.[13] Finding bin Laden topped his agenda.

In a series of transition briefings for Panetta, agency analysts laid out their leads on the reclusive al-Qaeda leader. One of the most promising was the courier al-Kuwaiti. If the CIA could find him, Panetta was told, they could find bin Laden. This immediately got Panetta's attention.

In March 2009, Panetta met with Obama and, in a wide-ranging conversation, explained that the CIA was actively searching for bin Laden's courier. Obama nodded politely, so Panetta moved on to the next agenda item. There would be more to say if the CIA actually found al-Kuwaiti.

A single phone call gave al-Kuwaiti away in August 2009.[14] It lasted less than a minute, but the spy satellites parked over Pakistan intercepted and recorded the call. It was logged into the National Security Agency's enormous databases. A keyword search alerted intelligence analysts. Soon America's electronic sleuths were tracking al-Kuwaiti through his mobile phone. A technical team mapped the locations of every phone al-Kuwaiti made a call to or received a call from. It showed red dots all over Afghanistan and Pakistan.

A covert ground team eventually spotted al-Kuwaiti himself in the Bilal Town section of Abbottabad, a prosperous enclave north of Pakistan's capital city of Islamabad. He liked to roam the busy streets of Abbottabad in a white sport-utility vehicle, with a distinctive red rhino emblazoned on its spare tire cover. It made him easy to follow.

Within weeks al-Kuwaiti was tracked repeatedly entering and exiting a mysterious walled compound. Seen from the sky, the compound was an imperfect diamond shape, with thick concrete walls ranging in height from ten to eighteen feet. Inside the protective walls was a three-story tower with concrete-block privacy walls screening its balconies. In another structure lived a veritable Noah's Ark of farm animals, including buffaloes, cows, and more than a hundred chickens.[15] A third structure seemed to shelter staff members, likely including al-Kuwaiti himself.

The walled compound, which CIA analysts estimated cost well over $1 million to build, had no telephone, Internet, cable television, or electrical wires attached. It seemed unlikely that the complex was simply the home of a wealthy Pakistani. After all, who would build thousands of square feet of living and working space without telephones or external electricity?

A CIA team gained access to Pakistan's official building-permit and ownership records. The paperwork indicated that the building permit for this specially constructed enclave was issued in 2005 and that the property was owned by al-Kuwaiti himself, under the name Arshad Khan. His brother was listed as a co-owner.[16] But neither man seemed to have the financial resources to fund such an elaborate structure. Nor was there any record of a mortgage on the land or buildings. So where would the al-Kuwaiti brothers find the financing for this concrete castle? CIA analysts wondered: Could this strange structure be bin Laden's lair?

The records held another surprise. The land for the bin Laden lair seemed to have been carved out of property owned by the Kakul Military Academy, Pakistan's answer to Sandhurst and West Point.

Panetta had previously ordered surveillance by satellite and drone aircraft. Now he weighed sending in a ground team to watch the Abbottabad compound from a nearby safe house and, in April 2009, intense surveillance began. At the time, the CIA's code name for bin Laden was "the Pacer."

Panetta was a member of "the principals," a group that included the heads of every agency and department involved in national security. Usually, the principals met at the White House. These meetings refined options to be presented to the president for action. Panetta pressed for action without delay. He didn't want bin Laden to slip away again.

At this point, in the spring and summer of 2009, Panetta was not necessarily recommending a ground attack. Any form of attack would do, he said, provided that it provably gets bin Laden, minimizes collateral civilian casualties, and can be carried out with minimal risk to U.S. forces.

What if it isn't him? It doesn't matter, Panetta responded. If it isn't bin Laden, then it's another very senior al-Qaeda leader. At the time, he didn't take a position on the type of attack. It could have been a Predator drone or a B-2 bomber cruise missile. A ground assault, it seems, was not even considered in 2009 or 2010. Secretary of State Hillary Clinton was supportive and Secretary of Defense Robert Gates was, too; he leaned toward a strike.

But Valerie Jarrett, who rarely attended principals meetings, was adamantly opposed. Obama himself was detached and noncommittal. Too many questions. Too many options. He wanted definitive intelligence.

In a search for answers for the president, the CIA intensified its surveillance. An undercover ground team was sent into Abbottabad and rented a house nearby. They soon learned there was another family living with the couriers, and that the composition of that family matched bin Laden's.

The covert CIA team tried various ruses to learn the identity of the compound residents. They offered free door-to-door child vaccinations in order to obtain DNA samples. The compound didn't answer its buzzer, though dozens of neighborhood children did get helpful injections. They even tried to smuggle a camera into the compound itself.[17] That, too, failed.

The first solid evidence that the al-Qaeda leader was, in fact, holed up inside came in the form of a recording of him speaking, picked up on a CIA microphone. The snippet was analyzed and it matched previous recordings of bin Laden's voice.[18]

Panetta again met with Obama in June 2009. The pressure on Obama to act was becoming harder to ignore. Panetta was eager.

Panetta and Obama did not meet often in the White House to discuss bin Laden or any other matter. As CIA director, Panetta visited the White House only nine times in more than twenty-four months, according to official White House Visitor Logs.

(By contrast, Jeremy Ben-Ami visited more than forty times over the same period, according to the same records. Ben-Ami is the executive director of J Street, a Jewish organization devoted to equal rights for Palestinians inside and outside Israel's 1967 borders.)

Panetta did his best to provide Obama with the detail and certainty he craved, despite the haziness inherent in the world of intelligence. Panetta showed the president aerial photographs of the compound, photographs of al-Kuwaiti emerging from his distinctive white SUV, and details of residents at the compound and a "pattern of life" that depicted their daily routine and habits, drawn from the ground team's reports.[19] The effort the CIA expended on the bin Laden operation was described as "extraordinarily concentrated"; but it was not enough for Obama.[20]

The president played for time. He kept demanding more proof, more certainty.

Obama, betraying a certain naïveté about the limits of intelligence, was concerned that there was no "slam-dunk" evidence indicating that bin Laden was actually there. Intelligence professionals often complain about the "CSI effect." This is what happens when elected leaders demand from intelligence services the kind of definitive technical evidence that is supplied to characters on that highly rated television drama. In real life, technical intelligence rarely delivers absolutely convincing proof.

From the perspective of some CIA staffers, the agency had done its job to "find and fix," jargon for determining the location and identity of a targeted individual. All that remained was to "finish the target"[21]—to kill or capture him.

The president wasn't so sure.

Deciding that the intelligence about bin Laden's location was definitive would force the president to make a number of difficult decisions. At this stage, those decisions revolved around what type of air strike to order and how best to manage its consequences.

Once Obama learned that there were women and children present at the site, he was even more reluctant to order military action. The president realized that an air strike could kill noncombatants, provoking enormous outrage in Pakistan.

So at this point it was easier to question the intelligence than to embark on what could turn into a calamitous adventure.

He waited and considered. Bin Laden could be actually somewhere else, or he could escape an attack unscathed. Obama needed no reminding that bin Laden had famously given a press conference in August 1998, cheerfully explaining that he had easily escaped an American cruise-missile strike. Obama didn't want history to repeat itself.

History repeating itself was fuel for constant debate in the months to come. "There wasn't a meeting when someone didn't mention 'Black Hawk Down,'" one staffer said. The botched helicopter rescue of hostages in Iran in April 1980 was another constant theme.[22]

Conversations became a vicious cycle. Panetta could give the president intelligence, but not certainty. Obama insisted on certainty.

At the White House, Obama advisors were told to "interrogate the data" to disprove that bin Laden was in the compound, while the CIA continued surveillance and data collection. The CIA effort was so wide-reaching and expensive that the agency had to make a secret request to Congress to reallocate millions of budgeted dollars to cover the costs.[23]

Late into the process, as Obama's indecision lingered on, Panetta took the unusual step of "red-teaming" the case. He brought the intelligence to other analysts at other agencies—people who had not been involved in the hunt for bin Laden and had no stake in any particular interpretation of the "mosaic"—and asked them for an independent critique of the analysis and an assessment of the likelihood that bin Laden was in the Abbottabad hideaway. The resulting "confidence levels" were between 40 percent and 60 percent. Obama seemed to want the certainty of numbers, even though those confidence levels had more to do with individual personalities and risk aversion than statistical analysis.[24]

Valerie Jarrett, skeptical from the start, made a point of being at virtually every White House meeting concerning bin Laden, except principals meetings. It is a measure of Jarrett's power and omnipresence that, regardless of her domestic affairs title, assistant to the president for Public Engagement and Intergovernmental Affairs, she came to involve herself in the Obama administration's most sensitive and secret foreign policy operation.

Eventually a "war caucus" emerged with Leon Panetta, Hillary Clinton, and Robert Gates favoring action of some kind.

Jarrett opposed the idea. She worried about a backlash against the president if the operation failed, or even if it succeeded. Clinton privately fumed about Jarrett's relentless presence and her injection of political considerations at every turn.[25]

The president remained studiously undecided. He refused to weigh in or commit himself on even small matters related to a possible strike on bin Laden. Such hesitance is usually a treasured trait among state lawmakers or senators because it preserves freedom of movement if a position should later prove unpopular. But it can be frustrating in an executive, maddening in a president. The bin Laden operation would require a long chain of decisions before the final "go" or "no go" decision. Delaying those staging decisions simply raised the risk that bin Laden would somehow slip away.

Throughout 2009 Obama demanded more and more certainty about U.S. intelligence concerning bin Laden. Jarrett repeatedly reminded Obama and other executive-branch officials that the president had campaigned on the "intelligence failures" of the Bush years. There was no need, she said, to hand our political rivals a set of intelligence failures of our own. As CIA covert teams successfully parried concerns about intelligence by extraordinary efforts that proved bin Laden was indeed in the Abottabad compound, a new set of delaying tactics emerged, embedded in the debate over what should actually be done.

After a series of meetings with Panetta, Gates, Clinton, and senior military officials, in January 2010, Obama, at last, ordered Vice Adm. Bill McRaven to develop a range of military options. McRaven, a former Navy SEAL, ran the Joint Special Operations Command that oversaw all of America's special forces.

• • •

In a secure facility at the Joint Special Operations Command (JSOC) headquarters in North Carolina, the commander of the group popularly known as "SEAL Team Six" was ushered in to meet with McRaven. The admiral wasted no time as the Team Six commander was read in, telling him simply that there was a high-value target that had to be captured or killed, and that the target was likely ringed by armed, trained protectors.

McRaven asked him to begin planning. The questions were few. Would the operation be in "denied [hostile] territory?" Yes. The compound coordinates were relayed. Satellite photographs were handed over. The conversation, in a secure room, lasted less than six minutes.

For security reasons, McRaven did not reveal that bin Laden was the target. The Team Six commander did not ask. It didn't matter, yet.

In a never-before-reported detail, the U.S. Army's Delta Force was briefly considered for the bin Laden operation, according to an official connected to the JSOC. While the secretive army unit had the equipment and experience needed, it was involved in other operations and could not be deployed for this one. Of course, some grumbled, McRaven was a SEAL. It is highly unlikely that McRaven's history played a role in the decision, say sources with knowledge. McRaven oversees all special forces and has never been seen to favor one team over another. "It would undermine his whole command," one said. "It is bullshit," said another. "It is a rumor that probably began with some bragging [master] chief." Inside its closed confines, the special forces world is always rife with rumors—part of its hypercompetitive atmosphere.

The SEALs had been running operations like this one since the global war on terror began on September 12, 2001. The special operations community—and especially the SEALs—had learned a lot in less than a decade. They became used to operating far from the sea, in urban terrain, and especially at night. The rapid tempo of covert operations had been a hard teacher. There were some instructive failures, especially in the Kunar and Kongreal valleys of Afghanistan. But the institutional knowledge— what the SEALs, in their internal communications, call "the lessons learned"—had never been more numerous or more intense. Sometimes JSOC is running as many as fifteen operations per day. Each "after action report" is carefully scrutinized and new training regimes devised. As a whole, the teams are constantly learning and learning quickly.

By February, the SEAL planners were hard at work in a building on the CIA's Langley campus. Dozens of issues needed to be addressed. How could the helicopters get in past Pakistan's radar? Use a stealthy chopper and schedule the mission during a time of "low loom"—little moon luminosity—so they could fly in the safety of darkness.[26] Standing behind that problem and solution were many more like it.

Fearing Valerie Jarrett would interfere and stop the planning, one official associated with the Joint Special Operations Command said that Panetta and McRaven kept the initial planning a secret.

While the SEALs worked on a ground assault operation, a parallel plan was being developed at the Pentagon. Obama directed the Chairman of the Joint Chiefs of Staff to develop a plan to bomb the Abbottabad site, as Panetta had originally suggested. As usual when senior military planners are involved, the Pentagon plan grew far more elaborate than a relatively simple missile strike from a drone aircraft. There were substantial doubts that the kind of Hellfire missile carried by the Predator 2B could succeed in leveling the target and that the drone simply wasn't heavy and strong enough to bear a substantial missile. In addition, planners were concerned that there might be an underground warren of tunnels or bunkers they couldn't see. Finally, a Predator is a subsonic aircraft that can be brought down by Pakistani war planes or surface-to-air missiles.

Once a drone attack was ruled out, the planners went to work on a more conventional air strike. In this case, they proposed a pair of B-2 stealth bombers carrying an array of two-thousand-pound Joint Direct Attack Munitions bombs, known as JDAMs. These "bunker busters" would definitely destroy the target and collapse any subterranean lair. The B-2s could also move undetected through Pakistani's radar grid.

The military brass were proud of their plan. They didn't see the flaws that soon became apparent when it was unveiled at the White House.

The table of the windowless White House Situation Room was crowded with papers and laptops for the March 14, 2011, meeting. The 5,000-square-foot room had been expanded at the direction of President Bush so that as many as four secret meetings could occur there simultaneously. On that day, the bin Laden meeting was the only one going on. The conference was so secret that White House schedulers did not list the topic of discussion in any internal communications.[27]

It was the first of five hot and contentious sessions in which the president and his national security team debated the options. There were essentially three possible plans: an air strike by drone or bomber, a special forces team insertion, or a wait-and-see approach. Each option, one participant said later, had many "sub-options."

The military planners went first, using their favorite weapon—the PowerPoint projector—to make their presentation, followed by the SEAL team planners.

The only decision that Obama made that day was this: Pakistan should be kept in the dark while America made its plans. It was an important decision, but many more lay ahead.

By month's end, McRaven was back at the White House to brief the president. Obama's military advisors were sharply divided about how to approach the situation. Secretary of Defense Robert Gates and Joint Chiefs vice chairman Gen. James Cartwright opposed what they called the "helicopter plan." They didn't see the need to put SEALs on the ground. Why risk American lives?

But the Pentagon's bombing plan had problems, too. There were serious concerns about using bunker-busting JDAMs. While the bombs could penetrate nearly thirty feet of packed earth and destroy any hidden underground bunkers, they would also rock Abbottabad like an earthquake. Flimsy Pakistani houses and apartment buildings could collapse, killing hundreds of civilians. And the bombing would certainly kill the women and children in bin Laden's lair. One CIA official was concerned about the proximity of the compound to other sensitive facilities. "All it has to be is about 1,000 yards off," he said, "and it hits the Pakistan Military Academy."[28]

Finally, bombing would not produce conclusive evidence that bin Laden was dead. "It would have created a giant crater and it wouldn't have given us a body," another intelligence official said.[29] Without DNA evidence, no one could be sure that bin Laden was actually dead. (Indeed, some CIA analysts had been speculating for years that bin Laden was dead already.) Eventually, the principals and the national security team came to view the Pentagon plan as "all downside," one participant said later.

The New York Times called the weeks of indecision prior to the raid "a nerve-racking amalgamation of what-ifs and negative scenarios."[30] The options were endlessly debated, meeting after meeting, another administration official close to the debate said.[31] Just as Obama wanted certainty in the uncertain world of intelligence, he wanted a perfect military option that guaranteed success with no negative side effects or appreciable risks. Without those things, he couldn't make a decision.

President Obama's national security team was particularly worried about Pakistan. That allied government was always vocally opposed to operations on its soil, in that nation's press at least. Al-Qaeda and other extremist groups remained popular in Pakistan and parties allied with them ideologically usually commanded more than one-third of the vote in parliamentary and provincial elections. In private, they usually asked for some wiggle room to deny knowing about the operation for internal political reasons.

In a never-before-reported account, Pakistan was more involved in the bin Laden operation than Obama's team admitted. When the CIA revealed that an ISI colonel had contacted the CIA in Islamabad and offered information about bin Laden, a debate followed. Was this a secret sign that the head of the ISI himself was pointing out bin Laden's hiding place or was the colonel actually the patriot who hated extremism that he claimed to be? Whatever the motivation, the CIA found bin Laden's hiding place within a month of the colonel's visit.

There was talk about devising a cover story that would allow Pakistan to be helpful while keeping its leaders from political harm. The story, according to an official with secondhand knowledge of the White House discussion, was that bin Laden was killed in a drone strike and that the U.S. later sent in a team to recover the body. That was believed to be less politically harmful than a commando team treading on Pakistan's soil. According to this official, Pakistan's Army chief of staff was alerted in December 2010, months before the operation. No concrete facts about the operation were passed on, but an informal approval was sought.

When the SEAL helicopter crashed into bin Laden's compound, the cover story was abandoned. "We completely fucked Pakistan," the official said.

The story could not be independently confirmed, but it has the virtue of explaining why the Obama administration did not press to end military aid to Pakistan when bin Laden was found eight hundred yards from its officer training facility.

Behind the scenes, Hillary Clinton was playing a critical role. She had a regular weekly meeting with the president. "Both of them held religiously to that schedule," Hillary's former State Department spokesman P. J. Crowley said.[32] She used that weekly breakfast meeting to build an enduring bond with Obama. While there was a lot of suspicion at first—their 2008 presidential primary fight had been brutal—she won over the president through "sheer, dogged hard work," Crowley said.

One measure of Hillary's new clout with Obama, Crowley added, was that she twice, in 2009 and 2010, got the president to reverse cuts in some State Department programs, over the objections of the White House budget office. This was a tough zero-sum game: The money had to come from other government departments' tight budgets. Yet she won.

Clinton used her weekly meeting to begin lobbying for a decisive blow against bin Laden. She knew her husband had paid a political price for failing to stop bin Laden before the September 11 attacks. She knew Obama's presidency could be mortally wounded if he had bin Laden in his gunsights and didn't fire.

But she also knew that this type of observation wouldn't win over the president. He liked arguments that sounded apolitical. So she gently but persistently pointed out that he must keep the decision-making process moving, if only to get the best thinking from his team. If people thought that the president was disengaged, their attention would shift to other projects that might command the attention of the Oval Office.

By 2011 Obama had been president long enough to realize that his team responded to cues from him, even unspoken or even unintended ones. He knew Clinton was right. So he agreed to keep making minor decisions, but remained uneasy about the big one at the end—deciding to kill bin Laden, and to risk losing American and Pakistani lives in the process.

Hillary was coordinating with Panetta, who continued to push all CIA officers and their covert assets for more and more reports. Panetta and Clinton had a deep and long-standing relationship. They trusted each other and knew that neither would use the bin Laden raid to upstage the other politically.

Hillary had also struck up a friendship with Gen. David Petraeus during his time as Iraq commander, and, later, in his capacity as commander of all military operations in the Middle East. It was a genuine friendship. Sometimes Clinton and Petraeus would dine together in a private upstairs room at Café Milano, a trendy Georgetown restaurant. Though the room was lined with wooden wine racks and views of Prospect Street, the two would rarely drink or walk over to the window. They were lost in conversation.

When Clinton's State Department aircraft broke down in the Saudi city of Jedda, she phoned Petraeus. He happened to be nearby, in the Saudi capital of Riyhadh. He ordered an unscheduled stop and brought Clinton and her team back to Washington on his plane.

By 2011, Petraeus was in charge of all military matters in Afghanistan, making him a key ally in diplomatic efforts there. Most important for the bin Laden raid, Petraeus was able to direct all military intelligence gathering in the Afghan-Pakistan region. With Petraeus, Panetta, and Clinton all coordinating, no intelligence about bin Laden got lost to turf battles among the CIA, special forces, military, and diplomatic corps. And they were united in their efforts to persuade the president to take decisive action.

Petraeus debated acting on his own and ordering an air strike on the bin Laden stronghold. The general believed he already had valid orders to conduct air strikes against any senior al-Qaeda figures. Clinton suggested that he raise the possibility directly with the president. An attack inside a Pakistani city, near its capital, would be seen as very different from a bombing raid in a tribally administered area on the frontier. It would be a major foreign policy decision, not simply a commander's prerogative. Petraeus quickly agreed.

Initially, as he had done before, the president indicated a willingness to act. He seemed moved by Petraeus's careful and carefully worded presentation.

But, Jarrett intervened, yet again, telling the president he would end up explaining to the American people and the Muslim world why so many civilians were killed. A bomb attack, she insisted, would hurt Obama.

Again Obama hesitated, this time openly delaying further meetings to discuss the issue with Panetta.

Obama also sought out the advice of Defense Secretary Robert Gates and members of the Joint Chiefs of Staff. Gates, like Panetta, was unable to push the president to act.

Gates was frustrated. He had told *Foreign Policy* magazine that he intended to retire before the start of 2012,[33] but he now began telling friends and coworkers that he might resign sooner because, among other reasons, he could no longer work for an indecisive president.

Ultimately, Panetta and Clinton convinced him to stay on and see the operation through, which he did. Gates retired on June 30, 2011.[34]

Perhaps sensing that the internal momentum was going against her, Jarrett shifted to support a helicopter-borne assault. One Defense official speculated that Jarrett's move was simply a play for time. It would take time for Panetta to persuade the military to act—the top brass still wanted to bomb—and this way the blame for any debacle would be shifted onto the military and the CIA. Plus the SEAL plan would take months to plan and the military opposition might eventually rule it out. At the same time, moving the helicopter option into a planning stage would make the president appear action-oriented.

Obama reluctantly agreed with Jarrett and now seemed to favor a ground assault. Though far riskier to American forces, it was far less likely to have negative political ramifications.

Then Panetta played his card. WikiLeaks had released a report from Guantánamo about Abu Faraj al-Libi.[35] It was only a matter of time before bin Laden realized his courier's identity and his own hiding place had both been blown.

We have to act now, Panetta said. Left unsaid was the risk that, if the president failed to act and the public learned about it, he would pay an enormous political price. Now he was talking Jarrett's language—and the president's.

Jarrett suggested that Obama should give Panetta the authority to move the plan forward if he thought it was wise. Jarrett seemed to be calculating that Panetta would hesitate to accept responsibility because he would "own" the operation if it went wrong. A high-profile failure like that might end Panetta's career.

It was a clever trap—a classic "heads I win, tails you lose" proposition. If the operation failed, Panetta would get the blame. If the operation succeeded, the president would grab the glory.

Jarrett miscalculated. Panetta was more worried about missing the opportunity to get bin Laden than hurting his own career. He felt secure in his reputation inside the Washington beltway and among the press corps. He gamely took the bait.

If Obama was surprised, he didn't betray his internal feelings. The president agreed that the operation would proceed under the CIA's legal authority, but would be carried out by the military.

Before the September 11 attacks, such joint operations were rare. The spy agency and the military were publicly criticized for working together to assassinate communist leaders and guerilla chieftains during the Vietnam War and, as a result, largely avoided working together in the decades that followed. The Afghan and Iraq wars changed the cultural and political calculus of both organizations. Within days of the September 11 attacks, the CIA and Special Forces teams were working side by side. By 2011, the two had conducted thousands of operations together. The bond was seamless and each was comfortable in the other's culture.

Clinton and Gates met with Panetta, warning the CIA director that he was stepping into a potential trap. He didn't care. Bin Laden was one hell of a prize. If it went south, the former congressman had allies all over Washington and at the major news outlets who could rally to his side, he said. Clinton volunteered that Panetta would not be alone. She would back him to the hilt. Gates also pledged his support.

Panetta did write himself a small congressional insurance policy. He later met with Rep. Mike Rogers (R-Michigan), whom he had known from his days on Capitol Hill. In the strictest secrecy, he confided part of the bin Laden operation to Representative Rogers. The powerful congressional baron immediately volunteered to back him if the mission went badly.

The trio of Clinton, Panetta, and Gates decided to enlist the support of White House chief of staff Bill Daley. The day after their meeting, Clinton spoke with Daley. She outlined the situation. Daley agreed to try to secure the president's full-throated support. Could the operation be delayed until he won the president's approval? Clinton said she was sure that Panetta would agree to a delay.

Hours later, Daley phoned Clinton. Jarrett was urging the president to remain noncommittal. Daley added that he, too, would fully support Panetta, even if it meant disclosing the president's indecision, should the operation fail.

Clinton told Panetta that he had Daley's backing, but not the president's. The risk would be Panetta's alone.

This approach had advantages and risks for Panetta and Gates. The operational planning and training could move forward seamlessly without a lot of second-guessing from the White House. But it came dangerously close to insubordination and would be judged as such if the mission failed.

Leaving the White House out of the loop did not leave the operation entirely up to the staff at the Joint Special Operations Command. Panetta's CIA continued to insist on operational changes. The CIA wanted its man on one of the two helicopters for the initial raid. It is officially a "CIA Op," McRaven was told by one of Panetta's deputies.

The agency also wanted to insert a CIA translator into the special forces mission. None of the assigned special forces spoke Arabic, Pashto, or any other local language. What if you need to talk to someone in the compound, or the police or the neighbors show up? It was a good point, but McRaven apparently wasn't persuaded. Had the CIA translator ever fast-roped out of a hovering helicopter one hundred feet off the deck in combat?

No, you're going to have to train him, he was told.

If McRaven sighed, the CIA deputy didn't hear it over the secure phone line.

Training began in earnest in April 2011. Just south of the Virginia state line, in a wooded wasteland, the SEAL teams practiced the raid on a full-scale mock-up of the Abottabad compound. After five days of drills, the team flew to a Nevada desert location for nighttime drills at another mock-up.

Admiral McRaven and a senior CIA official came to watch the SEAL "rehearsals" on April 21. McRaven was pleased with their progress. They knew that because he didn't order any additional drills.

The teams, and even the CIA translator, were ready. They had rehearsed the operation repeatedly. Men and materiel had been positioned at the forward staging area. The target remained under constant surveillance. Now all they needed was an order from the president.

On Monday, April 25, Panetta and Gates went to the White House. Obama listened closely to the briefing, asking few questions as they clicked through their PowerPoint slides. No final decision yet.

Leaving their secure base in Dam Neck, Virginia, the SEALs scoured their "cages" (storage units, to the rest of the world) for gear and joined a C-17 Globemaster at a Naval Air Station on April 26. Practicing "sleep discipline," most of the SEALs slept through the transatlantic flight and the refueling at Ramstein Air Base in Western Germany.

Nearly twelve hours later, the plane contacted air traffic control at Bagram Air Base outside Kabul, Afghanistan. It was just another military flight in a swarm arriving in Central Asia that day. By Wednesday, April 27, they were hauling their kit bags off the plane in Jalalabad, Afghanistan.

Meanwhile, back at the White House, the president had yet to give the "go" order. Instead, he wanted more meetings. The day after the SEALs arrived in Afghanistan, Obama met in the White House's Map Room with National Security Advisor Tom Donilon and his deputy, Denis McDonough, along with counterterrorism advisor John Brennan.

Panetta was concerned that time was running out. The Air Force's weather reports indicated "low loom"—relatively clear weather and low moonlight—for the next few days. They might have to wait a month or more for these conditions to return. It was now or never.

Yet a number of the national security team members wanted to wait. National Counterterrorism Center director Michael Leiter thought the intelligence was still too uncertain.

Ben Rhodes, a deputy national security advisor, spoke up in favor of going forward, which surprised the president and may have changed his mind. Rhodes isn't a hawk and strongly opposed President Bush's operations in Iraq and elsewhere. He had worked for years on Capitol Hill for Rep. Lee Hamilton (D-Indiana), who was known for pushing peace plans in Africa and Asia.

Rhodes had essentially bought into Panetta's view that the WikiLeaks documents would eventually reveal that the United States had learned the identity of al-Kuwaiti, bin Laden's link to the outside world. Additionally, Rhodes feared that the bin Laden operation itself would eventually leak.

But Obama was done for the night. It was just 7:00 P.M., but he was going to "sleep on it."[36] The room was silent. Given the nine-hour time difference, it was too late to order an assault that night. "I'm not going to tell you what my decision is now. I'm going to go back and think about it some more," Obama said.[37]

When he saw the looks on the faces of Panetta and Gates, he added, "I'm going to make a decision soon." When the president left the room, Panetta met Clinton's gaze. They were floored. Could the president really kill America's best opportunity to get bin Laden?

The next morning, Friday, April 29, top national security aides were summoned to the White House Diplomatic Reception Room. Before they could brief the president, he cut them off. He slammed the table, a dramatic gesture that seemed rehearsed, and said, "It's a go."[38]

Later that day, Obama told McRaven that he had approved the operation. The timing would be up to McRaven.

That would soon change. Hours later, a White House aide phoned McRaven and sought a twenty-four-hour delay. This delay was later explained to the press and the public as "weather related"—cloud cover over the target, or something like that.

But the official weather reports from the U.S. Air Force's combat meteorological service tell a different story. With some difficulty, I tracked down the weather reports that were used by the U.S. Army pilots to transport the U.S. Navy SEAL teams that day. The weather reports, drawn from weather stations in Bagram and Jalalabad, Afghanistan, were prepared by the U.S. Air Force Combat Climatology Center, as part of the Climate Analysis Support Flight of the 14th Weather Squadron in Asheville, North Carolina. While the skies were cloudy, there was no storm front moving in. Visibility, wind speed, and other weather factors were all within acceptable and safe parameters to operate helicopters that day. The bin Laden mission was not scrubbed because the weather had changed, but because the president had changed his mind. Again.

In reality, Obama was once more playing for time. He wanted to confer again with Jarrett and others.

On Saturday afternoon, McRaven and Obama spoke again. McRaven said the raid would occur on Sunday night. It was done. It would take an affirmative, deliberate command from Obama to stop it now.

On Sunday, May 1, White House officials canceled all West Wing tours. The concern was that visitors might wonder why so many high-level personnel officials were all in the White House at the same time.

As the president's top advisors were streaming in, the president left by helicopter at 9:42 A.M. for a round of golf at Andrews Air Force Base.[39]

While Obama chipped and putted, the White House Situation Room was filling up. By 11:00 A.M., the table was ringed by Secretary of State Hillary Clinton, Vice President Joe Biden, National Security Advisor Tom Donilon, Defense Secretary Robert Gates, Chairman of the Joint Chiefs of Staff Admiral Mike Mullen, Deputy National Security Advisor John Brennan, Director of National Intelligence James Clapper, and White House chief of staff Bill Daley.

Many others were present electronically. Panetta was on a secure video link from his CIA office in Langley. McRaven was on a secure speakerphone from Afghanistan. Also looped in over secure links were the secretary of defense's inner circle at the Pentagon and the U.S. Embassy in Islamabad, Pakistan, which houses the largest CIA station outside of the United States.

In a cubbyhole office in the West Wing, steps from the Situation Room, Brig. Gen. Marshall Webb, third in command at the Joint Special Operations Command, whom *The Nation* described as "a highly decorated military man almost no one has ever heard of,"[40] streamed a laptop video feed of the operation.

Everyone was there except Obama. By now he was well into his round of golf with staffers from the Department of Energy.

A little later, pool reporters noted the president abruptly stopped playing halfway through his customary eighteen-hole game and was hustled off the links at 1:29 P.M. They attributed it to the chilly, wet weather. Obama stepped out of his helicopter onto the South Lawn of the White House at 2:04 P.M. and made "an unusual beeline for his West Wing office."[41]

Obama arrived in the Situation Room just as Panetta was finishing the last briefing to the assembled officials that outlined the key stages of the attack. Obama was still in his golf clothes. Everyone else was dressed for history.

Minutes later, Panetta's voice boomed over the secure speakerphone. The helicopters, he said, had lifted off from Jalalabad. Fifteen minutes later, they had crossed safely into Pakistan.[42]

They would all listen to radio traffic for the next two hours, fearing that a Pakistani air patrol or radar operator would spot the two choppers, code-named "Razor 1" and "Razor 2."

It was a long, anxious wait. There were no communications from the SEALs. Strict radio silence.

Just before 4:00 P.M. Washington time, Panetta's voice came out of the speaker on the main table in the Situation Room. The SEALs' helicopters were nearing Abbottabad.

Obama abruptly stood up. "I need to watch this," he said. He knew the stakes. Presidencies are made or broken at moments like these. President Jimmy Carter did not recover from the deadly failure of "Desert One," an effort involving helicopters and other aircraft to rescue fifty-two American diplomats held hostage in Teheran.

With the fast-twitch muscle energy of an athlete, Obama bounded into the small cubicle where Webb was watching a satellite feed. Biden, Gates, and Clinton quickly followed, crowding in to stare at the tiny black-and-white laptop screen.

Contrary to what the White House spokesman would imply the next day, there wasn't a lot to see. The SEALs themselves were not wearing cameras or transmitting video from their aircraft. Once the choppers landed and the team began moving indoors, the video feed would show only roof tops. Indeed, the confused accounts came mainly from White House officials who simply were not in the room with the real-time video feed.

The bin Laden compound was akin to an isosceles triangle, carved out of the property of the Kakul Military Academy, Pakistan's West Point. The campus's main building sat some eight hundred yards from bin Laden's castle. The triangular compound was bordered with concrete walls ranging in height from ten to eighteen feet. The main building, a three-story tower, housed the archterrorist, his wives, and their children.

Razor 1 was supposed to deposit a SEAL contingent onto the roof of the bin Laden house. They would work their way down. Razor 2 was to deliver a blocking force that would "fast-rope" down into the compound and seize the other two buildings, clear, and hold them.

Contrary to the official story, Razor 1 did not immediately crash. As it approached the bin Laden compound, the helicopter's massive blades kicked up dust and threw plastic patio chairs against bin Laden's windows. The hand-built concrete structure rattled with the vibration from the American helicopter.

Also, contrary to the later White House narrative, the SEAL unit jumped from the bucking helicopter onto the roof and climbed down onto a balcony. It did not fight its way down the stairs. (Another unit would do that a few minutes later.)

But Razor 1 was certainly in trouble.

Back in the cubicle in the Situation Room, Obama, Webb, and the other officials were silent as the laptop video link showed the slow-motion distress. They could do nothing but watch and hope.

Razor 1's own propeller rotors had created a funnel of low-pressure air, causing the craft to sink. The buildings were forcing the air, churned by the blades, straight down and out at ground level—denying the chopper the lift it needed to stay aloft.

This problem was not discovered in many training exercises because the chain-link fences used at the North Carolina mock-up were not concrete walls; the fences allowed the air to move as if they weren't there at all, maintaining the helicopters' lift. The navy used chain-link instead of concrete because in the training exercises, the helicopter crews were coached to avoid the tops of fences, which can wreck an aircraft. No one realized air flow would be a factor.

There was nothing that the pilot, who was highly trained and experienced, could do. He couldn't change the laws of physics and, at less than fifty feet from the ground, didn't have the altitude to climb out of the low-pressure silo that his helicopter had created.

All he could do was try to land as safely and softly as possible. He chose the manure-topped animal pen. The Black Hawk dived nose-first into the spongy, smelly muck—scattering chickens and goats. None were harmed. Miraculously, no SEALs were seriously injured, either.

The rear tail rotor mashed its blades along the compound's outer concrete wall.

Razor 2's SEALs watched the chopper smash to earth. Did they take enemy fire? Massive mechanical failure? No one knew and no one was speculating on secure radio channels.

The now famous photograph of various leaders in the Situation Room watching in horror—Secretary of State Hillary Rodham Clinton holding her hand over her mouth—captures this moment, not the moment when bin Laden was killed. Though, as she said at the Naval Academy in April 2012, no one "could breathe for thirty-five minutes" during the raid, making it fairly representative of those tense moments.[43]

The SEALs would have to improvise if the mission was going to succeed, but it wouldn't be the first time. The teams are both careful planners and gifted improvisers.

Within moments, the SEALs inside Razor 1 radioed that they were unharmed and proceeding toward their objective.

Meanwhile, the team in Razor 2 landed safely and was moving forward.

There was no "forty-minute firefight," as the White House would later claim. Few shots were fired and the mission was completed in less than twenty minutes. Omar al-Kuwaiti emerged with an AK-47 and was instantly felled by a single shot from a SEAL. The bullet passed through him and killed his wife, who was standing a few feet behind. His brother Abrar would die within a minute when he, too, stepped out into the night with an automatic weapon.

The CIA translator and a bomb-sniffing Belgian dog named Cairo stood near the main gate. He and several armed SEALs were guarding the gate from approaching Pakistanis. The neighbors were not long in coming.

With the gunshots and the helicopter crash, the neighbors appeared. In perfect Pashto, the translator acted the part of a Pakistani policeman: "Go back to your houses. There is a security operation under way."

In the White House Situation Room, the president was in the dark. It was not *CSI* or *24,* with live full-color video from multiple angles. "I can tell you that there was a time period of almost twenty to twenty-five minutes where we really didn't know just exactly what was going on," Panetta would later tell *PBS NewsHour.* Once the operation began, there were few real-time reports. And once the SEALs were inside the buildings, virtually nothing was visible on the video link.

At 4:18 P.M. Washington time, the SEALs finally reached bin Laden.

Within two minutes, bin Laden, his son, and his protectors were dead.

In the White House's narrative, the next message from the SEALs said: "For God and country—Geronimo, Geronimo, Geronimo."[44] *The New Yorker* and other major media outlets soon repeated this account.

In reality, no one said: "For God and country." That bit of gilding the lily came into the narrative later, likely from the media operations team.

Instead, the radio traffic was strictly by the book. "Geronimo, Geronimo, Geronimo, third deck." Bin Laden had been spotted on the third floor.

The next transmission was also by the book: "Geronimo, E, KIA." Bin Laden, enemy, killed in action.

Obama's response was soft-voiced and slightly startled. "We got him."

Less than eight minutes had elapsed since the SEAL teams had landed. It was 4:26 P.M., Washington time. For the next twelve minutes, the mission shifted to an intelligence-gathering operation. From the perspective of career counterterrorism professionals, securing intelligence from the bin Laden compound was even more important than killing the man himself.

Proving that the SEALs had gotten their man was the first role of intelligence. Several DNA samples were extracted from bin Laden's corpse. These samples were carefully packed in a sealed container and flown back to a secure American facility in Afghanistan. The samples were compared against DNA strands taken from a Boston hospital, where, years earlier, one of bin Laden's sisters had undergone successful brain surgery. In hours, military intelligence knew that they had a match. The dead man was definitely Osama bin Laden.

Meanwhile, the SEALs searched the buildings for other forms of intelligence. With black Hefty-brand garbage bags, they gathered up computer disks, thumb drives, hard drives, digital cameras—any device that contained any kind of data at all. Others searched for files and documents, even a diary. They didn't have the time or the expertise to decide what to take. They took anything that might be valuable to technical intelligence analysts. Even a calendar with handwritten Arabic-language notes.[45]

The haul proved to be a treasure trove. It revealed the locations of al-Qaeda operatives from the Horn of Africa to the Khyber Pass. It also revealed an ongoing plot to assassinate President Obama and a separate plot to slay General Petraeus. Other pending plots included targeted attacks in New York and on America's railroad network.[46]

At 4:38 P.M. Washington time, after detonating the crashed helicopter, the teams departed for the return trip back to Afghanistan.

In the Situation Room, according to *The New Yorker,* Obama said: "I'm not going to be happy until those guys get out safe." No one present recalls the president saying those words out loud.

At 6 P.M. Washington time, the helicopters landed back in Jalalabad.

The daring operation, which had consumed almost two years of meetings and presidential worry, had succeeded beyond all expectations. No Americans were wounded or killed. Bin Laden was definitely dead. No neighboring civilians were harmed. And the only residents of the compound who were killed or wounded were either holding automatic weapons or standing beside people who were. One intelligence official with knowledge of the operation told me that it was "flawless, textbook."

But what happened next raised new questions about the president's priorities.

Less than an hour after the SEALs safely returned to Afghanistan and more than five hours before the American public was told of the raid, the president's counterterrorism advisor, John Brennan, alerted the Saudi government. Brennan's call, over a secure phone line, was personally authorized by the president.

Brennan spoke with the onetime head of Saudi intelligence. The president was concerned that the Saudi government might want the body of their former citizen. Bin Laden had lost his Saudi citizenship in 1994 when he was caught plotting to murder the Saudi monarch, but the bin Ladens had been close to the royal family for decades and remained a force to be reckoned with in Saudi politics.

Brennan briefly gave the details of the raid and explained Obama's plan to dump bin Laden's body from the deck of a U.S. aircraft carrier into the Indian Ocean. Did the Saudi government want the body or should the United States proceed as planned? The response was laconic: "Your plan sounds like a good one."

President Obama's next move shocked the intelligence community. Twenty-five minutes before midnight, on the night of the raid, he walked into the East Room of the White House. Alone with the cyclopean eye of the network pool camera and the cold type of the teleprompter, Obama told the world that bin Laden was dead.

The speech, which Obama wrote himself with the help of Ben Rhodes, is unintentionally revealing:

> Good evening. Tonight, I can report to the American people
> and to the world that the United States has conducted an opera-
> tion that killed Osama bin Laden, the leader of al-Qaeda, and a
> terrorist who's responsible for the murder of thousands of inno-
> cent men, women, and children.
>
> It was nearly ten years ago that a bright September day was
> darkened by the worst attack on the American people in our his-

tory. The images of 9/11 are seared into our national memory—hijacked planes cutting through a cloudless September sky; the Twin Towers collapsing to the ground; black smoke billowing up from the Pentagon; the wreckage of Flight 93 in Shanksville, Pennsylvania, where the actions of heroic citizens saved even more heartbreak and destruction.

And yet we know that the worst images are those that were unseen to the world. The empty seat at the dinner table. Children who were forced to grow up without their mother or their father. Parents who would never know the feeling of their child's embrace. Nearly three thousand citizens taken from us, leaving a gaping hole in our hearts.

On September 11, 2001, in our time of grief, the American people came together. We offered our neighbors a hand, and we offered the wounded our blood. We reaffirmed our ties to each other, and our love of community and country. On that day, no matter where we came from, what God we prayed to, or what race or ethnicity we were, we were united as one American family.

We were also united in our resolve to protect our nation and to bring those who committed this vicious attack to justice. We quickly learned that the 9/11 attacks were carried out by al-Qaeda—an organization headed by Osama bin Laden, which had openly declared war on the United States and was committed to killing innocents in our country and around the globe. And so we went to war against al-Qaeda to protect our citizens, our friends, and our allies.

Over the last ten years, thanks to the tireless and heroic work of our military and our counterterrorism professionals, we've made great strides in that effort. We've disrupted terrorist attacks and strengthened our homeland defense. In Afghanistan, we removed the Taliban government, which had given bin Laden and al-Qaeda safe haven and support. And around the globe, we worked with our friends and allies to capture or kill scores of al-Qaeda terrorists, including several who were a part of the 9/11 plot.

Yet Osama bin Laden avoided capture and escaped across the Afghan border into Pakistan. Meanwhile, al-Qaeda continued to operate from along that border and operate through its affiliates across the world.

And so shortly after taking office, I directed Leon Panetta, the director of the CIA, to make the killing or capture of bin Laden the top priority of our war against al-Qaeda, even as we continued our broader efforts to disrupt, dismantle, and defeat his network.

Then, last August, after years of painstaking work by our intelligence community, I was briefed on a possible lead to bin Laden. It was far from certain, and it took many months to run this thread to ground. I met repeatedly with my national security team as we developed more information about the possibility that we had located bin Laden hiding within a compound deep inside of Pakistan. And finally, last week, I determined that we had enough intelligence to take action, and authorized an operation to get Osama bin Laden and bring him to justice.

Today, at my direction, the United States launched a targeted operation against that compound in Abbottabad, Pakistan. A small team of Americans carried out the operation with extraordinary courage and capability. No Americans were harmed. They took care to avoid civilian casualties. After a firefight, they killed Osama bin Laden and took custody of his body.

For over two decades, bin Laden has been al-Qaeda's leader and symbol, and has continued to plot attacks against our country and our friends and allies. The death of bin Laden marks the most significant achievement to date in our nation's effort to defeat al-Qaeda.

Yet his death does not mark the end of our effort. There's no doubt that al-Qaeda will continue to pursue attacks against us. We must—and we will—remain vigilant at home and abroad.

As we do, we must also reaffirm that the United States is not—and never will be—at war with Islam. I've made clear, just as President Bush did shortly after 9/11, that our war is not against

Islam. Bin Laden was not a Muslim leader; he was a mass murderer of Muslims. Indeed, al-Qaeda has slaughtered scores of Muslims in many countries, including our own. So his demise should be welcomed by all who believe in peace and human dignity.

Over the years, I've repeatedly made clear that we would take action within Pakistan if we knew where bin Laden was. That is what we've done. But it's important to note that our counterterrorism cooperation with Pakistan helped lead us to bin Laden and the compound where he was hiding. Indeed, bin Laden had declared war against Pakistan as well, and ordered attacks against the Pakistani people.

Tonight, I called President Zardari, and my team has also spoken with their Pakistani counterparts. They agree that this is a good and historic day for both of our nations. And going forward, it is essential that Pakistan continue to join us in the fight against al-Qaeda and its affiliates.

The American people did not choose this fight. It came to our shores, and started with the senseless slaughter of our citizens. After nearly ten years of service, struggle, and sacrifice, we know well the costs of war. These efforts weigh on me every time I, as Commander-in-Chief, have to sign a letter to a family that has lost a loved one, or look into the eyes of a service member who's been gravely wounded.

So Americans understand the costs of war. Yet as a country, we will never tolerate our security being threatened, nor stand idly by when our people have been killed. We will be relentless in defense of our citizens and our friends and allies. We will be true to the values that make us who we are. And on nights like this one, we can say to those families who have lost loved ones to al-Qaeda's terror: Justice has been done.

Tonight, we give thanks to the countless intelligence and counterterrorism professionals who've worked tirelessly to achieve this outcome. The American people do not see their work, nor know their names. But tonight, they feel the satisfaction of their work and the result of their pursuit of justice.

We give thanks for the men who carried out this operation, for they exemplify the professionalism, patriotism, and unparalleled courage of those who serve our country. And they are part of a generation that has borne the heaviest share of the burden since that September day.

Finally, let me say to the families who lost loved ones on 9/11 that we have never forgotten your loss, nor wavered in our commitment to see that we do whatever it takes to prevent another attack on our shores.

And tonight, let us think back to the sense of unity that prevailed on 9/11. I know that it has, at times, frayed. Yet today's achievement is a testament to the greatness of our country and the determination of the American people.

The cause of securing our country is not complete. But tonight, we are once again reminded that America can do whatever we set our mind to. That is the story of our history, whether it's the pursuit of prosperity for our people, or the struggle for equality for all our citizens; our commitment to stand up for our values abroad, and our sacrifices to make the world a safer place.

Let us remember that we can do these things not just because of wealth or power, but because of who we are: one nation, under God, indivisible, with liberty and justice for all.

Thank you. May God bless you. And may God bless the United States of America.[47]

Some of the points President Obama made on this historic occasion only make sense in the light of contemporary American politics. President Bush had repeatedly emphasized that America is not at war with Islam—the terrorists, he said, had "hijacked Islam"—and no American commentator had made that claim in the Obama years. A logical explanation for including it here would be his desire to manage the response of ordinary Americans. The president seemed to fear that the public would view this as a victory over Islam, as opposed to being what it was: a victory over a terror master who had plagued America for decades.

In his speech, Obama made a repeated plea for national unity at the very moment of bin Laden's demise. He reminded the public how the nation came together in the wake of the September 11 attacks and, at several other points, urged citizens to come together.

This was a strange rhetorical position: Precisely whom in America did he think wouldn't be delighted by bin Laden's departure? Obama was at pains to remind us that bin Laden was a "mass murderer of Muslims" as well as other Americans and her allies. And he seemed to be pleading with antiwar activists that the United States didn't start this war and that the war must continue as a matter of national survival. Yet neither Muslim groups nor peace activists protested. Indeed, Obama's decision to remove bin Laden from this earth remains the most popular of his presidency, among people of all political stripes and all walks of life. So popular that Oscar-winning filmmaker Kathryn Bigelow of *The Hurt Locker* fame is making a film about it, *Zero Dark 30*—no doubt, in time for late fall special screenings to coincide with Obama's reelection campaign.

Perhaps he simply was mistaken about the likely public reaction.

Or perhaps, as seems more likely, he was signaling his own ambivalence about ordering the covert mission. He feared public protests partly because he heard the protests in his own head. Absent some confessional interview, it's impossible to know this for sure. Yet the strangely defensive tone and structure of the speech certainly suggested as much.

The strangest thing about the speech is that Obama delivered it at all. Why tell the world that bin Laden was gone and take away the element of surprise that would have allowed special forces to swoop in on other al-Qaeda leaders around the world? Why give away secrecy and surprise, the most coveted of military and intelligence advantages in war?

The ethos of secrecy has been a central value of the intelligence community since the beginning of time. In an out-of-the-way corner of a modest building that is home to the U.S. Navy SEAL-UDT Museum in Fort Pierce, Florida, hangs a simple wooden plaque that says, "In honor of undisclosed people who took part in an undisclosed action at an undisclosed place on an undisclosed date and who made an undisclosed achievement." This embodies the culture of secrecy that suffuses the special forces and intelligence operators.

There were compelling and powerful military reasons to keep bin Laden's death a secret. The identities of the individual SEALs (whose families would face the wrath of al-Qaeda) are officially top secret and had to remain so. Also, the equipment, tactics, and techniques of U.S. Special Forces are closely guarded military secrets. If these things became known (as they did), the SEALs would have to find newer, better equipment and develop new techniques and new tactics. That meant hundreds of hours of hard work and a costly toll of experiences, drawn from the Vietnam era to the present day, had just been reduced to rubble—in a few minutes of an imprudent speech. Giving away proven methods, as unknown to potential enemies as they are lethally effective, soon rendered them worthless.

President Bush established the precedent, during the War on Terror, of keeping America's greatest victories secret. He explained this doctrine in a speech to a joint session of Congress on September 20, 2001, just nine days after the September 11 attacks, considered by many to be his finest:

> Our response involves far more than instant retaliation and iso-
> lated strikes. Americans should not expect one battle, but a
> lengthy campaign unlike any other we have ever seen. It may in-
> clude dramatic strikes visible on TV and covert operations secret
> even in success.[48]

The June 2006 killing of Abu Musab al Zarqawi, the feared leader of al-Qaeda in Iraq who led the anti-American insurgency in that country, was not an occasion for a presidential victory lap. Nor did the March 2003 capture of Khalid Shaikh Mohammed, the operational planner of the September 11 attacks, merit a presidential speech or even a public acknowledgement from the White House. No one spiked the football when Ramzi bin al-Shibh, leader of the first attack on the World Trade Center was captured in September 2002, almost a year to the day after the 9/11 attacks.

In these cases, the intelligence services wanted time to explore and exploit the captured computers and cell phones that might lead to future victories. Intelligence teams wanted the same secrecy for the bin Laden raid, but they didn't get it.

The intelligence value of captured documents and hard drives was as incalculable as it was large. Inside the black trash bags the SEALs hauled away from Abbottabad were more than a hundred thumb drives, DVDs and computer disks, ten computer hard drives, five computers, and a mountain of documents.[49]

With the stolen fortune from bin Laden's fortress of solitude, the SEALs and other special operators could have launched surprise attacks on al-Qaeda leaders *for years to come.* Drone attacks could have killed many more. Every important al-Qaeda leader could have been killed or captured. The intelligence value of those raids would have uncovered al-Qaeda's secret means of moving money and men. It would have also revealed who, and in which Middle Eastern governments, were secretly helping al-Qaeda with funds, arms, or nuggets of intelligence. In short, the bin Laden operation, *if kept secret,* could have ended the existence of the al-Qaeda network. From the perspective of military and intelligence officials, the president's speech shoved away America's best chance at ultimate victory, perhaps forever.

Obama also gave orders that reduced the intelligence value of the mission. When the SEAL helicopters were ready to go, new orders came in. Bin Laden's wives were not to be captured. Another vital piece of intelligence—precious human intelligence—was simply thrown away. No reason was given.

But the larger question remains: Why did Obama give the speech?

This question is nearly impossible to answer with the president seeking reelection and many of his senior staff still in office. But telling clues abound. Top advisors anonymously told the press that they were concerned the news of bin Laden's demise would leak before any action could be taken.

It hadn't so far. Vice President Biden spoke to the Atlantic Council two days after the operation. "There was such an absolute overwhelming desire to accomplish this mission," he said, "that although for over several months we were in the process of planning it and there were as many as sixteen members of Congress who were briefed on it—not a single solitary thing leaked. I find that absolutely amazing." The crowd applauded wildly.

The details leaked only after the president told the world, touching off a mad race for political credit. Without that presidential speech, an incentive remained to keep the secrets, and none existed for leaking details. There would be legal penalties for violating the nation's secrecy laws but, if anything, public censure would be even greater. Who would dare put America's forces at risk and gamble with America's greatest military coup?

Obama's speech actually set off the leaks it was purportedly designed to prevent. It emboldened nearly everyone involved to grab their share of the glory. And it created unbelievable pressure for editors and reporters to implore the national security team for scoops—additional nuggets that make careers and drive ratings. The speech, though carefully scrubbed, turned incentives for secrecy into incentives for publicity.

Obama either didn't foresee that his speech would throw away the military advantages of secrecy and surprise, or he didn't care as long as doing so meant seizing political advantage.

Either reading raises grave questions about his leadership. A leader must weigh the likely outcomes of competing actions when making a key decision, and then make the decision that strikes the best balance between anticipated risk and reward.

A former White House official approached the subject this way: "I don't know why we didn't hold on to the news until October 2012." Indeed, that would maximize both the military and political advantages. Bin Laden would still be dead and scores more al-Qaeda leaders killed or captured. The president could have reaped the political benefit when the news was both startling and fresh for voters.

The mad scramble for credit began early Monday morning, less than twelve hours after Obama's speech alerted the world. Numerous claims, often made by officials not in the room during the operation, later had to be modified, retracted, or "walked back."

The administration mishandled the news of bin Laden's demise from the start, first by making it public and then by offering up so many wrong details that it irritated those who wanted to cheer them on.

In their hurry, the president and his men garbled key details and invented other "facts"—leading to days of having to correct what they invariably called "the narrative."

The senior White House staff and the president's press secretary ultimately had to retract or reverse many memorable details of that narrative, including the idea that bin Laden died in a firefight; that bin Laden or other men in the compound used multiple (or any) women as human shields; that a gun battle rang out for forty minutes; that the operation was a "kill, not capture" mission; and that the president and his staff were able to watch events unfold with a real-time video link.

Some of these misstatements were simply erroneous conclusions that the press jumped to, based on inartful statements from White House officials. Other statements were untruths advanced purposefully by White House officials who themselves were simply mistaken about key details of the bin Laden raid.

Let's examine each one in detail.

Bin Laden died in a firefight?
In fact, bin Laden was shot multiple times when reaching for an automatic weapon. He never fired a shot.

Wives as human shields?
Pursuing the question of how many women had been used as human shields, reporters zoomed in on the conflicting accounts. White House press secretary Jay Carney said, "I apologize. Even I'm getting confused."[50]

As the Tuesday, May 3 question-and-answer session with the press continued and the discrepancies and questions mounted, Carney became more disconcerted. He tried to stick to the official "narrative," but that became impossible. Reporters pushed for details about the wives as human shields, with one reporter demanding, "Bin Laden's wife was unarmed as well?" Carney let out a nugget of information not yet made public when he said, "That is my understanding." When the reporter followed up with a question about others who may or may not have been in the room with bin Laden, Carney simply said: "I don't know that."[51]

It was a press conference out of control. The questions, such as this one, kept coming: "In the narrative, which of those women was being used as a human shield, as [White House homeland security and counterterrorism advisor] Mr. Brennan suggested yesterday?" Carney gave up the pretense of providing facts about "the narrative," and said "[W]hat I would say about that is . . . to use your phrase, 'fog of war,' 'fog of combat.' [T]here was a lot of information coming in. It is still unclear. The woman I believe you're talking about might have been the one on the first floor who was caught in the crossfire [and killed]. Whether or not she was being used as a shield or trying to use herself as a shield or simply caught in crossfire is unclear. And we're working on getting the details that we can."[52]

Ultimately, it emerged that one woman (al-Kuwaiti's wife) was killed when she stood behind her husband, who was brandishing an AK-47. Bin Laden's youngest wife, Amal al-Sadah, was shot in the leg while approaching the two SEAL team members in her bedroom. Neither woman was used as a "human shield."[53]

40-Minute Firefight?

The Obama administration even had a hard time documenting how long the shootout lasted between the SEALs and bin Laden's men. The "firefight" was claimed to have occupied "most" of the forty-minute operation, as the senior Defense Department official originally told the press, or to have continued "throughout" the entire operation, as the White House press secretary said. Indeed, the operation wasn't even forty minutes long and the few shots that were fired came in the first few minutes.

Only seven shots were fired in all. One came at the start of the raid that killed al-Kuwaiti; one killed his wife; one killed bin Laden's son Khalid; one wounded bin Laden's wife; one missed bin Laden; two killed the terror leader. Hardly a firefight.

Real-time video link?

Not exactly. The SEALs do not wear helmet cams as some commentators imagined. The only video feed that Obama could watch was an aerial view of the compound's exterior.

Was it a kill mission?

On Monday, May 2, White House homeland security and counterterrorism advisor John Brennan said, "If we had the opportunity to take bin Laden alive, if he didn't present any threat, the individuals involved were able and prepared to do that. We had discussed that extensively in a number of meetings in the White House and with the president. The concern was that bin Laden would oppose any type of capture operation. Indeed, he did. There was a firefight. He therefore was killed in that firefight, and that's when the remains were removed. But we certainly were planning for the possibility, which we thought was going to be remote, given that he would likely resist arrest but that we would be able to capture him."

Brennan described the high tension in the White House Situation Room. In fact, he was not in the room where the video was being seen, but in the outer main conference room.

"It was probably one of the most anxiety-filled periods of time, I think, in the lives of the people who were assembled here yesterday," Brennan said. "The minutes passed like days, and the president was very concerned about the security of our personnel. That was what was on his mind throughout, and we wanted to make sure that we were able to get through this and accomplish the mission."[54]

Sen. Saxby Chambliss (R-Georgia) expressed irritation at the shifting "narrative" of the raid offered by the White House, the Pentagon, and the CIA. "Every day it seems like somebody is having to straighten out some fact," he told the *Atlanta Journal Constitution*. "You'd think that twenty-four hours after the fact, they'd be able to ferret things out a little more." Chambliss told the *National Journal*, "Twenty-four hours after it happened there should have been more clarification than what I heard coming out of Brennan."

One commentator, former Bush White House press secretary Dana Perino, who had spent years at the podium of the James S. Brady Press Briefing Room, couldn't understand how the administration hadn't managed to get its story straight.

"In a crisis or an unfolding news situation, first reports are almost always wrong," Perino said on the Fox News Channel. "And you can understand when you get the tide of the media calls coming in and you want to provide information as quickly as possible. You want to be responsive and you want to frame the argument first [before others do]. Sometimes though, if then you end up having to redefine that narrative, or correct things that you originally said, you end up sullying your original message. And I think that's what's happened to them.

"I am perplexed how they got so much wrong," she added. "I don't think it takes away from their achievement. I think that criticism will be relatively short-lived. However, for those people who might be critics of the administration, or have a little bit of distrust for the stories that are coming out of the White House, this will feed that. And it doesn't help build credibility."

Once Obama's speech set off the media feeding frenzy, it was all but unavoidable that some details would be mangled or mashed. It was yet another reason to delay a presidential announcement. Why let Obama's greatest foreign-policy victory be ruined by rushing headlong into a victory lap?

On Friday, May 6, Obama flew to Fort Campbell to thank the SEAL unit and helicopter pilots. This trip, too, tells us something strange about Obama's attitude toward the bin Laden mission.

Obama presented the team with a Presidential Unit Citation, the highest honor that the president can bestow on an entire military unit. "Our intelligence professionals did some amazing work," he said. "I had fifty-fifty confidence that bin Laden was there, but I had one hundred percent confidence in you guys. You are, literally, the finest small-fighting force that has ever existed in the world."

It is telling that the president was still telegraphing his past doubt about whether bin Laden was in the compound.

Obama received a framed American flag that was on board one of the back-up helicopters involved in the operation. The SEAL operators and the Night Stalker helicopter pilots had each autographed the back of it. On the front, it was engraved, "From the Joint Task Force Operation Neptune's Spear, 01 May 2011: 'For God and country. Geronimo.'"

As Obama held the gift in his hands, he told the assembled team that he planned to put it "somewhere private and meaningful to me."

Why private? Surely, this would be a piece of history that would attract legions of White House visitors eager for a look. Perhaps the president wanted to hide it because he wasn't sure it was something to be proud of. (The signatures are hardly a security risk; many of the names are not fully legible.)

Another comment by Obama also suggests ambivalence about the covert mission. Speaking to Steve Kroft of CBS's *60 Minutes*, Obama said there was no need to release the photos of Osama bin Laden's dead body. "We don't need to spike the football."

Isn't a presidential speech following a military victory just another end-zone dance?

Months later, a Chinook helicopter over Afghanistan was shot down. Thirty American special operators were killed, including twenty-two from SEAL Team Six. It was the largest loss of life among the SEALs on a single day in the history of the teams. Many of their surviving comrades wondered: Did the president's victory lap put a target on their back?

We may never know. While revealing the details of covert kills can have political benefits, it also has costs measured in human lives.

The leadership questions are large. Why did Obama decide to put Americans at risk by revealing the bin Laden operation? As a leader, how did he strike the balance between risk and reward?

Considering the false starts and second-guessing before the operation and the ever-changing official story that gave away the advantage of surprise in fighting al-Qaeda and put Americans, in and out of uniform, at risk, Obama's handling of the bin Laden mission may be the single biggest blunder of his presidency. Far from being an example of decisive leadership, it is a case study of a leader who puts his personal needs ahead of his constitutional duties.

CHAPTER 5

ISRAEL'S DILEMMA

You're sick of him? I have to work with him every day.

—Barack Obama, talking about Israel's prime minister
Benjamin Netanyahu, with French president Nicolas Sarkozy[1]

Barack Obama's difficult chemistry with Israel's prime minister Benjamin Netanyahu began years before they ever met—and the catalysts for that bubbling compound were two rabbis, one of whom the future president never met.

That admixture is so volatile that, people who have met both leaders fear, it is always about to explode. And, often, it did.

It raised the question that is the measure of any manager: Can he work with people of differing philosophies toward a shared goal? As we saw in chapter three, Obama had difficulty working with Republicans when a national debt crisis loomed. Netanyahu presented the same problem in a different way; Obama had to work with a skilled leader possessing a divergent outlook while the Arab Spring and the Iranian nuclear program threatened the future of Israel, the region's stability, and America's oil prices.

Obama's challenge could hardly be greater. Israel is America's most important ally in the world's most dangerous region.

Long before he was elected president—and long before he actually met Netanyahu—Obama was signaling that he held a sharply different view of Israel compared to any of his post–World War II predecessors, either Democrat or Republican.

In the years before he was elected president, Obama developed rigid views about Israel while learning comparatively little about its complex history and present dangers. He had met the Palestinian activist and scholar Edward Said in 1982 and soon become close to him, Said's Columbia University's archive had just been opened to researchers and reveals long, favoring letters to Said from Obama. They dined together, sent each other letters, made phone calls, and posed for photographs together over the next two decades. They were friends and Obama sought his approval. Rev. Jeremiah Wright and Rev. Jesse Jackson, both Obama mentors, also shaped his thinking on Israel. Once he was president, he did not modify his positions very much. So what did Obama think about Israel?

A little noticed speech in the middle of the country was the first clue.

In the heat of his fight with Hillary Clinton for the Democratic Party nomination in February 2008, Obama walked into a hotel ballroom in Cleveland to raise money without raising eyebrows. The crowd packed into the ballroom was mostly Jewish. Obama must have known that he would be asked about Israel. He knew he would have to be careful. The press, both mainstream and religious, missed the importance of Obama's words.

In his prepared remarks, Obama contrasted what he said was the open-mindedness of Israelis to discuss a broader spectrum of possibilities for peace, against the relative closed-mindedness of the American Jewish community: "One of the things that struck me when I went to Israel was how much more open the debate was around these issues in Israel than they are sometimes here in the United States."[2]

When Obama said these words, he had only been to Israel once, for a jaunt beginning on January 9, 2006. He stayed less than forty-eight hours.

"He was touched," said Lee Rosenberg, then an AIPAC board member, who traveled with him on his 2006 trip. "[Obama] got an appreciation of the people in Israel."[3]

It is hard to see how. Crammed into the whirlwind trip were two nine-hour plane flights to and from Israel, a lengthy helicopter flyover of the West Bank, and two nights alone in the darkness of his hotel room and a few short meetings with peace activists and security officials. If he met any ordinary Israelis, it was while waiting in line at David Ben Gurion Airport.

Yet, here Obama was in Cleveland, holding forth like an old hand.

Nor would his travel companion and guide explain Obama's sudden knowledge of Israel. Rosenberg, who had discussed Obama's trip with reporters in 2006, refused to comment or expand on his earlier remarks when I contacted him in 2012, even off the record. "It's not my thing," he said.

Another aspect of Obama's 2006 trip to Israel is instructive. Shortly before he arrived, Israeli officials ordered the destruction of a Palestinian man's home after he intentionally rammed his truck into a public bus, hurting twenty-four commuters. The man's statements, following his arrest, left no doubt that he considered the attack to be a protest against the elected government's policies in the West Bank. Obama's staff crafted a response that didn't quarrel with Israel's decision to bulldoze the terrorist's house, a decision that was later reversed by an Israeli judge. But Obama objected, "saying he doubted that bulldozing houses deterred terrorism and that the man's relatives were being punished for a crime in which they played no part. But, then he added, 'I'm not going to say *that* in public.'"[4]

Obama's second, and only other pre-presidential trip to Israel, would occur months after the Cleveland fund-raiser. It also lasted two days, starting on July 22, 2008. By then, he had a Secret Service detail that made informal contacts with ordinary Israelis nearly impossible. Yet he kept repeating in his campaign speeches the line about Israeli public opinion being broader than American views of Israel.

Obama would continue to speak and write as if Israeli public opinion had remained in a time capsule that was sealed sometime in 1993. That's because, for him, it was. Many of the American Jews who had influenced his thinking about Israel, as we will see, had not visited the Jewish state in many years and still favored the left-wing peace plans that the overwhelming majority of Israelis are now actually skeptical of.

They were skeptical of the bold peace plans of the 1990s because those peace plans had failed—years before Obama's brief visits.

The 1993 Oslo Peace Accords sharply shifted the attitudes of the majority of Israelis, first by raising hopes and then by dashing them. Signed by Israel's elected government officials and the leaders of the Palestine Liberation Organization in September 1993, the wide-ranging agreement recognized an independent Palestinian government in the West Bank and Gaza Strip, provided for the withdrawal of Israel's military forces (except in certain strategic zones), and provided for Palestinian access to water, electricity, highways, and other Israeli infrastructure networks. Virtually every demand made by the Palestinians was addressed. Yet, other Palestinian groups, including Hamas, refused to abide by the accords and, indeed, refused to recognize Israel's right to exist as an independent Jewish state. Violent attacks culminated in the "intifada" that raged for years— killing or wounding hundreds.

As the Palestinians failed to follow the Oslo Accords, Israeli public opinion soured on those accords. Many began to wonder, for the first time, did the Palestinians actually want peace? By May 2000, only 39 percent of Israelis surveyed by Tami Steinmetz of the University of Tel Aviv's Center for Peace Research favored the Oslo Accords, and less than one-third thought that the agreements would bring peace in the coming years. As terrorism surged, the decline in support continued. By May 2004, the Center for Peace Research found that only 18 percent of Israelis thought that the Oslo Accords would eventually result in peace.

By the time of Obama's first visit in 2006, most Israelis and Americans had grown to distrust Palestinian claims. Still, Obama was stuck in that pre-1993 time warp, encouraged by a clutch of radical thinkers that acted as if the Oslo Accords had never been tried, let alone had failed.

If there was any doubt about Obama's outdated thinking, he dispelled it in his February 2008 Cleveland talk: "There is a strain within the pro-

Israel community that says unless you adopt an unwavering pro-Likud approach to Israel, that you're anti-Israel."[5]

At the time, the head of Likud, the lead opposition party, was Netanyahu, who enjoyed a big lead in Israeli opinion polls. Likud would return to power in the next elections, in February 2009—suggesting that more Israelis agreed with the Likud position on peace than not. Likud emphasized security over concessions when bargaining with the Palestinians. And Likud had governed Israel as recently as September 2005—hardly a right-wing fringe party.

What Obama, on the 2008 campaign trail, was saying, was that he was not planning to see eye-to-eye with Israel's future prime minister.

Obama's words were also a surprising intervention into another democracy's internal politics. "Imagine Netanyahu saying that just because you don't take a pro-Democratic [party] position does not mean that you are anti-American," asked one of Netanyahu's aides. He remembers thinking at the time: This is "just not done."

As events unfolded, Obama and Netanyahu would be increasingly at odds, with radically different views on Israel, the future of the Palestinians, and the growing threat from the Islamic Republic of Iran. It wasn't simply a personality clash; it was a conflict of visions.

What was Obama's vision of Israel and where did it come from?

Immediately after Obama stepped down from the podium in Cleveland, he was, as usual, besieged with requests for autographs.

With one autograph seeker that night, he shared a moment that speaks volumes about his views on Israel. Requesting an autograph for her two sons, the woman began spelling their names: "Meyer, M-E-Y-E-R," and "Heschel, H- . . ."

The future president interrupted: "Like Abraham?"[6]

Rabbi Abraham Joshua Heschel, through his modern disciple Rabbi Arnold Jacob Wolf, helped forge Obama's thinking on Israel.

Escaping from Europe just ahead of Nazi storm troopers, Rabbi Heschel arrived in New York City in 1940 and quickly became a leader in nearly every progressive crusade. He marched with Martin Luther King

Jr. and against the Vietnam War, erupting in anger at Robert McNamara during a meeting at the war's height. He had doubts about Alger Hiss's guilt, but no doubt about America's warmongering imperialism.[7]

Heschel's private secretary was a rabbinical student named Arnold Wolf. Once Wolf became a rabbi in his own right, he, too, took up progressive causes. Former *New Republic* magazine editor Peter Beinart wrote admiringly of the rabbi: "Wolf stood at the vanguard of the liberal activism that helped shape organized American Jewish life."[8]

Heschel and Wolf were initially Zionists who supported the state of Israel.

Then Israel made the mistake of winning the 1967 Six Day War against the combined armies of Egypt, Jordan, and Syria, and the 1973 Yom Kippur War, which began with a surprise attack on Judaism's holiest day.

These Israeli victories meant that Israel was no longer the underdog in many progressive minds, including theirs. After the 1967 war, Heschel became increasingly critical of Israel's control of the West Bank and the Gaza Strip. He died before Israel's victory in 1973, but, as usual, Wolf followed the lead of his mentor and launched an organization called Breira ("the Alternative")—the first collection of American Jews to openly support the creation of a separate Palestinian state. It was a beginning of a break with mainstream American Jewish organizations.

Though Breria dissolved in a hail of criticism and funding problems in 1977, Wolf's views did not change. He spent most of the 1970s as a Jewish chaplain at Yale University, where he worked alongside legendary liberal activist Rev. William Sloane Coffin, who held similar views on the Arab-Israeli conflict. Wolf did not stop by simply adopting a pro-Palestinian position. He wrote an infamous essay headlined "Overemphasizing the Holocaust" in 1979. It ended by saying: "'Never again' means nothing more or less than 'Jews first—and devil take the hindmost.'"[9]

In the 1980s, Wolf returned a brotherhood award from the National Council on Christians and Jews, received in 1962—because Ronald Reagan had received the same award. He later explained to the *Chicago Sun-Times* why he returned his award: "If Ronald Reagan is a humanitarian, then I am not."[10]

Reagan received this humanitarian award for his years of work pressuring the Soviet Union to allow Russian Jews to immigrate freely to Israel.

Shortly before his death, the ever-quirky Wolf celebrated his bar mitzvah with the words, "Thirteen is too young, that's why I am doing it at eighty-three." His brand of Reform Judaism did not recognize the bar mitzvah practice in his early days. He confided to the *Jewish Daily Forward* that he was nervous about the ceremony because it would be the first time that he would be chanting the Torah in public.

For many years, Wolf ran the KAM Isaiah Israel Temple, steps from Obama's Hyde Park home. In that progressive enclave near the University of Chicago, the two men had spent perhaps thousands of hours together from the early 1990s onward.

They had a lot in common: a passion for civil rights, social justice, and radical politics. While Wolf had earned his radical credentials over decades of sit-ins, walk-outs, and marches on police lines, Obama was also developing his radical résumé. He audited a class at Columbia University taught by famed writer and Palestinian activist Edward Said, spoke at protests at Harvard Law School, and attended a church where the radical anti-Israel sermons of Rev. Jeremiah Wright echoed off the walls.

Wolf saw in Obama a way to rekindle the fraying alliance between Jews and blacks that had worked together so successfully in the civil rights fights of the 1950s and 1960s. Wolf's congregation enthusiastically agreed. "This is a congregation, where the question wasn't, 'Are you going to vote for Obama?'" said Wolf's successor Darryl Crystal. "The question was, 'What state are you going to help canvass?'"[11]

Wolf publicly supported Obama from his very first run for political office.

At a fund-raiser in Wolf's home for Obama's 1996 campaign for the Illinois Senate, Wolf said: "Mr. Obama, some day you will be vice president of the United States."

Obama laughed. "Why vice president?"[12]

The largely Jewish crowd laughed.

• • •

Through Rabbi Wolf, Obama met Rashid Khalidi, a Palestinian activist who often spoke at Wolf's synagogue. Khalidi favored establishing an independent Palestinian state and confining Israel to its 1967 borders. Obama seemed to agree.

Obama was introduced to Rabbi Wolf by Newton Minow, a powerful Chicago lawyer, fiery liberal, and chairman of the Federal Communications Commission in the Kennedy administration. At the FCC, he famously attacked the idea of commercial television and set the stage for the creation of the Public Broadcasting System and National Public Radio. Minow shared Wolf's views toward Israel. He opposed Israel's 1982 incursion into Lebanon, when the Jewish state was seeking to stop terrorist attacks launched from there. Minow spoke at a press conference held by Americans for Peace Now, a left-wing group largely hostile to the policies of Israel's elected government, and thundered against the government of Israel.

Minow later served on the advisory council of J Street, a vocal opponent of Netanyahu's policies.

J Street's policies are radical. Its executive director, Jeremy Ben-Ami, has repeatedly called for Israel to be "more democratic" and grant equal voting rights to the Palestinians living inside its borders—effectively ending Israel's identity as a Jewish state. Ben-Ami understands the implications of his views. At a 2011 J Street conference, he declared that Israel cannot be simultaneously peaceful, democratic, and Jewish. He would be happy with only the first two.

J Street officially opposed a bipartisan congressional resolution condemning the United Nations' Goldstone Report, which accused Israel of war crimes without any believable evidence. It also arranged meetings for Goldstone on Capitol Hill. (Goldstone later backed away from the conclusions of his U.N. report.) J Street also opposed Israel's blockade of the Gaza Strip, which allowed food and medicine through but not guns or explosives. Egypt assisted Israel in maintaining the naval patrols along the Gaza coast. J Street opposed sanctions on Iran, which is defying sanctions to build nuclear bombs and long-range missiles to carry those devices. J Street also opposed using the U.S.'s U.N. Security Council veto to stop anti-Israel measures in the world body.

At a recent J Street conference, Ben-Ami boasted that he had met with Obama or White House officials more than forty times—making him one of the president's most frequent visitors.

Ben-Ami didn't point out that he visited the White House more often than the then-CIA director Leon Panetta, who had visited only nine times between 2009 and 2011, according to White House Visitor Logs.

Another confidant of the Obamas is federal judge Abner Mikva, who also served on a J Street board with Wolf and was a member of Wolf's synagogue. Mikva is openly hostile to Israel's prime minister: "Netanyahu speaks excellent English and that is the only positive thing I can say about him."

Rabbi Wolf was also friendly with two other prominent Jews who had a big impact on the development of Obama's views toward Israel: Bettylu Saltzman and her father, Philip Klutznick. Saltzman played a prominent role in Americans for Peace Now and also serves on J Street's advisory council. She was vice president for the New Israel Fund and, notes Beinart, "seethes with hostility toward the mainstream Jewish groups."[13]

She met Obama in 1992, and helped raise money for all of his campaigns for public office.

It was Saltzman who introduced Obama to David Axelrod, who rose to become Obama's chief strategist. Axelrod was a longtime donor to the New Israel Fund, a nonprofit that finances nearly every radical group in Israel, including some groups that have called for an end to Israel as a Jewish state. The New Israel Fund describes itself as "the leading organization committed to democratic change within Israel" with the objective of "social justice and equality for all Israelis."[14] The New Israel Fund virtually always sides with the Palestinians over the elected government of Israel.

Axelrod took a similar anti-Israel line when he told ABC's Jake Tapper in March 2010: "It was an insult," when the Israeli government announced approval of new housing units in an Arab section of Jerusalem upon Vice President Joe Biden's arrival in Israel. "What it did was it made more difficult a very difficult process. We've just gotten proximity, so-called proximity talks going between the Palestinians and the Israelis, and this seemed calculated to undermine that, and that was—that was distressing to everyone who is promoting the idea of peace—and security in the region . . . this was not the right way to behave . . . I think the Israelis understand clearly why we were upset and what, you know, what we want moving forward."[15] Axelrod's statement closely tracks with that of the New Israel Fund, J Street, Peace Now—and President Obama.

The so-called "insult" was a municipal planning and zoning board decision to advance a Jerusalem building project in the seventh of what is about a twenty-five-stage planning process, during Biden's visit. "The PM had no idea about it, any more than president [Obama] knows about planning decisions in Chevy Chase," said a close aide to Netanyahu.

The neighborhood is in the heart of municipal Jerusalem, said one aide, "that everyone in their right mind knows will be a part of Israel in any conceivable agreement and which in fact, according to the Al Jazeera leaks that came to the surface the following year, the Palestinians had already conceded in negotiations with the previous Israeli government."

An Israeli official adds, "So the whole issue was a manufactured crisis on building in Jerusalem."

There is ample evidence to support this view. Axelrod's broadside came after the issue was discussed and resolved between Biden and Netanyahu the previous Thursday. So there was no "insult" and no "crisis" at the time. The matter was resolved.

Yet the Obama administration created a "crisis" with Israel anyway, starting with an infamous forty-three-minute phone call to Israel's prime minister from Obama, a public rebuke from Hillary Clinton on Friday, and Axelrod's attack on the Sunday talk shows.

Israelis were shocked that Obama and his senior officials would use such strong language to fault an ally.

And it wasn't the first time. The previous November, Obama had "strongly condemned" Israel for building in another Jerusalem neighborhood, Gilo, which is home to forty thousand people and would also be part of any peace deal.

Before running for president, there is ample evidence that Obama shared Wolf's views of Israel. Obama said he read and admired the work of two of Israel's most famous peace activists—David Grossman and Amos Oz.[16]

Grossman wrote *The Yellow Wind,* a sympathetic and controversial nonfiction book about the plight of Palestinians in the so-called "occupied territories," that faults Israel for harsh police tactics and economic deprivation of its Arab population.

Amos Oz is widely hailed as one of Israel's greatest writers and his many books have appeared in both Hebrew and English. Nor is there any doubt about Oz's political views. Throughout his writings over the years, he has repeatedly said that he prefers Jewish socialism to Jewish religion. At fifteen, he became a Labor Zionist—a left-wing socialist who envisions Israel as home to a Jewish proletariat—and chose to live on a kibbutz: "Tel Aviv was not radical enough—only the kibbutz was radical enough."[17] In his book *How to Cure a Fanatic,* Oz writes about religious fanaticism as "the plague of many centuries."[18]

Grossman and Oz clearly colored Obama's thinking. In his 2006 book, *The Audacity of Hope,* he devotes a single paragraph to Israel. But it is a revealing one. Seemingly referring to his February 2006 helicopter expedition over Israel and the West Bank, Obama writes that Israeli and Arab villages are impossible to tell apart. He also establishes an equivalence, which also appears in the works of Grossman and Oz, between the suffering of Israelis and Palestinians. While it can be difficult to trace intellectual influences, the moral equivalence between the suffering of the Jews (and others) in the Holocaust and the plight of the Palestinians was made in President Obama's 2009 Cairo speech. (Interestingly, one of the boats in a pro-Palestinian flotilla that unsuccessfully tried to leave Greece in 2011 to run the "Gaza blockade" was named *The Audacity of Hope,* according to *Al Jazeera*.)[19]

Wolf's influence is evident, too. Before Obama's presidential run, Wolf explained Obama "was on the line of Peace Now."[20]

When Wolf died in December 2008, President-elect Obama called him a "dear friend," and said "Rabbi Wolf's name is synonymous with service, social action, and the possibility of change."

What was the possibility of change that Obama and Wolf both shared?

When campaigning for the U.S. Senate in 2003, Obama asked Jack Levin, whom he had gotten to know while he was a Harvard Law School student, to organize a fund-raiser. Since Levin was inviting mainly Jews interested in Israel, he asked Obama to write a position paper laying out his thoughts on the Jewish state.

Obama resisted.

Levin explained that most of the crowd would be Jewish and that many of their questions would be about Israel.

Obama wasn't eager to put his views in writing: "I don't want to put out any position papers yet, because it just makes it easier for people to attack me."[21]

Why did Obama believe that stating his positions on Israel would lead to attacks from Jews who were major donors to the Democratic Party? Levin apparently didn't ask him.

When Obama eventually wrote the paper, Levin was pleased with it. While no copy of the 2003 paper is publicly available, Levin summarized the content for *The Jerusalem Post* in 2008 as: "hitting all the bases: addressing the right of Israel to defend itself, defending the legitimacy of the security barrier, condemning Hamas and recognizing the need for a fair and just peace."[22]

The exact wording of that long-lost position paper, providing specifics on precisely how Obama would achieve a "fair and just peace," might reveal why Obama feared attacks on his views.

Lester Crown, a billionaire who has backed both Obama's U.S. Senate and presidential campaigns, conceded in 2008 that Obama's views on Israel are a little hard to define: "He obviously doesn't look at it in the same historical context as I do. I am sure the subject hasn't been anywhere near as important to him, so he doesn't have the depth of knowledge."[23]

At the time, Lester's son, James, was Illinois finance chairman for Obama's presidential campaign.

Obama's next-door neighbor in Hyde Park, Illinois, was a Jewish immigrant from Germany named Henry Gendler. While he generally found Obama to be friendly, he said, "When it came to Israel, it was not like that."[24] Gendler said: "When Israel started to become the topic, he became very cold. He always told me that we need a more 'balanced' approach, which in America is a code word for [not] being too pro-Israel."[25]

Obama's seemingly pro-Israel statements during the 2008 campaign, Gendler thought, were not genuine: "Now it is like he wants to hug and kiss Israel every five minutes. That's completely not the Barack I had as a neighbor. That started this year [2008], when he was trying to get elected."[26]

Another Jewish neighbor of Obama's, Ron Gidwitz, knew Obama and called him "friendly" and "warm." They worked together to reform Chicago's schools. But Gidwitz, who cares passionately about Israel, decided to support Sen. John McCain over Obama in 2008.

Generally, progressive Jews tended to give Obama the benefit of the doubt, while Republican-leaning Jews, like Gendler and Gidwitz, tended to be more wary. They had known Obama for years and thought his views on Israel were outside of the American Jewish mainstream.

The neighbors were right to be wary.

Once in office, Obama's real views on Israel emerged.

Shortly after he was sworn in as president, Obama announced subtle, but strong changes in America's policy toward Israel.

This was no accident. Every member of his team involved in shaping policy toward Israel was, in one way or another, a disciple of Rabbi Abraham Heschel and Rabbi Arnold Wolf, and an ideological enemy of Prime Minister Benjamin Netanyahu.

Anti-Netanyahu comments from Obama's team, and others close to them, are in great supply. Netanyahu is "one of the single most obnoxious individuals you're going to come into (contact with)—just a liar and a cheat," Clinton's onetime White House Press Secretary Joe Lockhart said.[27]

Obama and his aides charted a collision course with Netanyahu from the administration's first days. Obama "decided to come out louder, harder, and faster than almost any of its predecessors before understanding what the situation was," former peace negotiator, Aaron David Miller, said.[28]

At first, Obama picked Washington establishment figures with mainstream (if slightly left of center) views on Israel to guide his Middle East policies. Former U.S. senator George Mitchell was named special envoy for the Palestinian-Israeli peace process and reported directly to Obama, not to Secretary of State Clinton. Mitchell was an experienced negotiator, both in the Senate and in the British-Irish peace talks; his direct pipeline to Obama gave him unusual clout. His experience and his access to Obama should have given him the space to succeed, if anyone could. Yet, he found the Palestinians to be unrealistic and intransigent, the Israelis to be fearful and incremental, and President Obama to be unpredictable and overly ambitious.

"He hit a brick wall. Or maybe he thought he was tilting at windmills," said Dan Levy, a research fellow at the New America Foundation and a veteran of the peace talks.[29] He knew Mitchell well.

Throughout 2010 and the early months of 2011, administration officials had been debating the merits of a major speech by the president that would force the peace process forward. Hillary Clinton had switched sides—supporting and opposing the idea of a presidential address—so many times that insiders were left confused. Influential White House speechwriter Ben Rhodes was in favor of the speech (perhaps because he would likely write it), believing that both the Palestinians and the Israelis were locked into their narrow perspectives and that a properly worded speech would jolt them into seeing the big picture. Mitchell and others believed that even small gains would be hard won and that soaring words wouldn't move minds.

Obama sided with Rhodes and others who believed a speech could transform the Middle East stalemate.

The timing and setting of the president's speech were repeatedly moved and delayed, from January 2011 at the White House, to eventually a hall at the State Department in May 2011.

Mitchell resigned the day that Obama spoke at the State Department. "He quit because he failed," said Hebrew University of Jerusalem expert Shlomo Avineri. "And he failed because he received a mission impossible from President Obama."[30]

Mitchell's departure alarmed even the *Huffington Post:* "There is a recognition that there is precious little prospect of getting a negotiated effort relaunched because Mitchell is the guy . . . you want in the room."[31]

The power of a presidential speech was about to be tested.

•   •   •

Far from fostering peace, Obama's speech prompted the collision that he and his aides had set in motion from Day 1: Israel's statehood, Obama said at the State Department on May 19, 2011, "cannot be fulfilled with permanent occupation" of "Palestinian lands." He continued: "Israel and Palestine should be based on the 1967 lines with mutually agreed swaps, so that secure and recognized borders are established for both states."[32]

The 1967 borders zigzag through Israeli neighborhoods up and down the country and divide its capitol, Jerusalem. Israeli foreign minister Abba Eban, a famous dove in peace talks, refers to the 1967 lines as "Auschwitz borders" because they squeeze Israel into a space less than nine miles wide at its narrowest point and put strategic hills just outside of Israel from which Palestinians could fire bullets, mortars, and rockets into Israeli suburbs below. Indeed, sniper fire from Palestinian roofs was a near-daily occurrence until the Israelis built concrete walls in crowded cities, depriving the snipers of their prey. Next, the Palestinians turned to rocket attacks, launched from the very Gaza Strip neighborhoods that Israeli Defense Forces had unilaterally retreated from in 2005. Even this partial restoration of the 1967 lines—in the vicinity of the Gaza Strip—resulted in thousands of rocket attacks that forced some 1 million Israelis into bomb shelters. In suburban neighborhoods inside Israel, rockets from Gaza have killed at least ten civilians.

Netanyahu had resigned from the Sharon government over the 2005 withdrawal and, predicted that a wider retreat would trigger rocket attacks on Israel's major southern cities, such as Ashkelon, Beer Sheva, and Ashdod, and encourage more terror. He proved to be prophetic.

Obama's 2011 speech at the State Department was a sharp break with more than forty years of presidential precedent. When Obama said, "We believe the borders of Israel and Palestine should be based on the 1967 lines with mutually agreed swaps," he was being far more radical than even President Johnson was in the days after the 1967 war.

Obama's announcement was a change in U.S. policy and an unpopular one at that. With the weight of accumulating contrary evidence, Obama's spin doctors were forced to find a new spin.

Hours after the State Department speech made headlines across

America and Israel, the frantic phone calls began. Many came from prominent donors, others came from Israel.

Netanyahu's top advisors were shocked by the surprise change in American policy. They had been informed "less than twenty-four hours earlier," one senior advisor told me.

Secretary of State Clinton, U.N. ambassador Susan Rice, and White House officials tried to mollify them. Tension was especially high because Obama and Netanyahu were due to meet in the Oval Office on Friday afternoon, less than twenty-four hours after the president's State Department speech.

An Obama White House spokesman expressed surprise at Netanyahu's objections to Obama's proposal.

When opposition to Obama's plan surged in Congress, the White House scrambled to explain itself. At first, the official line was that it wasn't a change in policy at all. President Clinton had used a similar formulation—a wording that had been crafted by many of the same advisors, who were now advising Obama. But, American public policy had shifted, in tandem with Israeli public opinion, since the Clinton era. And, in fact, Clinton had never mentioned returning Israel to its 1967 borders, only the idea of "land swaps."

The policy of the U.S. government was put into writing by President Bush in 2004. He wrote that Israel's borders would be subject to negotiation at any final peace with the Palestinians and would not be imposed by America on that tiny democratic nation, that population centers (including "settlements" of any size) would be part of Israel, and that the Palestinians would live in a separate state, not in Israel. In short, Israel would not revert to its 1967 borders and the Palestinians would have no "right of return."

The Bush policy was articulated in a 2004 official letter to then–Prime Minister Ariel Sharon and endorsed by overwhelming majorities in both houses of Congress. The policy was publicly supported by most Democrats, including then-Sen. Hillary Clinton. Presidential letters of this type are considered binding and both future U.S. presidents and foreign governments usually rely on them. Bush's letter was not a new policy, but a written articulation of one that existed for more than forty years.

Every American president since the 1967 war has essentially opposed the idea of returning to the pre-1967 war boundaries.

Returning to the 1967 lines, President Johnson had said, "is not a prescription for peace but for renewed hostilities." This statement appeared just days after the war's end.

"The U.S. has not developed a final position on the borders. Should it do so it will give great weight to Israel's position that any peace agreement with Syria must be predicated on Israel remaining on the Golan Heights [which are miles outside the 1967 lines]," President Ford wrote in a letter to Israel's prime minister in September 1975.

Following the 1978 Camp David accords, which established formal but cold peace between Egypt and Israel, President Carter told Congress that border negotiations in the future would begin with U.N. resolution 242, which is as close as Carter would come to hinting at the 1967 prewar borders. It was barely a hint. The U.N. resolution contemplates that Israel should withdraw from undefined "territories"—and not "all territories"— to "secure and recognized borders" without any reference to the 1967 lines. "The reason for this language was specifically to rule out return to indefensible 1967 lines, which is why the Arabs opposed [U.N. resolution 242] at the time," one Israeli government advisor told me. "They later accepted it and tried to reinterpret it."

Noting that "the bulk of Israel's population lived within artillery range of hostile armies," President Reagan opposed reverting to Israel's earlier borders in September 1982.

The president who came the closest to Obama's position was Clinton, who, in January 2001, floated the possibility of "territorial swaps," but never mentioned the 1967 borders in this context.

While conceding that there might be some exchanges of territory between the Palestinians and the Israelis, President George W. Bush wrote, in April 2004, that "realities on the ground" meant that reverting to the 1967 borders would be impossible, that all populations centers would have to be incorporated into Israel, and that Palestinian refugees couldn't move to Israel and all previous peace talks "have reached the same conclusion."

•   •   •

The Friday afternoon meeting needed to go well.

The dueling calendars of the president and the prime minister would provide plenty of opportunities for sniping, if either side chose to do so. Obama was slated to speak on Sunday at the American Israel Public Affairs Committee's gala dinner. AIPAC is one of America's most powerful lobbying organizations and the premier forum for supporters of Israel to debate Middle East policy. Many of the attendees are major donors to both presidential and congressional campaigns. If they were displeased with the president's new position, they would be well placed to make their displeasure known. On Monday, Netanyahu would also speak before AIPAC and on Tuesday he would address a joint session of Congress. Advisors to both Obama and Netanyahu knew the official schedules of both men. If the meeting didn't go well, each leader had already scheduled appearances at which he could retaliate.

The stakes were high.

But the Friday meeting in the Oval Office didn't go well.

When Netanyahu met Obama, he had prepared a careful, detailed brief, one advisor told me. It was supposed to calmly present the case for the logic of American policy of the past four decades.

Obama was angry; he wanted to lecture, not to be lectured. And, an Obama advisor said, he didn't like the idea that he had misspoken. He wasn't ready to admit that he had been wrong.

Netanyahu knew that Obama could not simply "walk back" a speech he had just given. The prime minister was realistic. Yet, an Israeli official explained, "he wanted to explain why he was deeply troubled by the speech and change in U.S. policy. He was looking for clarifications."

Clarification was not forthcoming.

The meeting dragged on for some forty-five painful minutes. White House pool reporters and photographers were clamoring to get into the Oval Office for a previously scheduled photo op. The photo op was behind schedule and network executives were getting nervous. Following the president's State Department speech, the joint appearance was guaranteed to make news. But, the newsmakers were running late and commercial breaks were looming.

When the Oval Office doors finally opened to admit the camera crews, the mood was tense. This wasn't going to be the feel-good session that the press was expecting.

Obama and Netanyahu had moved to a preplanned spot near the Oval Office fireplace. Instead of harmony, reporters heard dueling and discordant remarks from the two leaders.

Netanyahu decided to say to the world all of the things that Obama wouldn't let him say in the meeting, one advisor who was present told me.

Netanyahu realized he had a global audience and did his best to present Israel's case in common-sense terms. He explained sixty-three years of Israeli history and Israel's right to defend itself. He emphasized Israel's ongoing willingness to make "generous compromises," but was emphatic that Israel would never go back to the "indefensible" 1967 lines. He lectured Obama and warned, "A peace based on illusions will crash against the rocks of Middle Eastern reality."[33]

Obama had trouble making eye contact with Netanyahu. Nor did his face hide his emotions as his ill-conceived "peace" initiative crashed in front of him. "He was like watching the [space shuttle] Challenger explode," one Israeli advisor, who had grown up in the United States, told me.

Obama might have avoided the indignity of Netanyahu's history lesson if he had given Netanyahu's personal history a little more attention. Israel is such a fragile and young country that Netanyahu is actually its first prime minister to be born in the state of Israel. His father (who died in 2012) is a well-regarded scholar, writer, and editor, who is known for his view that Zionism needs to break with its passivist and socialist impulses and forthrightly defend the right of Jews to live and the right of Israel to exist. Netanyahu was a member of Israel's elite Special Forces, saw combat in both the 1967 and 1973 wars, and was shot rescuing hostages on a hijacked Sabena plane. The 1967 borders are not an abstraction for him or a line on a map delimiting a piece of ground that he has never seen. They are hills and homes where fellow soldiers died and civilians and children were extinguished. He knows the loss from terrorism at an intimate level. His brother, legendary commando leader Yonatan, was the only one who died on a world-famous raid on the Entebbe Airport, where Jewish passengers were held captive by leftist terrorists and Ugandan soldiers. Netanyahu has twice been elected Israel's prime minister and, in that capacity, visited with Presidents Clinton, Bush, and Obama. He has also held nearly every important portfolio in the Israeli cabinet including foreign ministry (twice, once as deputy foreign minister in the early 1990s, famously making Israel's case during the Gulf War and at the Madrid peace conference, and again as foreign minister from November 2002 to February 2003), finance minister (where he launched far-ranging reforms of Israel's tax and welfare policies), and U.N. ambassador (where he vigorously defended Israeli policy from European socialists and Arab extremists). So, he is no stranger to verbal combat, either.

He also knows American politics extraordinarily well. He lived for years in the United States and speaks English fluently.[34] He has two degrees from the Massachusetts Institute of Technology. He has friendships that go back decades with congressmen, senators, diplomats, generals, and journalists. He has appeared on virtually every major program on every American network, both on television and radio. He has spoken to every major Washington- and New York–based think tank and, in many parts of the United States, may be more popular than Obama himself.

Netanyahu has also surrounded himself with advisors who know America well. One advisor (Ron Dermer) grew up in Miami Beach, Florida, where both his father and brother served as mayor. Israel's Ambassador, Michael Oren, was born and grew up in America, and is a noted historian who specializes in America's policy in the Middle East. Two of Oren's historical books (*Power, Faith and Fantasy* and *Six Days of War*) were bestsellers in the United States.

It would be hard to imagine a foreign rival better positioned to triumph over Obama in the American media and to compete with Obama for the hearts of his countrymen.

In short, Netanyahu was well positioned to separate Obama from his own political supporters, while Obama—who has few long-term relationships with Israelis, who have seen Obama's public standing in their country collapse to low double-digits in most Israeli polls—doesn't share similar leverage among Netanyahu's voters. This was not a case of mutually assured destruction. Given the asymmetry between Netanyahu and Obama, the president was reckless to believe that he could prevail.

Nevertheless, Obama's advisors—and the president himself—believed that they did have leverage over Netanyahu. Two previous prime ministers from Netanyahu's Likud party had lost their positions when they confronted an American president—Yitzhak Shamir in 1992 and Netanyahu himself in 1999. But the Obama administration had clearly misread Israeli politics. Not only had the failure of the 1993 Oslo Accords soured Israelis on the peace process, but also Obama didn't have the credibility in Israel that Clinton once enjoyed. Israelis had ruefully noticed that Obama's first television interview as president with a foreign broadcaster was with Al Jazeera, that his father was a Muslim, and that the president himself had attended Muslim schools in Indonesia. Obama's first trips to the Middle East were to two Muslim states, Turkey and Egypt, and he had not even included a courtesy stop to Israel on either trip. Finally, Israelis knew that the Kadima party, now in opposition, had green-lighted the 2006 withdrawal from the Gaza Strip, leaving behind "settlements" and getting rocket attacks in return. Few expected Obama's settlement freeze to yield better results.

Yet he went ahead with his antagonistic State Department speech and then, incredibly, agreed to keep a long-scheduled personal meeting with Netanyahu (which had been set months earlier) and followed standard White House routine to allow network cameramen to be present. Even worse, neither the president nor any member of his inner circle had seen the conflict coming or planned to manage the likely outcome.

Obama would have been better prepared for his showdown with Netanyahu if he, like General Patton, read his antagonist's book. In the preface to his book, *A Durable Peace: Israel and Its Place Among the Nations,* Netanyahu wrote, "I am neither detached nor objective when it comes to securing the future of the Jewish state. In fact, I plead unabashed and passionate partisanship in seeking to assure the Jewish future. This is the conviction that guided me as the prime minister of Israel between 1996 and 1999, and this is the conviction that will guide me for the rest of my life."[35]

In the Oval Office press conference, Netanyahu clearly kept returning to Israeli's "red lines."

Where are the red lines? Netanyahu made it clear: "We don't have a lot of margin for error. Because, Mr. President, history will not give the Jewish people another chance."[36]

That Netanyahu would draw these red lines should not have surprised Obama. *A Durable Peace* contains the same position that Netanyahu voiced in his Oval Office conversation and in his many speeches before and since. "I am convinced of one thing: The Jewish people will not get another chance. There are only so many miracles that history can provide a people, and the Jews have had more than their share. After unparalleled adversity, the Jews came back to life in the modern State of Israel. For better or worse, the Jewish future is centered on the future of that state. Therefore we must be extra careful not to toy with Israel's security and jeopardize its defense, even as we pursue peace with our neighbors, for what is at stake is the destiny of an entire people."[37]

Nor was it the first time that such a meeting between the president and the prime minister ended with raised voices and hurt feelings.

At their first meeting on May 18, 2009, Obama blundered over Netanyahu's red lines. When Obama flatly demanded that Netanyahu stop Israeli settlements in "occupied territories" and return to its 1967 borders, Netanyahu agreed to a temporary freeze on new construction in certain disputed areas. It was a big concession by the leader of the Likud party. Obama's team believed it was just an appetizer.

Still, Netanyahu considered Obama's move to be a strategic mistake. A senior Israeli official summed up the prime minister's thoughts this way: "We thought settlements were a bogus issue that was going to muck up negotiations and put the entire onus on Israel despite Palestinian rejection of both [Prime Minister] Barak's peace offer in 2000 and [Prime Minister Ehud] Olmert's in 2008. Suddenly Israel was in the dock, Palestinians were avoiding negotiations and we were to blame." In short, even the Palestinian leadership had assumed that Jewish neighborhoods (critics call them "settlements") would be part of Israel in any final peace, so to raise the issue now was pointless and phony. More importantly, the temporary freeze shifted the burden to Israel—even though it was the Palestinians who had walked away from peace negotiations.

Despite his strategic sense, Netanyahu agreed to a "temporary" freeze on new construction in settlements of the West Bank—in the hopes of winning over the president, not the Palestinians. The freeze did not apply to Jerusalem. Secretary of State Hillary Clinton later hailed Israel's action as "unprecedented." Obama was silent on the issue.

Obama didn't offer any concessions of his own. The president seemed to believe that the rightness of his position was so obvious that he could command Netanyahu's assent simply by stating it. He seemed completely unprepared for the prime minister's response, even though that response would surprise no one who knew him.

"The question is, which bright spark advised the president to demand a settlements freeze without working out what the next step should be when Netanyahu inevitably said 'No'?" former head of the Council on Foreign Relations, Leslie Gelb, said. "Why wasn't George Mitchell in the room? Where was Jones?"[38]

Obama had appointed George Mitchell as his envoy and retired Marine general Jim Jones as his national security advisor.

Gelb is wrong that Mitchell and Jones were not involved in planning the meeting and the agenda. Both were in conversations with Israeli government officials. Mitchell had actually suggested the idea of a "settlement freeze" in the 2002 Mitchell Report that influenced the Bush administration's Road Map in 2003.

The meeting was one-on-one between Obama and Netanyahu. Later in the meeting, Uzi Arad and Ron Dermer came into the room along with Jones and White House spokesman Robert Gibbs. At a later stage in the meeting, Rahm Emanuel walked in. Netanyahu remembered Rahm from the Clinton administration and, a senior Israeli official said, "he may have been pressing for a confrontation" with Rahm.

Obama was only prepared to push his agenda, not actually navigate the complexities of the region. He failed to anticipate Netanyahu's likely objections or even be prepared for them. And, Obama insisted that Netanyahu deal with the settlement issue first. But, in early 2009, Netanyahu was more worried that nuclear missiles from Iran would annihilate Israel, or in the words of a prominent Iranian mullah on state-run television, "finish the job that Hitler had begun."

Obama's response was breezy and not reassuring. The president believed that then-negotiations with Tehran would defuse the crisis and that Israel's fears were exaggerated: "I am prepared to make what I believe will be a persuasive argument, that there should be a different course to be taken."[39]

Four of Obama's most influential aides had ties to former Congressman Lee Hamilton. All four, both separately and jointly, had pushed the president to demand a freeze on settlements from Netanyahu in May 2009.

Rep. Lee Hamilton, an Indiana Democrat and onetime chairman of the House Foreign Affairs Committee, was a member of the liberal freshman class that swept into Congress in 1965. He quickly distinguished himself as a dove, criticizing Johnson's prosecution of the war in Vietnam, President Reagan's support of the Contras in Nicaragua, and, after he left Congress in 1999, was a vocal critic of the Iraq War. While his views on Israel were complex, the one constant theme that emerges is that Israel must make bigger concessions in order to secure peace with its neighbors. Many of Obama's advisors on Israel were alumni of Hamilton's office, either in Congress or at the Iraq Study Group. Obama's senior director for the Middle East and North Africa at the National Security Council had worked as a legislative analyst for Hamilton. Mara Rudman, who served as chief of staff for special envoy Mitchell, had also worked in Hamilton's congressional office. Denis McDonough, the National Security Council's chief of staff, had worked for years for Hamilton. McDonough had an unusually close relationship with the president and sometimes briefed him outside of the presence of the national security advisor. Obama's chief foreign policy speechwriter was Ben Rhodes; he had worked for Hamilton at the Iraq Study Group, where he cowrote the group's report along with Hamilton.[40]

Significantly, Hamilton had long advocated for opening a diplomatic dialogue with Hamas, the terrorist group that runs large sections of the West Bank and Gaza Strip.

Obama quickly endorsed the four Hamilton alumni's position. White House strategists decided that Vice President Joseph Biden should float the idea at an AIPAC conference on May 5, 2009. He did so unambiguously, saying that the Jewish state must "not build any more settlements."[41]

Then came Obama's first meeting with Netanyahu some two weeks later, after which Obama went public, saying, "Settlements have to be stopped in order to move forward."[42]

•   •   •

That was just the beginning. Obama continued to press the settlements issue, making it a centerpiece of his famous Cairo speech a month later: "The United States does not accept the legitimacy of continued Israeli settlements. This construction violates previous agreements and undermines efforts to achieve peace. It is time for these settlements to stop."[43]

Netanyahu responded with a speech at Bar-Ilan University in Tel Aviv. "We want peace," he said. But first Israel demanded that the Palestinians formally recognize Israel's right to exist as an independent Jewish state and that it forswear all alliances, military or otherwise, with state sponsors of terrorism such as Iran and Syria or the terrorist proxies of those states including Hamas and Hezbollah. Settlements were a side issue that could be addressed in peace negotiations once Israel's preconditions were met. Netanyahu added: "There is a need to have people live normal lives and let mothers and fathers raise their children like everyone in the world. The settlers are not enemies of peace. They are our brothers and sisters."[44]

The difference between Netanyahu's and Obama's views on Israeli settlers could hardly have been more divergent.

Meanwhile, inside the White House, aides were debating how to toughen the antisettlement stance that Netanyahu had just agreed to. The main priority was making the settlement freeze permanent, not temporary. But other antisettlement options were also being discussed. One involved rewriting America's free trade agreement with Israel to bar goods and services made by Israelis outside of its 1967 borders. This would be costly and complicated to administer. Aside from a handful of farm goods produced in the "so-called occupied territories" by Israelis, most of the products were parts of goods or services that were completed inside Israel's 1967 borders. What if one computer programmer, living a few miles outside of Jerusalem in the territories, worked on computer codes that were also written by Israelis living in the pre-1967 portions of Jerusalem? What if a plastic product was made in Tel Aviv and assembled east of the 1967 lines? Would it make a difference if they used Arab labor for that assembly? After all, Palestinians are able to sell into the U.S. market under the U.S.-Israeli free trade agreement.

Another option considered: Instructing the Internal Revenue Service to deny tax deductions to American nonprofit groups that qualified under the IRS code as 501(c) 3 "tax-exempt organizations," which gave some of their funds to poor Israelis eking out a living on a "settlement." This, too, was thorny. Do you include or exclude "settlements" that are essentially suburbs and that would almost certainly be counted as Israeli territory in any final peace agreement? If you treated all settlements as equal, then more difficult questions arise. What about funds destined for an orphanage or elementary school? What about charitable operations that aid Palestinians and Israelis alike?

After months of meetings and memos, these policy options were eventually discarded. They weren't dropped because the administration's opposition to settlements had softened but because they were bureaucratically difficult to administer and would likely be strongly opposed by Congress.

Additionally, the free trade ideas might be seen as a violation of the agreements that the United States had signed at the World Trade Organization because they reduced the volume of tariff free trade and used trade policy to interfere in the internal affairs of an independent nation.[45]

A temporary settlement freeze was agreed to in November 2009 and ran until September 2010. While the Obama administration got the headline it wanted in the exhaustive negotiations stretching from May to November of 2009, the Netanyahu government got the details it sought. That included exempting from the construction halt all buildings in East Jerusalem, essential government buildings—such as schools and hospitals—and all buildings whose foundations had already been laid. Each of these limits to the construction ban had their own internal logic: government buildings can take years to approve through Israel's zoning and planning process—one of the most onerous in the world—and it wouldn't make sense to stop construction midway through, when wind and weather might wear the internal skeleton of large public projects. So, the "settlement freeze" was, in practice, very narrow.

The Obama administration and many peace activists were disappointed. Peter Beinart, in his book *The Crisis of Zionism,* captures the feeling of frustration: "All in all, according to Peace Now, construction began on 1,518 West Bank housing units in 2008. In 2009, the number was 1,920. In 2010—the year of the "freeze"—it was 1,712."[46]

The peace activists were wrong that the freeze had no effect; they just misjudged Israeli reaction to it. People rushed to build before the freeze formally began and then returned to construction after it was over. Israel suffers from a shortage of affordable, middle-class housing, and demand is almost always greater than supply.

Netanyahu had won, again.

When the ten-month settlement freeze ended, Netanyahu pointed out that the Palestinians had not been buoyed by the settlement freeze and had not used the freeze to remove anti-Israeli messages from its school textbooks or radio broadcasts. Israel had gotten nothing in return for agreeing to Obama's brainstorm.

By March 2010, the settlement freeze was breaking down. The exemptions that Israel had won meant the freeze had no practical effect on construction.

During her weekly meeting with Obama, Hillary Clinton complained that Israel had announced new construction plans in the neighborhood of Ramat Schlomo—during Vice President Biden's visit to Israel. It was an "insult" and one that continues to smolder to this day.

Clinton told Obama, to his amusement and approval, that she had angrily scolded Netanyahu for forty-three minutes over a secure telephone line. She believed that the Israeli government had broken its deal regarding a settlement freeze.

Netanyahu explained that the freeze specifically exempted East Jerusalem and, besides, Ramat Shlomo is mostly inside the 1967 lines.

But the administration was spoiling for a fight. Officials continued to believe that their criticism could bring down Netanyahu's Likud-led government and that new elections would enable them to work with a more pliable Israeli leader.

Two days after Hillary's dressing down, Axelrod appeared on ABC's Sunday morning program *This Week*, where he went public with the administration's feeling of insult over the new construction announced upon Biden's arrival in Israel.

As the freeze was nearing its agreed-upon end date, the Obama administration officials urgently sought an extension. Netanyahu resisted.

In the end, the new partial ban lasting three more months was debated, but the Obama administration backed away from the deal. In the end, there was no extension.

And, in the events of 2009 and 2010, Obama had lost something important, too. Netanyahu was now much less likely to agree with Obama's next big idea.

That idea, it turned out, involved shrinking Israel's borders back to May 1967.

As the president's speech took shape, Obama's advisors took special precautions to keep the section regarding Israel and its 1967 lines a secret. When "speechwriters began circulating drafts inside the administration, they left the Israel section blank."[47] That meant that when Netanyahu's expected counter-volley came, none of the president's supporters would be prepared to come to his defense. Obama would be alone—against a very skilled adversary.

In December 2010, the Palestinians announced that they would seek a U.N. Security Council resolution demanding that Israel "immediately and completely cease all settlement activities."

The wording was no accident. It had come from a speech by Obama's secretary of state.

The Palestinian move would have immediately earned a veto by the United States in the U.N.'s Security Council in any previous post–World War II Administration.

The Obama administration was divided and largely leaning toward not using the veto to stop the Palestinian resolution at the United Nations. Clinton and Secretary of Defense Robert Gates were leaning against a veto, as was U.N. ambassador Susan Rice. Deputy National Security Advisor Ben Rhodes was passionately opposed to a veto.[48]

The argument that seemed to be winning the day was simple—and simply wrong. The "Arab Spring" was toppling Arab dictators that had long been friendly toward the United States in the winter of 2010 and the spring of 2011, including the leaders of Tunisia and Egypt. Mass demonstrations were also building in Bahrain, Lebanon, Syria, Yemen, and smaller movements were breaking out in nearly every member of the twenty-two-nation Arab League. Vetoing the Palestinian resolution at the United Nations, Clinton and other officials believed, would signal that America was opposed to Arab interests. The problem? None of the Arab protests cited Israel-Palestine as a concern. The protestors were concentrating on government corruption, food prices, and youth joblessness. Israel was not on their minds.

The pressure to use the veto at the United Nations was entirely outside of the Obama administration—it was coming from the Congress, where both Democrats and Republicans, were demanding action. Major donors were threatening to leave over the issue.

Reluctantly, the administration yielded and used the veto.

Less than twenty-four hours before Obama's State Department speech, a senior National Security Council (in charge of the Middle East portfolio) was permitted to phone an official in Netanyahu's government.

It was late Wednesday night in Israel. The message was shocking and brief. It was more of a telegram than a discussion.

Netanyahu and his senior officials quickly discussed it. Dermer phoned another senior National Security Council official "to argue against making what Israel thought would be a big mistake."

Dermer suggested changes, including ruling out the so-called "right of return" that would allow Palestinians to flood into Israel, or demanding that the Palestinians be forced to recognize Israel's right to exist as an independent Jewish state or being specific about Israel's security needs, such as the need to maintain a long-term Israeli military presence along the Jordan River. The American official was not able to make any changes to the president's prepared remarks.

Still, it was clear that Obama and his team had settled on the issue and wouldn't be talked out of it. Dermer got the message: "The administration wasn't going to make any refinements."

Hillary Clinton phoned Netanyahu the next day, roughly an hour before Obama's speech. She seemed to have delayed her call long enough to send the message that it was too late to fine-tune the president's remarks.

At lunchtime in Washington on Thursday, May 19, Obama walked up to the lectern at the State Department.

An official State of Israel press release accidentally elevated the tension. "Prime Minister Netanyahu expects to hear a reaffirmation from President Obama of U.S. commitments made to Israel in 2004, which were overwhelmingly supported by both houses of Congress. Among other things, those commitments relate to Israel not having to withdraw to the 1967 lines which are both indefensible and which would leave major Israeli population centers in Judea and Samaria beyond those lines."

The Obama administration reacted sharply to the word "expects." It is the kind of word that the State Department uses when addressing human-rights abuses in Burma. Inside the State Department, it had kind of a stylized usage. Who, they said, was Netanyahu to "expect" anything?

The Israeli government had a fine and finely parsed response. "Expects," according to Dermer, is a translation for the Hebrew word *metzapeh,* could also be translated as "anticipates." While the Hebrew statement was being tweaked, the earlier English-language was forgotten in the rush to catch a flight to Washington. In the normal course of events, the English version would have been scrutinized for possible misreadings like this one.

In fact, "expects" in English has two senses: an anticipatory one and a more commanding one. A child could expect (hope for) ice cream after dinner, while not being able to demand it. The Obama administration was misreading English.

The Obama administration, which had come to expect criticism from Netanyahu, had simply gone looking for a fight.

It was a fight that Obama lost. Peter Beinart, who favors Obama's Israel policy, recognized that the president was losing ground: "It was merely the beginning of one of the most extraordinary humiliations of a president by a foreign leader in modern history."[49]

But, for now the Obama administration pretended otherwise. Netanyahu was not given a joint press conference, or even a photo op, during his second visit to the White House on May 20, 2011.

Two days later, on Sunday, May 22, Obama went before AIPAC and tried to make his formulation about the 1967 lines palatable to the American Jewish establishment, declaring, "The parties themselves—Israelis and Palestinians—will negotiate a border that is different than the one that existed on June 4, 1967. That's what mutually agreed-upon swaps means . . ."[50]

Obama was in full retreat.

Following Obama's speeches at the State Department and at AIPAC, donations to Obama's reelection campaign fell sharply. One Democratic fund-raiser told *New York* magazine that some $10 million had disappeared that weekend.

As with House Speaker John Boehner and the House Republicans generally, Obama seemed to believe that the problem of dealing with Netanyahu could be solved with power, not persuasion. Obama had long-held ideological beliefs and, like many intellectuals, believed that a hard shove would move the world into the right place. Professors, who generally lack power, have a hard time grasping how much power presidents actually have—it is never as much as they imagine. And they have a harder time recognizing the power dynamics among personalities. Obama misjudged both.

Persuasion only works when it flows in the direction of self-interest and, as Obama had to be repeatedly told, self-interest is how people see their own interests and those of the people they are responsible for—not how you see their interests.

In the end, Obama couldn't compel Netanyahu to surrender his lifelong beliefs about Israel, or to risk his reelection, on plans that Obama had formulated years earlier in the spirited company of Rabbi Wolf and his comrades. In the real world, leaders cannot afford to experiment with dreams.

It is the hallmark of a poor leader to even try.

The following day, Netanyahu enjoyed a rare honor for a foreign leader. He addressed a joint session of the U.S. Congress. Both Democrats and Republicans repeatedly rose to interrupt the prime minister's remarks with standing ovations. The applause was loud and heartfelt.

CHAPTER 6

FAST AND LOOSE AND FURIOUS

Thank you, Reverend [Al] Sharpton. I appreciate your kind words, but I am especially grateful for your prayers—and for your partnership, your friendship, and your tireless efforts to speak out for the voiceless, to stand up for the powerless, and to shine a light on the problems we must solve, and the promises we must fulfill.

—Attorney General Eric Holder, April 11, 2012[1]

The key test for any leader is what to do when a subordinate repeatedly fails and then repeatedly tries to cover up his role in the failure.

Attorney General Eric H. Holder Jr. may be President Obama's favorite cabinet member. The first black president likes to watch ESPN with the first black attorney general in the White House residence. They have much in common: strong mothers who pushed them to rise, elite educations, a decades-long hostility to gun rights, and a shared passion for racially polarizing preachers—and they have worked side by side for almost four tumultuous years.

Yet Holder has caused much of that tumult. He fought for more than a year to try the September 11 mastermind, Khalid Shaikh Mohammed, in civilian court in lower Manhattan. Congress and the public overwhelmingly opposed the controversial effort. He declined to prosecute a number of New Black Panther party members caught on video intimidating voters at a polling place in Philadelphia. Then he dropped the ongoing prosecutions of several federal officials who had leaked U.S. government secrets to *The New York Times* and other news outlets. These leaks compromised America's security by revealing operational secrets of the war on terror and led to the shutdown of the most successful multinational program to disrupt al-Qaeda's finances. Computer records clearly revealed the identity of the leakers. The case was overwhelming, but Holder declined to prosecute it, a decision that surprised career officials.

As a result of these and many other controversial decisions, more than 120 members of Congress and three senators have called for Holder to resign—an unprecedented number in American history. A similar number have endorsed a no-confidence resolution condemning his job performance. And, if the chairman of the House Oversight and Government Reform committee, Rep. Darrell E. Issa (R-California), prevails, the attorney general may face a congressional censure.

Presidents have removed attorney generals for far less.

Nevertheless, the strong bond between Obama and Holder remains. There are two secret reasons for the durability of this relationship: the role of Valerie Jarrett and a political debt from 2008.

Jarrett is exceptionally close to the attorney general. She told the *American Lawyer* magazine in 2008, "There isn't a day that we [Jarrett and Holder] don't talk."[2] When not in direct contact, Jarrett serves as an essential intermediary between Holder and the White House on many projects.

She described Holder's role in Obama's first presidential campaign in all-encompassing terms: "He is the utility man for Team Obama, playing a variety of positions: surrogate, fund-raiser, strategist, and source of wisdom in the ways of Washington."[3]

In the early days of the Obama campaign, when the junior senator from Illinois was seen as a long shot against Hillary Clinton, Holder's presence sent a vital message. Since he had been deputy attorney general under President Clinton, his perceived shift to the Obama camp gave the candidate credibility. That was essential to Obama.

Holder's endorsement of Obama may have been the product of revenge. As deputy attorney general, he had essentially approved a presidential pardon for Marc Rich, a Wall Street trader whose former wife, Denise Rich, was a significant Democratic donor. Rich had fled to Switzerland to avoid charges that he bought or sold oil from Iran in violation of the U.S. embargo against that nation. In his written recommendation on a presidential pardon to Clinton, Holder concluded that he was "neutral leaning towards favorable."[4]

Congressional investigators harshly questioned Holder at a February 2001 hearing before the House Committee on Oversight and Government Reform. He never forgot it. "I have been angry, hurt and even somewhat disillusioned by what has transpired over the past two weeks with regard to this pardon."[5] He blamed the Clintons for his perceived mistreatment, adding that his wife was livid and believed the Clintons owed her husband "more loyalty than he was shown."[6]

But Obama's debt to Holder didn't end there. He raised tens of thousands of dollars for Obama and spent countless hours on campaign conference calls and meetings at the young campaign's national headquarters, then above a pizza parlor on Capitol Hill. They were like combat veterans whose shared suffering forged a link that could be better felt than described.

And he saved Obama from the biggest crisis of his 2008 campaign: Rev. Jeremiah Wright. Holder worked closely with Valerie Jarrett and Michelle Obama on the March 18 speech Obama gave in Philadelphia about race relations, which was meant to defuse the furor surrounding Reverend Wright's racial remarks.

But a single undercover operation, and the cover-up that followed, defines Holder's tenure as attorney general. And the longer Obama has permitted Holder to hold a top federal post, the more questions have been raised about his judgment and leadership abilities.

Loyalty is gravity for Obama: It keeps the universe intact, and its pull goes in both directions. Yet gravity can also destroy. A leader has to balance loyalty's attractive and destructive qualities. Regarding Holder, can Obama tell the difference?

The ill-fated sting known as Operation Fast and Furious began while Holder was attorney general. His now-former deputy attorney general, Gary Grindler, had direct knowledge of the operation and it seems likely that the attorney general did as well. Holder has denied direct knowledge, but congressional investigators think the denials are "Clintonian" and false. More importantly, Holder has denied investigators access to the more than seventy thousand pages of documents that might prove his innocence.

Fast and Furious led to the deaths of hundreds of innocent people on both sides of the U.S.-Mexico border, notably a brave U.S. Border Patrol agent named Brian Terry.

This complex and controversial tale remains largely untold. Many accounts have focused on Holder's culpability. As the evidence of wrongdoing has accumulated—whistleblowers threatened, key witnesses transferred away from the reach of congressional subpoenas, documents hidden or delivered only when their denial became politically or legally untenable—Obama failed to act.

At no time did Obama publicly demand Holder's resignation or even request that he fully cooperate with congressional investigators. Nor has he removed Holder's subordinates, even after they were caught lying to Congress. Indeed, many of those officials who were caught lying have even been advanced in terms of pay or power, though the administration denies the transfers were promotions.

It is the biggest Obama administration scandal the public has never heard about.

Outside of the Arizona border town of Nogales lies Peck Canyon, a deep, dry gulch that runs between Arizona's Atascosa and Mexico's Tumacacori mountains; it is so rugged and remote that parts of it can only be traveled on foot.[7] It has long been a secret highway for the lawless. Over the centuries, Apache raiders and Mexican renegades used to creep out of its cracks, launch surprise attacks, and then disappear without a trace. "During the day Peck Canyon is beautiful, peaceful, and quiet," a local television station reported. "But once the sun goes down, things are very different out here due to the illegal smuggling that takes place here literally every night."[8]

This is no exaggeration. Some one hundred violent crimes were reported in or near the canyon in 2011 alone. And that number is believed to be low, because most victims were illegal aliens who usually decline to report crimes to American authorities.[9]

Border Patrol agent Brian A. Terry was part of a four-man Border Patrol Tactical Unit that worked its way into the folds of Peck Canyon the night of December 14, 2010. They were hoping to intercept a "rip crew," a roving armed band that attacks migrant workers and illegal immigrants, along with rival gangs and drug smugglers.[10]

Terry loved the Border Patrol. He was gung-ho and so serious and effective that his fellow agents nicknamed him "Superman."

Around 11:15 P.M. that night, Terry and his fellow agents spotted the five-man rip crew on the floor of the canyon. Through thermal binoculars, the team saw them skulking past scrub oaks in knee-high grass, according to the affidavit of FBI special agent Scott Hunter.[11] They could see that every one of them was armed with what appeared to be military-style automatic weapons.

The Border Patrol agents were armed with "less than lethal" guns that fired high-speed bean bags. They were no match for the bad guys.

One of them called down to the suspects, "Border Patrol! Drop your weapons!"

The outlaws had no intention of being arrested. They raised their weapons, searching the rocks above. They had night-vision goggles and soon spotted the border agents above them. Their gun barrels were moving toward the agents.

The agents only had seconds to react. The agents "deployed" their nonlethal bean bags. The high-speed bags landed with a thump. The rip crew fired.[12] Flashes of flame darted from their uncleaned gun barrels.

Within seconds, a bullet punched Terry in the back, according to a shooting incident report from the Border Patrol. "I'm hit," he said as he fell.[13] He wasn't dramatic, just relaying a fact his team needed to know.

As the "medium caliber bullet" penetrated "the skin and soft tissues of the left lower back, the bullet passed forward, rightward, and upward to penetrate the spinal column and cord at the level of L2," the Pima County medical examiner wrote in his report. "The bullet continued on to perforate the aorta, mesentery, small intestines, distal stomach, and left lobe of the liver before causing subcutaneous hemorrhage of the anterior midline abdominal wall, 22 inches from the top of the head."[14] The bullet entered his back, climbed his spine, severed it, and bounced across vital organs in his midsection.

"I can't feel my legs," Terry said. "I think I'm paralyzed." These appear to be his last words.

The internal bleeding was catastrophic. Seconds later, Terry died in the arms of a fellow agent.[15]

When the weapon that killed Terry was seized and its serial number traced, investigators were shocked: It was part of a secret U.S. Department of Justice program that made no effort to follow the guns that were handed to Mexico's deadliest drug lords.

Details about what happened next are hard to come by. The Justice Department sealed all court records after the indictments for the Terry killing without explanation. Justice Department spokeswoman Debra Hartman of the U.S. Attorney's San Diego office would only say: "Yes, our office is handling the case and can't comment further."[16]

The sealing of the Terry case court records is just one of a dizzying number of efforts, congressional investigators believe, to conceal the facts of the case, from small (Justice department officials initially denied the agents shot bean bags,[17] not bullets) to large (Holder's role in approving Operation Fast and Furious itself).

The original idea of Fast and Furious was to encourage Arizona gun shops to illegally sell guns to "straw purchasers," who either trafficked them into Mexico to be sold to known Mexican cartel members, or sold them to middlemen along their path southward.

Federal agents from the Bureau of Alcohol, Tobacco, Firearms, and

Explosives (known as "ATF") allowed and oversaw these sales, knowing where the weapons would ultimately end up. They could have arrested the traffickers or straw purchasers at any time and seized the weapons. Instead, they did not bother to make arrests, consistently arguing that the plan was to build bigger cases against the cartels and to identify their high-level officers and gun-acquisition techniques. Agents call such sting operations "gunwalking."

Even in the handful of cases when ATF agents actually arrested their targets, they quickly released them. ATF special agent Hope MacAllister arrested the lead target in Operation Fast and Furious, Manuel Fabian Celis-Acosta, in May 2010. She questioned him for less than an hour and let him go. He wasn't tracked or followed. Before she let him go, MacAllister wrote her phone number on a ten-dollar bill and passed it to him. She asked him to stay in touch. He never did.

Fast and Furious was developed as the answer to a unique ATF problem: the agency couldn't find any cases of cartels buying guns from legitimate dealers. Given the strict federal laws on gun purchases, it is nearly impossible for cartels to buy guns from ordinary retailers. Gun sellers are licensed by the federal government and a valid identity card (usually a driver's license) is required to buy a gun.

Those licenses are then checked against a database. If a would-be buyer has had a criminal conviction, a domestic-violence charge, or a history of mental problems, the law requires that the sale be stopped. Gun retailers are extremely vigilant. They don't want to risk losing their business or their freedom in exchange for a $200 gun sale. And gun sellers generally see themselves as on the side of law and order and see their business as a way of helping people protect themselves from criminals. They don't want to arm criminals. As a result, virtually all guns involved in crimes in the United States come from the black market—not licensed gun dealers.

Nevertheless, senior Justice Department officials wanted to prosecute a case involving licensed gun dealers. (Why not focus on black market gun sales, which is the source of virtually all guns used in crimes in the United States? That question would come up again, after innocents had died on both sides of the border.) To make their case involving legitimate gun dealers, the ATF had to persuade gun-store owners to sell large quantities of weapons to straw purchasers, who would pass all the background checks (they had valid photo ID and no criminal histories). This wasn't easy. It is illegal for anyone to act as "straw buyer," to purchase a weapon actually intended for someone else, and illegal to sell a gun if the seller believes the buyer will transfer the weapon to a criminal. Firearms store owners didn't want to go anywhere near any illegal activity. Many refused to cooperate. Others initially agreed to cooperate with the sting, but then objected when they saw the scale of the illegal gun sales. The ATF agents pressured them to keep making the illegal sales.

The government had to allow a string of lesser crimes in order to trace the firearms and catch major criminals. Or, at least, that was the theory.

Yet the operation was dangerously flawed from the start. There were no tracking devices hidden on the guns. So agents watched, from a distance, the guns disappear into the trunks of cars.

The straw purchasers often eluded the agents. They suddenly turned off of a highway or vanished into buildings. So the illegal guns kept getting away—ultimately arming Mexican kill squads.

No one at the ATF or the Justice Department shut down the program before congressional investigators discovered it in 2011.

Since the bureau kept losing the guns it was supposed to track, supervisors decided to make a minor change in the operation. Later in the operation—which went on for almost two years—the ATF switched from watching gun runners to having its own agents act as straw purchasers and deliver the guns to known Mexican criminals. They were supposed to watch those criminals. Instead, those lawbreakers vanished, too.

The secret operation was a total failure. The gun-tracking program failed to follow guns or result in a single criminal conviction. But the illegal guns kept appearing at crime scenes in Mexico and, increasingly, in the United States.

Police labs use ballistic tests to compare the unique grooves inside a gun barrel and the minute marks made on a bullet as it passes down that barrel. That's how they are able to quickly and conclusively show that a particular gun is a murder weapon. And virtually every firearm legally sold in the United States, and indeed almost everywhere in the world, has a unique serial number. That number allows police to examine the gun's history of ownership, much like a title on a car. Ballistic tests and serial numbers kept connecting murder weapons to ATF's secret operation.

Mexican gangsters, like many criminals, tended to drop their weapons near murder scenes so they couldn't be arrested with a gun linking them to a shooting. This bit of human nature made it practically impossible for ATF to definitively track illicit guns in the first place. The operation was flawed from the start.

Another flaw in the operation: The ATF asked gun-shop owners to alert the ATF if there were any increased purchases of Mexican criminals' "weapons of choice"—and defined those weapons so broadly to include virtually all semiautomatic rifles and many types of pistols, which some 4 million of Americans own and shoot. A semiautomatic rifle fires one bullet per trigger pull, a category that includes most of the nation's estimated 100 million hunting rifles. The ATF wanted to know whenever someone bought more than a few at a time.

The ATF responded by encouraging the sales. One buyer, identified as Jaime Avila, and several of his confederates, bought hundreds of guns for their "personal use," including 575 AK-47 type semiautomatic rifles.[18] These guns can be modified to be fully automatic machine guns.

One federal agent, who requested anonymity because he feared retaliation from the Holder Justice Department, called the program "insane."

Another agent, who also remained anonymous out of fear of reprisals, told CBS reporter Sharyl Attkisson: "The numbers [of missing guns] are over 2,500 on that case by the way. That's how many guns were sold—including some 50-calibers they let walk."

A 50-caliber round is the size of a Magic Marker and can punch a hole as big as a golf ball in a manhole cover.

There are civilian uses—many shooting enthusiasts use them to hit targets over a mile away—and the military uses the round in its sniper programs in Afghanistan. But the cartels weren't innocent hobbyists. They were using the military-grade rounds to kill hundreds of innocents. In at least one case, cartel members used Fast and Furious weapons to take out a Mexican helicopter.

The federal government was working overtime to arm and equip these mass murderers.

By the spring of 2010, ATF officers in Phoenix were in open revolt. They had gotten into law enforcement to save lives and punish wrongdoers, not to arm them.

The project supervisor, ATF Phoenix Group VII supervisor David Voth, tried to quell the rebellion by writing, in a March 2010 e-mail, that the failing operation was a top Justice Department priority. It came directly from Washington, he said. Then he threatened uncooperative agents:

> Whether you care or not people of rank and authority at HQ are paying close attention to this case and they also believe we (Phoenix Group VII) are doing what they envisioned the Southwest Border Groups doing. It may sound cheesy, but we are "The Tip of the ATF spear" when it comes to Southwest Border Firearms Trafficking. We need to resolve our issues at this meeting. I will be damned if this case is going to suffer due to petty arguing, rumors, or other adolescent behavior. If you don't think this is fun you're in the wrong line of work—period ... Maybe the Maricopa County Jail is hiring detention officers and you can get paid $30,000 (instead of $100,000) to serve lunch to inmates all day.

Most agents fell in line. One did not.

Special Agent John Dodson was supposed to buy guns from a Federal Firearms licensee, whose name Voth redacted in documents.

Anxious about violating the law, one gun-shop owner demanded a letter in writing. Against orders, Dodson gave it to him. The June 10, 2010, letter said, in part:

> Per Section925(a)(1) of the Gun Control Act (GCA) exempts law enforcement agencies from the transportation, shipment, receipt, or importation controls of the GCA when firearms are to

be used for the official business of the agency. Please accept this letter in lieu of completing an ATF Form 4473 for the purchase of four (4) CAI, Model Draco, 7.62 × 39 mm pistols, by Special Agent John Dodson. These aforementioned pistols will be used by Special Agent Dodson in furtherance of the performance of his official duties. In addition, Special Agent Dodson has not been convicted of a misdemeanor crime of domestic violence.[19]

Like the gun-store owner, Dodson was concerned about the undercover buy. Though the Fast and Furious operation was described as a "sting" to catch Mexican cartel gun buyers, it looked to Dodson as if, in fact, the ATF was simply funneling guns to the cartels. He was essentially committing a crime "in furtherance of the performance of his official duties."

And that made him nervous.

So did the orders from his supervisor. Voth ordered Dodson to use taxpayer money to buy firearms from gun dealers "off the books," and then allow Mexican cartels to buy them from him. That, too, was a federal crime.

Later, Dodson, on his own initiative, spent six hot summer days at a desert stakeout, waiting for a buyer to pick up the guns. When the buyer finally appeared, Dodson called for help to make an arrest. His supervisors told him to let the guns "walk." He was told to leave the scene. There would be no arrests.

He was stunned.

That wasn't the only arrest stopped by higher-ranking officials. For months, ATF agents had been following 50-caliber weapons heading toward the Mexican border. From a stakeout, they watched the money and illegal guns change hands. They had probable cause for an arrest and evidence that would all but certainly lead to a conviction.

The agents repeatedly begged, by phone and radio, for permission to arrest the Mexican cartel members with the weapons in their hands, according to congressional testimony. The ATF brass refused. The answer was unambiguous: "Negative. Stand down."[20]

With no arrests allowed and guns that were only effectively traced after they had been used at murder scenes, many ATF agents began to wonder: Why does the Justice Department want us to do this?

•   •   •

President Obama and Attorney General Holder had been publicly worrying about the threat of illegal guns since the earliest days of the administration.

During a joint press conference with Mexican president Felipe Calderón in April 2009, Obama said, "Our focus is to work with Secretary [Janet] Napolitano, Attorney General Holder, our entire Homeland Security team, ATF, border security, everybody who is involved with this to coordinate with our counterparts in Mexico to significantly ramp up our enforcement of existing laws. In fact, I've asked Eric Holder to do a complete review of how our current enforcement operations are working and make sure we are cutting down on the loop holes that are causing some of these drug trafficking problems. Last point I would make, is that there are going to be some opportunities where I think we can build some strong consensus. I'll give you one example and that is the issue of gun tracing, the tracing of bullets and ballistics and gun information that had been used in major crimes."[21]

It seemed to many in the gun-rights community that Obama and Holder were laying the groundwork for claiming that the government's gunwalking program justified another round of gun regulation. Citing border security and the fight against illegal drugs as justification, Obama and Holder were already seeking to increase government oversight of gun ownership. But opposition from the public and Congress was steep. Fast and Furious may have been designed to show that their opponents were wrong.

That suspicion, which so far has not been proved with "smoking gun" evidence, is surprisingly widespread. Everyone from ATF agents to congressional investigators repeats it. As one congressional staffer connected to the investigation said, "Nothing else makes any sense."

The missing link in this story is that Eric Holder and President Obama were looking for justification for a new rule they planned to issue by executive order, which bureaucrats at the ATF call a "demand letter."

ATF was gathering "evidence" to support the new regulations, which would put further restrictions on gun-store owners.

In his fact-finding quest, Mark Chait, ATF assistant director for field operations in Washington, sent this e-mail to ATF agent Bill Newell on July 14, 2010. Newell was in charge of ATF's Phoenix office.

"Bill—can you see if these guns were all purchased from the same (licensed gun dealer) and at one time. We are looking at anecdotal cases to support a demand letter on long-gun multiple sales. Thanks."[22]

Indeed, Obama issued this executive order, which has the force of law, and cited exactly the justification that Chait mentioned:

> The international expansion and increased violence of transnational criminal networks pose a significant threat to the United States. Federal, state, and foreign law enforcement agencies have determined that certain types of semi-automatic rifles—greater than .22 caliber and with the ability to accept a detachable magazine—are highly sought after by dangerous drug trafficking organizations and frequently recovered at violent crime scenes near the Southwest Border. This new reporting measure—tailored to focus only on multiple sales of these types of rifles to the same person within a five-day period—will improve the ability of the Bureau of Alcohol, Tobacco, Firearms and Explosives to detect and disrupt the illegal weapons trafficking networks responsible for diverting firearms from lawful commerce to criminals and criminal organizations. These targeted information requests will occur in Arizona, California, New Mexico, and Texas to help confront the problem of illegal gun trafficking into Mexico and along the Southwest Border.

House Republicans later passed a 2013 appropriations bill that included a "rider" preventing the Justice Department and ATF from enforcing that new policy. The White House quickly issued a statement calling that rider one reason Obama intended to veto the bill.

Did the White House know about the deadly failure of Operation Fast and Furious? The evidence is overwhelming that it did.

The Phoenix ATF office had already briefed White House officials, in detail, from the earliest stages of the program. In September 2010,

Kevin O'Reilly was national security director for North America at the White House. O'Reilly was asked to provide a presidential briefing in advance of President Obama's trip to Mexico. So O'Reilly called Bill Newell, his friend, to get the details—the same Bill Newell who was in charge of Operation Fast and Furious in Phoenix.

Newell sent the information in an e-mail to O'Reilly that said, "You didn't get this from me."

Congressional investigators, working for Rep. Darrell Issa (R-California) and Sen. Charles Grassley (R-Iowa), later uncovered the e-mail exchange. The e-mails were the subject of a July 26, 2011, hearing in a House office building.

When Congressman Trey Gowdy (R-South Carolina) asked Newell, "What does that mean, 'You didn't get this from me'?"

This July 2011 hearing was the first time anyone publicly documented that a White House official was familiar with Operation Fast and Furious.[23]

Newell answered, "Obviously he was a friend of mine and I shouldn't have been sending that to him."[24]

The ATF agents in Arizona had also kept Eric Holder fully briefed, it appears. He bragged about the program at a Cuernavaca, Mexico, conference for Mexican and U.S. law enforcement officials on April 2, 2009, saying, "Last week, our administration launched a major new effort to break the backs of the cartels. My department is committing one hundred new ATF personnel to the Southwest border in the next one hundred days to supplement our ongoing Project Gunrunner."[25]

Documents dating from summer 2010, released during a series of congressional hearings, show the detail of Holder's knowledge.[26] At least five briefing memos on the subject were delivered to Holder's office from aides and supervisory agents in the field, but the attorney general has maintained that he "never read" them.

Agent Dodson, only concerned about the ATF abetting the murderous capabilities of the Mexican cartels, had no idea about Obama's and Holder's political maneuvering.

He went to his supervisor, Voth, and Voth's assistant, George Gillett, for answers, but the conversation quickly escalated into a "screaming match" heard by the entire Phoenix office. Dodson told his bosses angrily: "Why not just go direct and empty out the ATF arms room to the cartels. Don't you know these guns will be used to kill people?"

Dodson "argued with a superior asking, 'are you prepared to go to the funeral of a federal officer killed with one of these guns?' Another said every time there was a shooting near the border, 'we would all hold our breath hoping it wasn't one of 'our' guns.'"[27]

They would not have to hold their breath for long.

On December 14, 2010, one of the guns, an AK-47, placed in the hands of a Mexican criminal, did exactly as Dodson had warned. It killed Agent Brian Terry.

Investigators combed Peck Canyon and, in the brush, found the murder weapon where it had been thrown when the "rip crew" fled. When the story of Terry's murder flashed across local television screens, ATF agents started arriving. One detective at the scene recalled, "All these ATF guys were showing up. We were trying to catch suspects and rope up the crime scene, and all the ATF guys were saying they needed the serial numbers! They needed the serial numbers!"[28]

The need for serial numbers was obvious within the ATF: If the murder weapon was one of "their" weapons, they had a problem.

Indeed, they did.

On the day after the Terry murder, an ATF agent, whose name has been redacted in the official record, sent an e-mail. "The two firearms recovered by ATF this afternoon near Rio Rico, Arizona, in conjunction with the shooting death of U.S. Border Patrol agent Terry were identified as 'Suspect Guns' in the Fast and Furious investigation." The gun serial numbers were edited out of the e-mail. The e-mail continued: "I initiated an urgent firearms trace request on both of the firearms and then contacted the NTC to ensure the traces were conducted today."

While the agent was eager to help trace the guns, Eric Holder and his top lieutenants were not. The cover-up had begun.

•   •   •

Voth was on top of things in Phoenix. He e-mailed Bill Newell, the ATF agent in charge of all operations in Arizona, who had briefed the White House on Fast and Furious before Obama's trip to Mexico. Fewer than twenty-four hours had passed since Agent Terry's murder. "We are charging [Jaime] Avila [who purchased the alleged murder weapons along with hundreds of other guns] with a stand-alone June 2010 firearms purchase. This way we do not divulge our current case [Fast and Furious] or the Border Patrol shooting case."

Newell replied. "Great job."[29]

He knew ATF had a public-relations disaster on its hands. Taking a page from Voth's playbook, he held a news conference that he hoped would get his agency ahead of the story and show its operations were successful and results-oriented. He announced indictments of a number of illegal gun purchasers whom the ATF had known about for more than a year, but had declined to prosecute because, according to January 2010 ATF documents, they were "not from any member of the targeted group of straw purchasers identified in this investigation. Rather, they were Hispanic individuals (both male and female) whose association with our target group is currently unknown."

This was all the ATF had. But they were desperate to make a splash.

During the news conference, a reporter asked Newell if the ATF had purposely allowed guns to fall into the hands of Mexican cartel members. "Hell no," Newell said.[30]

He was lying, as congressional investigators would later prove.

The ATF indictments of low-level random Mexican gun purchasers did not succeed in diverting attention from the Terry murder investigation or Operation Fast and Furious. On January 27, 2011, Sen. Charles E. Grassley (R-Iowa) sent a letter to Kenneth Melson, acting director of the ATF in Washington, D.C.

Referring to Newell's press conference, the senator quoted Newell as saying: "We strongly believe we took down the entire organization from top to bottom that operated out of the Phoenix area."

Grassley said that statement raised "a host of serious questions" because he knew the ATF had been aware of those gun purchasers before Agent

Terry's murder. The senator also said he was concerned that the "ATF may have become careless, if not negligent" in its gunwalking programs and that he had heard the two AK-47s used in the shootout in Peck Canyon were purchased through the program on January 16, 2010, in Glendale, Arizona. Grassley said had, in his possession, "detailed documentation which appears to lend credibility to the claims and partially corroborates them." He demanded immediate answers from Melson.[31]

Grassley contacted agents in Arizona. He had heard about efforts to silence anyone who answered his questions and told Melson to put a stop to any efforts to stonewall him or retaliate against people cooperating with the investigation, writing:

> As you know, I wrote to you on Thursday, January 27, regarding serious allegations associated with Project Gunrunner and the death of Customs and Border Protection Agent Brian Terry. Although the staff briefing I requested has not yet been scheduled, it appears that the ATF is reacting in less productive ways to my request. I understand that Assistant Special Agent in Charge (ASAC) George Gillette of the ATF's Phoenix office questioned one of the individual agents who answered my staff's questions about Project Gunrunner. ASAC Gillette allegedly accused the agent of misconduct related to his contacts with the Senate Judiciary Committee. This is exactly the wrong sort of reaction for the ATF. Rather than focusing on retaliating against whistleblowers, the ATF's sole focus should be on finding and disclosing the truth as soon as possible.[32]

The cover-up didn't last long. *The Arizona Republic* broke the story, on February 1, 2011, that the AK-47 used to murder Terry was part of an ATF operation.[33]

It was quickly becoming clear at the Justice Department that Grassley's allegations could not be ignored. Still, Melson did not respond to Grassley's request. Instead, Melson asked a deputy at the Justice Department to keep Grassley at bay.

In a February 4, 2011, letter that would become infamous, Holder's assistant attorney general Ronald Weich wrote to Grassley that the allegation "that ATF 'sanctioned' or otherwise knowingly allowed the sale of 'assault' weapons to a straw purchaser who then transported them to Mexico—is false." He said that the ATF "makes every effort to interdict weapons that have been purchased illegally and prevent their transportation to Mexico." He went on to say: "I also want to assure you that ATF has made no attempt to retaliate against any of its agents regarding this matter." He said the Department of Justice wanted "to protect investigations and the law enforcement personnel who directly conduct them from inappropriate political influence," and asked Grassley to end his investigation, saying, "we respectfully request that Committee staff not contact law enforcement personnel seeking information about pending criminal investigations, including the investigation into the death of Customs and Border Patrol Agent Brian Terry."

He asked that any further inquiries be directed to him in "this office."[34]

As the Justice Department tried to put a stop to Grassley's investigation in Washington, Holder's people in Arizona went into overdrive to shut down any cooperation by agents who had direct knowledge of Operation Fast and Furious.

Agent Dodson, who had so vociferously warned his superiors that their program would "kill people," was stripped of his role and assigned to lesser duties. He was ridiculed as a "nut job," "wing-nut," and "disgruntled." The word went out: "Contact with Dodson was detrimental to any ATF career."

Other agents who testified before Congress about the failed operation have seen their lives and careers disrupted, and have been financially saddled with legal bills. Agents Larry Alt, Orlindo James Casa, and Carlos Canino (ATF's acting attaché in Mexico) no longer work for the ATF in Phoenix; they were all transferred. Agent Forcelli, who had tried to protect Dodson, was demoted to a desk job after he testified.

While the agents on the ground testified to the details of Operation Fast and Furious, its leaders stonewalled. And the stonewalling started at the top.

Obama denied that he had supported the secret operation. He gave an interview to the Spanish-language cable channel Univision on March 23, 2011. "Well, first of all, I did not authorize it. Eric Holder, the attorney general, did not authorize it. There may be a situation here in which a serious mistake was made. If that's the case, then we'll find—find out and we'll hold somebody accountable."[35]

Yet Obama never launched his own investigation and the president never held anyone personally accountable—including Holder.

So Congress stepped in. Congressman Darrell E. Issa, the chairman of the House Committee on Oversight and Government Reform, held hearings to question Eric Holder. Representative Issa was trying to do what the president would not do: get to the bottom of a sting operation that killed a U.S. border patrol agent and hundreds of Mexicans.

Holder was not about to accept any accountability. Holder's responses to questions show him to be a careful avoider of facts on a Clintonian scale, parsing what the meaning of "is" is. The entire exchange is striking:

> Issa: "When did you first know about the program officially, I believe, called Fast and Furious? To the best of your knowledge, what date?"
>
> Holder: "I'm not sure of the exact date, but I probably heard about Fast and Furious for the first time over the last few weeks."
>
> Issa: "Now that you've been briefed on it, the president has said on March 22 that you didn't authorize it. Did your deputy attorney general, James Cole, authorize it?"
>
> Holder: "I'm sorry. That would be?"
>
> Issa: "The deputy attorney general, James Cole."
>
> Holder again acted puzzled: "Did he—I didn't hear. Did he?"
>
> Issa completed the question: "Did the deputy attorney general authorize it?"
>
> Holder finally gave a less than clear answer: "My guess would be no. Mr. Cole, I don't think, was in the—I—I think—I don't think he was in the department at the time that operation started."

Issa went on to ask: "How about the head of the Criminal Division, Lanny Breuer?"

Holder: "I'm not sure."

Issa: "Did he authorize it?"

Holder: "I'm not sure whether Mr. Breuer authorized it. I mean, you have to understand the way in which the department operates. Although there are—there are operations, this one has become—has gotten a great deal of publicity."

Issa later asked: "Do you stand by this program? In other words—and it's not a hypothetical, really—if you knew this program, knew about this program 90 days ago, 180 days ago, would you have allowed it to continue? And if not, then what are you going to do about the people who did know and allowed it to continue?"

Holder: "Well, what I have told people at the Department of Justice is that under no circumstances in any case that any investigation that we bring should guns be allowed to be distributed in an uncontrolled manner."

Issa: "So that would be cognizant with the March 9 letter from Deputy Attorney General James Cole in which he says that we should not design or conduct undercover operations which include guns crossing the border. If we have knowledge that guns are about to cross the border, we must take immediate action to stop the firearms from crossing the border, and so on. That's— that's your policy today."

Holder: "That has—that is our policy. That has totally been the policy that I tried to impose."

Issa: "And isn't Fast and Furious inconsistent with that policy?"

Holder: "Well, that's one of the questions that we'll have to see whether or not Fast and Furious was conducted in a way that's consistent with what Jim wrote there, what I have said today. And that's what the inspector general is, in fact, looking at."[36]

As the hearings continued, Issa brought in Assistant Attorney General Weich, who had written that letter to Grassley on behalf of ATF acting director Kenneth Melson. In that letter, Weich had categorically denied that the Justice Department "knowingly allowed the sale of 'assault' weapons to a straw purchaser who then transported them to Mexico." Issa asked Weich if he had written the letter. Weich squirmed and said, "These letters are the product of the Justice Department."

Issa pushed him and pointed out that he had signed the letter. He asked if he really did claim Grassley's allegations were "false." Weich didn't directly acknowledge that he had made the statement in the letter he had signed. He answered vaguely about taking responsibility.

Issa responded by asking him again if his assertion to Senator Grassley, that the Justice Department was not allowing the sale of assault weapons to Mexican drug cartels, was false. Weich wiggled again, "Obviously, there have been allegations that call into serious question that particular sentence."

Issa tried yet again to get a clear-cut answer: "I will just take your agreement that those documents indicate that that statement that you signed that someone prepared for [your] signature were false?"

Weich continued to resist answering. "Congressman, I am not prepared to say that at this time." He went on to say, "Everything that we say is true to the best of our knowledge at the time we say it." Of course, documents have emerged that directly contradict Weich, Holder, and other ATF officials, requiring the truth to be adjusted. Anticipating this, he said, "As more facts come out, obviously our understanding of the situation is enhanced."[37]

The cover story had to keep changing as more facts became public.

Holder and Weich were not the only officials to mislead about Fast and Furious under oath. Lanny Breuer, assistant attorney general for the Criminal Division at the U.S. Department of Justice, knew about the ATF "gunwalking" sting early on. His biography at Covington & Burling (where he was Holder's colleague) quoted *Washingtonian* magazine calling Breuer "one of the cleverest [lawyers] in Washington."[38] If the ability to mislead the public while under oath is clever, then *Washingtonian* was right. Yet the truth about how these guns were ending up in the hands of the Mexican drug cartels was not as important as public relations. Breuer met with his aide, the aptly named James Trusty, and expressed concern that "the bad stuff that could come out" about guns walking.[39]

Breuer and his aides came up with a clever diversion for questions about Operation Fast and Furious by using another operation called "Wide Receiver," which had occurred under President George W. Bush, in an attempt to shift blame and save the ATF, Holder, and Obama from embarrassment if something bad happened on their watch.[40] Wide Receiver was also a gunwalking sting operation, but there are important differences. It involved the knowledge and cooperation of the Mexican government, it involved many fewer guns, no Americans were killed, and arrests were made and convictions sought. More importantly, the operation was a mixed success and the career staff learned to distrust such risky undercover operations. Fast and Furious repeated all of the mistakes made in Wide Receiver and added many new ones. Nevertheless, Breuer repeatedly cited it as evidence that the Bush administration had done similar things. He was trying to muddy the lens of accountability.

Breuer also was involved in the drafting of Weich's February 4 letter to Grassley that broadly denied that the ATF allowed guns to walk into the arms of Mexican criminals; e-mails reveal he was shown at least four separate drafts, forwarding one to his own personal Google e-mail account and telling one of his aides, "as usual, great work."[41]

When Grassley asked Breuer about the letter, he brazenly misled the senator, saying, "At the time, I was in Mexico dealing with the very real issues that we are all so committed to." In reality, he was defending Operation Fast and Furious to incredulous Mexican officials. Breuer was clever enough to first mislead about the Justice Department gunwalking and then also mislead about the letter denying it.

In a Nixonian move, that now infamous February 4 letter was formally withdrawn by the Department of Justice on December 2, 2011.[42] Its accuracy was no longer "operative."

When Eric Holder appeared again to testify before Congress, Rep. Jim Sensenbrenner (R-Wisconsin) asked him about the February 4 letter. He was reminded that misleading Congress is a criminal offense. "Nobody at the Justice Department has lied," Holder said. When Sensenbrenner pressed him about what constituted lying, Holder said, "It all has to do with your state of mind."[43] Holder had worked for President Clinton.

The congressional hearings kept coming and so did the spin from Obama's Justice Department. Chairman Issa opened oversight hearings on July 26, 2011, stating, "President Obama has been keen to talk about who didn't know about the program and who didn't authorize it. These answers will not suffice. The American people have a right to know, once and for all, who did authorize it and who knew about it."[44] Bill Newell testified that day, but his testimony, as Issa later put it, "lacked clarity and completeness." In that hearing, he minimized his friendship with Kevin O'Reilly, the White House staffer whom he had unofficially briefed on the gunwalking program.

After Newell's e-mails to O'Reilly were made public, giving lie to his previous testimony, he released a twelve-page "supplemental statement" that acknowledged his July 26 testimony was not forthright. Unfortunately, neither was his supplemental statement.

Among the misleading statements, he wrote, "To the best of my knowledge, at no time during the operational phase of the 'Fast and Furious' investigation did any of the whistleblowers contact [them] with concerns regarding the investigation."

In fact, whistleblowers and other witnesses were kept away from congressional investigators. The Obama White House sent Kevin O'Reilly, in a surprise reassignment, to Iraq for a "State Department assignment," beyond the reach of a congressional investigators.[45] Grassley and Issa have repeatedly asked to interview O'Reilly, and Grassley told me that he is willing to testify. Obama administration officials have refused to make O'Reilly available.

One of the reasons Eric Holder repeatedly cited for not taking further action on the Fast and Furious scandal is that it will interfere with an investigation by Cynthia Schedar, acting inspector general at the U.S. Department of Justice. Schedar never interviewed any of the major players at the top of the Department of Justice, and certainly not her boss and close friend Eric Holder. After more than a year of delaying, Schedar left office on July 29, 2011, having produced no report at all. But she was able to throw a significant monkey wrench into the Grassley and Issa investigations. Her "investigation" was another convenient cover story.

Investigators traced the gun used to murder Agent Terry to a gun store tucked into the corner of a strip mall in Glendale, Arizona. Andre Howard, owner of the Lone Wolf gun store, was told—not merely permitted—by ATF agents in the fall of 2009 to sell guns to anyone who wanted to buy them, without regard to the law.[46] He normally would have refused to sell to anyone with a fake ID, or who used rubber-banded stacks of cash to buy weapons. The ATF insisted. Following federal orders, he sold 50-caliber rifles and AK-47s as fast and furiously as he could.

Still, Howard was nervous. He kept expecting to hear of arrests, as the fruit of this operation to trace these obviously criminal buyers, but the arrests never came. "Every passing week, I worried," he said. He feared he might be inadvertently participating in a criminal operation. He demanded a letter from the ATF explaining in writing what they wanted him to do, which Special Agent David Voth provided.

Howard became especially concerned when Jaime Avila bought a variety of guns including AK-47s, FN 5.7 pistols, a Barrett 50-caliber rifle, and various handguns, paying about $48,000 in cash for them. His store was wired for sound and video camera that recorded the transaction. He expected the ATF to follow up, but never heard anything. Increasingly concerned, he sent a copy of the paperwork to the Phoenix office.

Avila was eventually stopped, but not by the ATF. Immigration and Customs Enforcement officers caught him with dozens of weapons at the Arizona border. The officers checked with ATF and were stunned to be told that Avila needed to be released so that the ATF could track him. Congress has asked the Justice Department why Avila was released, but Justice has refused to answer this simple question.

The afternoon following the murder of Agent Terry, ATF agents showed up at the door at Lone Wolf. Bill Newell had ordered a trace of the serial numbers on the AK-47s. Howard had watched the news of the border agent's murder on television, and seeing the agents in his shop, said, "I was scared to death." He watched as the agents scanned his paperwork to look for a match. They found it. Howard said, "Both of them were in shock, too. You could tell they were sick."

More than sick, Howard was scared. Fearing he might be framed to take some of the rap, he started secretly recording his conversations with the ATF agents. The recording of the conversation he had with ATF agent Hope MacAllister is especially revealing. MacAllister was concerned that everyone's stories should match and Howard, a simple gun shop owner, was clearly aware that the scandal reached into the top levels of government and involved the Department of Homeland Security, the FBI, and others.

> Howard: "[Dodson's] more toxic than you realize. I can tell you because I asked him, 'How much of this f———g file did you release?'"
>
> MacAllister: "Mmm-hmm."
>
> Howard: "He said basically the underlying case file. I said, 'Okay, who'd you release it to? F———g [Sen.] Patrick Leahy! Okay? Wasn't just [Sen. Chuck] Grassley, it was Leahy, alright? Leahy, as we both know, has adjourned this inquiry right now, okay, with no plans to reconvene it. So your people were successful to that end."
>
> MacAllister: "Right."
>
> Howard: "Obviously that's good. However these idiots from . . ."
>
> MacAllister: ". . . The House?"
>
> Howard: "Yeah, and that I don't know. What is troublesome with this [is] I expected [Rep.] Darrell Issa's signature to be on this [but] it wasn't. He's your biggest thorn. He hates Holder."
>
> MacAllister: "Yeah. Where's he out of?"
>
> Howard: "Darrell Issa?"
>
> MacAllister: "California."
>
> Howard: "Lamar Smith, you know's, out of Texas, I don't know. Holder has to respond to this tomorrow."

MacAllister: "Yeah, he's gonna respond."

Howard: "I know he is. And I assure you the media isn't gonna like his response, because basically it's gonna mirror what he's told Grassley."

MacAllister: "Yeah."

Howard: "He can't deviate."

MacAllister: "Well if, I mean, I've seen a rough copy of what our U.S. attorney here has sent up. Whether or not he has the balls to actually use it or not, I doubt it. But, I mean, it's pretty aggressive. The way I see it, our local U.S. attorney is extremely aggressive. [But] when it gets to D.C...."

Howard: "Who, [Assistant U.S. Attorney] Emory [Hurley]?"

MacAllister: "No, the U.S. attorney."

Howard: "Burke, yeah, used to work under Clinton... Talking about [Dennis] Burke?"

MacAllister: "Mmm-hmm."

Howard: "Yeah, well ..."

MacAllister: "But the problem is, once it gets to D.C., it just gets ... well, you know."

Howard: "Discombobulated—that's a good term for it. Yeah, I get that."

Though the Lone Wolf gun shop story is interesting by itself, Cynthia Schedar's role makes it even more so. To protect himself from the growing scandal, Howard gave copies of the tapes to congressional investigators. ATF officials had already started painting Howard with guilt. ATF officials are quoted in *The Washington Post,* blaming Lone Wolf for "selling guns to the cartels," without disclosing that Howard was doing so at the direction of, with the approval of, and, indeed, at the request of the ATF.[47] They were setting him up, just as he feared.

Staffers for Senator Grassley provided copies of the tapes to the DOJ Inspector General's office to help further its investigation. Schedar, however, used the tapes to warn Holder's top officials. She provided the targets of her investigation with copies of the tapes, thus compromising her own purported investigation as well as those being conducted by Grassley and Issa, who wrote her, saying:

> Your decision to immediately disclose the recordings to those you are investigating creates at least the appearance, if not more, that your inquiry is not sufficiently objective and independent. It appears that you did not consider the significant harm that providing these recordings to the very individuals under investigation could cause to either our inquiry or your own. You did not consult with us about the recordings even though the congressional inquiry and reactions to it are discussed at length.[48]

Schedar is no longer at the Justice Department. She received no formal reprimand for her actions.

Obama has replaced her with Michael Horowitz, a close friend of Lanny Breuer. With his strong personal ties to many top names in the scandal, it is questionable if Horowitz has willingness to conduct a thorough and independent investigation.

Given that much of the sworn testimony of Obama administration officials has been shown to be misleading, incomplete, incorrect, and false, it is not surprising that Eric Holder told Congress at a December 8, 2011, hearing that he will not comply with requests for any more documents about Fast and Furious or the Justice Department's response to the scandal.[49] After more than a year of investigation, the DOJ has still failed to turn over seventy-four thousand requested documents to the House Oversight Committee. As of early May 2012, Holder had failed to fully comply with Issa's congressional subpoena. Thirteen of the subpoena's twenty-two sections may as well have been written in invisible ink: the attorney general seems to have completely ignored them.

Holder has dismissed as racist anyone who has questioned the truthfulness of his Justice Department. He told *The New York Times,* "This is a way to get at the president because of the way I can be identified with him, both due to the nature of our relationship and, you know, the fact that we're both African American."

Holder added that the "more extreme elements" are people who want "payback," and said, "They want to go after some high-level official in the administration."[50]

Eric Holder may feel like a victim; but, of the real victims, he has said little.

Holder finally wrote an apology of sorts to Brian Terry's family for his death, but only after Sen. John Cornyn (R-Texas) pressed him during a November 2011 Senate Judiciary Committee hearing. The apology, though, appears to have been an attempt by Holder to fix his public image: He leaked the apology letter to the newspaper *Politico* before Terry's mother had the chance to read it. It was more about public relations than contrition.

Most of the dead have been Mexican nationals. So far, no one in the Obama administration has apologized to the government of Mexico. Speaking to *The Daily Caller* in January 2012, Issa said Holder's department "has blood on their hands." Holder hasn't even acknowledged this tragic reality.

The Department of Justice has provided no accounting for the more than two thousand missing guns—not to mention grenade parts that it "lost track" of. The ATF admits some twenty-eight weapons were used to commit violent crimes in Mexico. Mexican authorities put the number at higher than 170 and counting.[51] That may well be an undercount. The Obama administration has yet to process many of the Mexican government's requests to trace guns in American databases.

One such case is the kidnapping, torture, and murder of the brother of Mexico's attorney general for the state of Chihuahua. Mario Gonzalez Rodriguez was abducted in October 2010, forced to make a video statement, then shot with an AK-47 variant, much like the one that was used to murder Agent Terry.[52] Mexico's attorney general, Marisela Morales, has asked the United States for information about Operation Fast and Furious, but the Obama administration has stonewalled her as effectively as it has blocked inquiries in Congress.

All Eric Holder can say is, "Unfortunately, we will feel its effects for years to come as guns that were lost during this operation continue to show up at crime scenes both here and in Mexico."

Under questioning by Rep. Ted Poe (R-Texas) during a December 8,

2011, hearing, Holder finally admitted the deadliness of Operation Fast and Furious.

"More people are going to die, probably," Poe suggested.

"Unfortunately I think that's probably true," admitted Holder.

Sadly, Holder's prophecy has proved to be true. February 2011 saw yet another tragedy as U.S. Immigration agent Jaime Zapata was gunned down south of the Texas border. Later that year, his death was linked to a Fast and Furious gun.

Still, the bureaucrats in charge of the operation that led to so much death and suffering and who have misled and blocked investigators have been rewarded, not punished.

Melson's stonewalling as acting director of the ATF and obfuscation in congressional hearings has earned him a position in the ATF Office of Legal Affairs.

Senator Grassley called for Lanny Breuer's resignation for lying to Congress, yet he retains his position as assistant attorney general for the Criminal Division at the Justice Department.

Bill Newell got a promotion, moving from the field office in Phoenix to a bigger job at the Office of Management in Washington, D.C.

David Voth and his deputy George Gillette, who had gotten into the screaming match with Agent Dodson, also moved to management positions in Washington, D.C.

Hope MacAllister, one of the officials who ordered Dodson and others to stop tailing suspects who had bought ATF guns, was given a Lifesaving Award for her efforts.[53]

Those few who weren't promoted have moved on without the stigma that should come from having participated in a deadly government-sponsored failure. Ronald Weich announced his resignation in April 2012. He will be the next dean of the University of Baltimore's School of Law.

Dennis Burke resigned as the U.S. Attorney for Arizona, but officials have publicly claimed his resignation had nothing to do with Fast and Furious.

Holder continues as attorney general, despite this and many controversies that would have ended any career not personally safeguarded by the president of the United States.

Holder's race-driven worldview has been responsible for many lapses in judgment. These include calling the United States a "nation of cowards" with regards to race and refusing to prosecute baseball bat-wielding Black Panther thugs who intimidated voters in Philadelphia. Responding to criticism that he was ignoring a serious act of voter intimidation, he said: "To describe it [the Black Panther voter intimidation case] in those terms I think does a great disservice to people who put their lives on the line, who risked all, for my people."[54] Meanwhile, Holder praised the notorious Al Sharpton for his "partnership," "friendship," and "tireless efforts to speak out for the voiceless, to stand up for the powerless, and to shine a light on the problems we must solve, and the promises we must fulfill."

Holder also has an unfortunate tendency to let ideology drive his decisions, without regard for the law or political implications. Despite opposition from nearly every corner, Holder doggedly insisted on attempting to try terror mastermind Khalid Shaikh Mohammed in a civilian trial in Manhattan. He hadn't done his political homework before announcing on November 14, 2009, "After eight years of delay, those allegedly responsible for the attacks of September 11 will finally face justice. They will be brought to New York—to New York—to answer for their alleged crimes in a courthouse just blocks away from where the Twin Towers once stood."[55] He didn't back down for more than a year. A military tribunal for KSM, which had been canceled in January 2009, was begun again in April 2012.

Where was President Obama during all of this?

When the gun-running scandal first became public, Obama said Holder had "assigned an inspector general to look into how exactly this happened. And I have complete confidence in him, and I've got complete confidence in the process to figure out who, in fact, was responsible for that decision and how it got made."[56]

When Obama took office in 2009 he promised "a new level of transparency, accountability and participation for America's citizens."[57]

In light of the string of proven falsehoods throughout the Justice Department, Obama must feel some sense of disappointment in Holder's performance. But he has not removed him.

Every leader has to terminate subordinates who fail in their appointed tasks, especially when they fail to tell the full truth. By any measure, Holder's tenure as attorney general has been studded with stunning failures. Yet he remains on the job.

The attorney general, like all presidential appointees, famously serves "at the pleasure of the president." Either Holder's service continues to please the president, in which case Obama has not been properly monitoring his team, or Obama is unable to manage personnel effectively by taking corrective action. Either way, Obama fails to lead.

CHAPTER 7

WHAT KIND OF LEADER IS OBAMA?

Again and again, we've seen him make tough choices when easier ones were available. His values and his record affirm what is best in us.

—Barack Obama, speaking at the 2004 Democratic National Convention about the leadership qualities that make a great president.

Campaigns and candidates will spend much of 2012 debating the key decisions of the president, but the more fundamental question is: What kind of a leader is Barack Obama?

To answer this question, you have to look behind his biggest achievements (passing health care reform and killing Osama bin Laden) and his biggest implosions—failing to broker a budget deal with Congress to avert downgrading America's credit rating, wrecking the relationship with America's most vital ally in the Middle East, and refusing to discipline or remove his attorney general, Eric Holder, who repeatedly misled Congress and defied congressional subpoenas regarding the Fast and Furious operation that led to the deaths of hundreds of Americans and Mexicans.

It is in the details of these successes and setbacks that the character of his leadership emerges. In each and every one of these cases, the president was indecisive and dilatory. When he achieved success, he did so by surrendering his leadership to a subordinate (House Speaker Nancy Pelosi, Secretary of State Hillary Clinton, then-CIA Director Leon Panetta, or Adm. William McRaven). While strong leaders delegate the details of implementation to subordinates, they set the direction and define the goals of big decisions. Reforming health care was initially not the president's idea and every pivotal decision in its rocky path to passage was made by Pelosi—sometimes over Obama's objections. In the bin Laden raid, the president had to be repeatedly pressed to make decisions and he canceled the mission three times in 2011 alone. Without the steeling determination of Panetta and Clinton, bin Laden would still be alive today and when Obama belatedly did decide to approve the mission, he wrote internal memos to shift the political risk onto his subordinates—the antithesis of leadership.

His greatest failures also reveal his leadership qualities. Faced with record federal budget deficits, the largest national debt in American history, and the looming threat that international bond ratings agencies would lower their estimates of America's creditworthiness and drive up interest rates, the president spent months attacking his political rivals. When offered a "grand bargain" that would reform entitlements, close tax loopholes to raise some $800 billion, and stave off financial crisis, he sabotaged the historic deal days before it was to be announced.

In negotiating with Israel's prime minister Benjamin Netanyahu, he was unable to work amicably with America's closest ally in the region and shocked people in both countries with a surprise announcement that would turn over Israeli neighborhoods to the very people who had been bombing and shooting Israelis for decades. When forced by public opinion to retreat from his unprecedented position on Israeli's borders, his evident contempt for Israel's elected leader deepened. As a result, Netanyahu sadly said that Israel now has better relations with Canada than with the United

States—a statement that would be unthinkable at any other time since Israel's birth in 1948.

As America's first black president, he seems unable to discipline America's first black attorney general. While America's top law enforcement officer continues to defy lawful subpoenas and to lie under oath to congressional committees, Obama has not appointed a special prosecutor to investigate Holder's role in the growing scandal or to demand his resignation. Meanwhile, in an unprecedented move, more than two hundred current members of Congress have publicly demanded Holder's resignation. Even as a growing number of congressmen and senators have publicly raised the possibility of impeaching and removing Holder, the president has remained silent.

It's time to measure Obama's leadership against the standards demanded of any leader, from platoon sergeant or corporate manager to chief executive or president of the United States. It's time to assess what "leading from behind" really means.

A leader is bigger than his autobiography. In his 2004 speech at the Democratic National Convention, he introduced himself to a national audience for the first time. It is here that we first meet all of the tropes of his initial appeal, from overcoming the difficulty of having a "funny name" to his parents hailing from different races and different continents. It's an appealing speech and a revealing one. At every turning point in his career, from his election as the first black president of the Harvard Law Review to his election as the first black president of the United States, Obama appealed for support based on facts over which he had no control— his parents, his name, his childhood overseas, his race. Even the drama of his missing father—another factor outside of his control—became the central reason for the publication of his first book, *Dreams from My Father*. At every stage, he put himself forward as a symbol of impersonal forces rather than as a sum of personal achievements. A leader's life story matters; it is the raw material that allows him to empathize with others and to understand his changing competitive environment. Yet a leader must rise out of circumstances that he did not make and make his own imprint on the world. He is not merely the set of things that have been impressed upon him; he is also the slew of things that he has made through his own unique efforts. If he is no more than what the world has done to him, he is a follower, not a leader.

By contrast, President Reagan rarely mentioned his absent father and President Clinton sometimes mentioned his drunken and deceased father; each leader commanded the public's attention with his vision, and his past achievements. Neither president relied on autobiography to captivate the public; they used it selectively to connect with the public and to steer to ambitious goals.

One of the things that makes Barack Obama unusual is that he uses his biography as a kind of demand. He often appears like a victim demanding justice, using his life story to compel political support. This is fine in a candidate, especially one with no record as an executive. Throughout his storied career, Obama was always a member of a committee (in the Illinois Senate and the U.S. Senate), or a junior member of the faculty (at the University of Chicago Law School), or an entry-level employee at a community-organizing outfit or financial newsletter business.

He never had to stand alone as a leader who solely decides. He never ran the community-organizing entity. He was never dean at any law school. He was never chairman of any permanent Senate committee. He never owned a business or ran a state as governor. So, as the presidential nominee of America's oldest political party, he had to campaign for America's affection on the basis of his biography.

As president, he has to transcend his biography. He has to do, not just be. Yet, again and again, he retreats to biographical details. When asked to decide whether to support Nancy Pelosi's drive for health care reform by then–Chief of Staff Rahm Emanuel and warned of its massive political risks, he explained his decision to follow the House Speaker by citing his historic election. When challenged by Minority Speaker John Boehner, he again cited his life story and his election.

Biography is not a guide to present or future decisions; it is, at best, a record of past ones.

A leader has clear principles and sticks to them. Announcing clear goals and driving toward them is the core of what effective presidents do.

Sometimes, presidents shift tactics or make strategic compromises, but their goals remain burning stars that both friends and foes can steer by. President Clinton campaigned on reforming welfare and ultimately signed a sweeping overhaul of America's safety net into law when Congress met his well-defined parameters. President Reagan never wavered in his desire to shrink the size and cost of government, but agreed to raise the federal gasoline tax in 1982 in exchange for future spending cuts that were supposed to be twice as large as the new revenues. While his effort failed when Congress refused to make the agreed-upon spending cuts, he circled back to his goals with the 1986 tax reforms. While President George W. Bush was adamant about his plans to hold terrorists indefinitely without recourse to civilian trials, his policy was overturned by the U.S. Supreme Court in 2006. Nevertheless he persuaded Congress to give him military tribunals in order to detain who he saw as dangerous men. Whatever the merits of these presidential policies, no one could argue that they weren't clearly outlined and followed despite great adversity and opposition.

Obama campaigned on ending earmarks among other issues. In his first days in office, Pelosi breezily dismissed this reform. Obama did not persist. The issue was quietly dropped and never raised again by the president.

While Obama campaigned on closing the detention centers at Guantánamo Bay, when foreign governments were reluctant to take custody of the terrorists held there, and Congress was unwilling to have those terror suspects tried in civilian courts inside the United States, the Obama administration briefly tried bribing Pacific and Caribbean nations to take the detainees. When that failed to move many detainees, the effort to transfer them was abandoned altogether.

Again and again, whenever the president ran into any opposition to his stated goals, he would either give up or announce new contrary policies. Even the sharpest dividing line between the Obama and Bush administrations—the conduct of the war on terror—has all but been erased. Guantánamo Bay's six detention camps remain open. American soldiers remain at war in Iraq and Afghanistan, albeit in smaller numbers. Even the pace of the military withdrawal broadly matches the plans laid out by the Bush administration. While Obama famously outlawed "torture," the Bush administration also had a stated anti-torture policy and abided by all international treaties regarding the treatment of detainees. Killing terrorists with drone attacks, already on the rise in the last two years of the Bush administration, has tripled in the Obama years.

As a candidate, Obama repeatedly said that he would not raise taxes on Americans earning less than $250,000 per year. The historic health care reforms that he signed into law in 2010 contained tax increases of 2.5 percent on gross income for every wage earner making more than $11,000 per year.

When enlisting the public's support for his health care reforms, Obama often said that Americans could keep their doctors and their current health insurance plans. Yet, in ObamaCare, health insurers will be forced either into state-run exchanges or out of business and many doctors have vowed not to participate. These provisions make it all but certain that the president's goals will not be met.

A leader stays in the room. In complex negotiations, Obama has a consistent pattern of sullenly stalking out of the room when he encounters difficulty or opposition. When challenged by Pelosi over the course of health care reform, he strangely declared that "I am not a stupid man," and exited the room. During tense negotiations with Boehner, Obama again literally walked away. When pressed to make a decision regarding the bin Laden mission, Obama stood up from the conference table and left the room. When Netanyahu publicly staked out a position differing from the president's own, only live television coverage stopped him from walking off. Instead, he often refused to make eye contact with the Israeli prime minister and turned his body to ignore his fellow leader as much as possible.

Tellingly, Obama even walks out on meetings with his own senior officials. While Secretary of Energy Steven Chu was briefing the president on the progress of the British Petroleum oil spill, Obama stood up. All he offered by way of explanation was: "Steve, I'm out."

A leader puts principled compromise ahead of personality clashes. President Reagan negotiated eight budgets with House Speaker Tip O'Neill, President Clinton negotiated six budgets with House Speaker

Newt Gingrich, and President George W. Bush negotiated two budgets with House Speaker Nancy Pelosi. In each case, a sharply defined ideological president had to compromise with a strongly partisan leader of the opposite political party. By contrast, Obama has not successfully negotiated a single budget deal with House Speaker John Boehner. Working well with rivals to achieve shared goals is a key test for any leader. Especially on budget matters, every modern president has forged a compromise with leaders of the opposing party—except Obama.

A leader keeps his word. Obama made what could have been an historic bargain with Boehner to reform the federal budget. At great political risk to himself, Boehner had agreed to some $800 billion in new revenues through closing tax loopholes. Obama agreed and the two men actually shook hands. Then, when the political winds seemed to shift slightly, Obama broke the agreement and demanded another $400 billion in new revenues—violating Boehner's trust and bringing the bargain to an end. Without a belief in the sanctity of the president's word, both Republican and Democratic leaders in Congress have found it impossible to make budget deals with the president. As a result, the United States has gone more than seven hundred days without an approved federal budget—the longest time since the passage of the 1974 Budget Control Act.

A leader takes risks for a cause larger than himself. In both of Obama's signature successes—health care reform and killing bin Laden—Obama pushed the risks onto other leaders while claiming the credit for himself. Pelosi repeatedly took risks to pass health care reform, as illustrated in chapter 2, while Obama and his senior officials either retreated from the political scrum or tried to sabotage her efforts. Once the bill was passed, Obama signed the measure into law and repeatedly trumpeted the bill as his own. In fact, the White House never even supplied Congress with draft legislation, which is nearly unheard of for a landmark law in the history of post–World War II presidents. At the start of the 2012 campaign, Obama adopted the critics' moniker of "ObamaCare" as his own, even deploying it in yard signs, T-shirts, and Web videos. During the planning of the bin Laden raid, Obama penned memos for the record laying the responsibility on then-CIA Director Panetta and Admiral McRaven. Once the mission was a success, he broadcast a worldwide speech that same evening in which he took credit for the raid. Later, in a series of television and print interviews, Obama repeatedly took credit for the operation. The Obama campaign has distributed videos commandeering credit for dispatching bin Laden while questioning whether his 2012 Republican rival would have made the same decision.

A leader elevates with vision, and has realistic plans for achieving that vision. After the historic Republican sweep in the 2010 congressional elections, Obama summoned his senior staff and unveiled an ambitious legislative agenda to be pushed through Congress over the Thanksgiving and Christmas holidays before the new Republican majority could be sworn in on January 3, 2011. As documented in chapter 3, even his senior aides were incredulous. The legislative list was long and would have been difficult even if they had two years and large Democratic majorities in both houses of Congress. It was simply not going to happen—and it did not. The president's lack of realism, at least temporarily, unnerved his staff and surprised his allies.

A leader makes timely decisions. The hardest task of any leader is not making the right decision, but in making the right decision in time. In the timeless expanse of the faculty lounge or the university library, many inventive options can be cautiously weighed, carefully calibrated, and fully considered. But a leader must act as sand races through the hourglass. Time relentlessly presents and subtracts alternatives.

Yet, over and over, the president is vexed by indecision and slow to decide, if he ever decides at all. Throughout the long months of 2009, Obama was repeatedly urged to either back a troop surge in Afghanistan or order a rapid withdrawal. When he finally announced a decision at West Point in December 2009, he split the difference between two stark alternatives and ordered a modest surge. Since the fighting season in Afghanistan runs from April through October, the president's delays robbed the military of clear direction during an entire year of brutal war.

When pro-democracy demonstrations broke out in Iran, the president dithered for months about whether to support the dictators or the democrats. When he finally made some public remarks, he limited himself to a vague call for humanitarian restraint by the regime's cruel security services. Unlike President Reagan who called on the last leader of the Soviet Union to "tear down this wall," Obama never called for a democratic transition in Iran.

When more than 3,000 Syrians were gunned down demanding democracy in 2011, one demonstrator pointedly held up a sign in English and in Arabic: "In Israel, the police use rubber bullets." Yet nothing could move the president to make a decision to speak out about the slaughter of innocents in that Arab nation.

When the Deep Water Horizon–British Petroleum oil spill in the Gulf of Mexico created the biggest environmental catastrophe in more than two decades, Obama couldn't decide for weeks whether to accept the help of Dutch and other European navies.

A leader removes unethical or failing subordinates. For the first time since the Nixon years, the U.S. attorney general has lost the confidence of nearly a majority of Congress and is tainted by what ultimately could be found to be criminal activity. And, for the first time since the Jefferson years, the sitting attorney general is credibly connected to the unlawful death of an American citizen. Yet Obama has made no move to remove him or to appoint a special prosecutor. By this standard, it is hard to know what wrongdoing a presidential appointee has to be accused of to lead the president to dismiss him. Leaders who fail to enforce standards or to fire errant subordinates may be "leading from behind," but they are actually not leading at all.

A leader calms and unites. Perhaps the biggest single hope and change that led voters to elect Obama in 2008 was the idea that he would be a racial healer. This hope was not simply that electing the first black man to the presidency would be an historic and transformative act, but also that his soothing words would be a balm at times of racial division. Yet in two instances in which national racial controversy loomed, Obama inserted himself into local issues and chose sides, rather than calling for peace.

When Harvard professor Henry Louis "Skip" Gates was found by a Cambridge, Massachusetts, policeman to be entering a house through a window, he was questioned by the uniformed officer. Rather than immediately explain that he had mislaid his keys or that the house was his own, the millionaire professor berated the beat cop and accused him of "racism." When the president was asked about it by a reporter, Obama immediately escalated the event and sided with Gates. It would have been wiser to say that he did not have all the facts, or that it was a local issue and not a national one. But, the president wondered aloud about race and police procedures, impugning the policeman's character. Black and other minority officers quickly came to the patrolman's defense. It also emerged that the officer personally conducted diversity training seminars. Once the situation was inflamed by the president himself, he hurriedly announced a "beer summit" and invited the officer to the White House.

A more egregious case followed the death of Florida teenager Trayvon Martin. Once again, a local controversy was building that pitted a black victim against an armed Hispanic man. Again, the issue was more complicated than black and white. George Zimmerman was defended by his black neighbors, has black relatives, and has spent time teaching black inner-city youth to read. Not exactly your typical member of the KKK. Nevertheless, Obama weighed in on a local issue before he had all of the facts, saying, "If I had a son, he'd look like Trayvon." While the circumstances of this tragic incident are complicated and not yet fully known, this time the president's remarks demonstrably made things more dangerous. Citing the president, the New Black Panther Party literally called for "blood" and murderous attacks while using racial epithets. The Zimmerman family went into hiding while other families, wholly unconnected to the incident, were terrorized in their homes on the mistaken belief that they were housing Zimmerman. A string of racially motivated brutal beatings occurred in cities and towns across the United States, with the assailants often shouting, "This is for Trayvon."

A president with Obama's unique biography and obvious gifts as a speaker could have appealed for calm and drained the crisis of its racial dimension. He could have reminded the public that justice will ultimately be done under our system of laws, however slow it may seem in coming. But the president, who rarely misses an opportunity for a major address, did not give a timely speech from the White House that called for unity, not division, and for peace, not vigilantism.

Instead, he allowed his attorney general to travel to a conference held by Rev. Al Sharpton and deliver remarks praising one of the most racially divisive men in American politics. Sharpton has still not apologized for the Tawana Brawley hoax or the Crown Heights violence—where Sharpton pointedly pushed tempers to the boiling point and attacked innocent policemen as "racists."

A leader inspires and brings out the best in people. In fact, Obama seems to have a "divide and conquer" strategy of governing. In his first year in office, he spent a considerable amount of time blaming and criticizing his predecessor, who was constitutionally ineligible from seeking the presidency again. During the 2010 congressional midterm election season, Obama used virtually every public speaking opportunity to attack Republicans who, at that point, were powerless minorities in every elected branch of government. After the Republicans won control of the House of Representatives, Obama spent much of the next year attacking the very leaders with whom he had to work. In foreign affairs, the president has repeatedly and publicly criticized foreign allies who are vital to America's security; the tempestuous relationship with Netanyahu was documented in chapter 4. In addition, Obama all but ruptured the "special relationship" with the United Kingdom by returning its gift of a bust of Winston Churchill and insulting the Queen by publicly interrupting her at a banquet and presenting as an official gift an iPod loaded with Obama's speeches. Relations with Canada were soured when that nation elected a conservative prime minister and further damaged when the Obama administration sought to use regulatory delays to slow timber imports from America's largest trading partner in an apparent violation of our free trade treaty with that nation.

By contrast, Obama has promised to "re-set" relations with Russia and promised to give them additional concessions after the election.

A leader sacrifices short-term gain for long-term benefit. President Obama's speech immediately following the death of bin Laden allowed dozens of senior al-Qaeda leaders to escape by robbing America's intelligence and military services of the advantage of surprise. If the president had kept the archterrorist's demise a secret, for even a few weeks, our nation's special forces could have exploited the intelligence gathered in bin Laden's compound to swoop in on terror leaders around the world. Instead, his globally televised address spread the news of bin Laden's end faster than al-Qaeda's couriers—alerting our enemies to move before they could be killed or captured. The element of surprise is the most significant advantage in warfare. Wars are lost and won by it. To give away a perhaps war-winning advantage for a temporary peak in the polls is a decision that no other wartime leader has ever made in American history.

A leader focuses on the most important problems even if they're the hardest—before they become crises. On the day he was sworn into office in 2009, the scope of America's economic suffering was obvious and obviously getting worse. Gas prices were rising, home prices were falling, and joblessness was accelerating. The president championed a "stimulus" bill that largely went to maintaining payrolls of local, state, and federal unionized workers, and led an unprecedented effort to take over two of America's major automakers to save the jobs of workers represented by the United Auto Workers union. Obama did little to save nonunion jobs. He did not offer tax relief for nonunion employers and used the regulatory colossus to stop Boeing from opening a nonunion plant in South Carolina. Nor did he relax the regulatory burdens for new hires.

The president announced three major initiatives to allow home buyers to refinance their troubled mortgages. But, the plans were so complex that comparatively few managed to qualify for relief. In addition, new regulations were passed as part of the Dodd-Frank measures that made it harder for banks to make loans to marginal borrowers or owners of properties whose values had declined. This led to a tightening of credit that made loans harder to secure and homes harder to sell. A glut of unsold and foreclosed homes remains, depressing home values in most parts of the country. In addition, Dodd-Frank includes provisions against "speculators," investors who might otherwise buy up unwanted houses.

As for gas prices, Obama could have ordered a temporary suspension of the federal gasoline tax, which raises gasoline prices by slightly more than 18.4 cents per gallon. In addition, Obama could have temporarily suspended costly and complicated fuel reformulation rules that boost gas prices. Green-lighting onshore and gas and oil production would have increased domestic energy production and over the next few years reduced prices at the pump. Instead, Obama announced a temporary ban on drilling in the Gulf of Mexico. While domestic energy production has ticked upward, all of that production has occurred on private land over which the president has no control. Oil and gas production on public land, which the president does control, has declined sharply. So far from taking measures to reduce gas prices, the president's policies have increased them.

What made solving these problems difficult for the president was that addressing them required him to take on his own political party, which tends to oppose efforts to even temporarily suspend taxes or to temporarily ease regulations.

Instead, the president spent the bulk of his first two years in office ignoring these difficult but important issues, and to devote his time to passing health care reform, which had been on the progressive wish list for almost a century.

Leading from behind is not leading at all. Among paratroopers, the commander is the first man out of the aircraft. On a football team, the quarterback is at the center of every line of attack. In the hurly-burly of American capitalism, the entrepreneur and the executive take the greatest risks. Americans expect no less of their presidents. Harry S. Truman famously said, "The buck stops here." That's a classic example of leading from the front. Obama's slogan seems to be, "I'll take the credit but not the blame." That's leading from behind.

ACKNOWLEDGMENTS

I would like to thank my researchers and assistants, Martin Morse Wooster, Lisa Merriam (of Merriam Associates, LLC), and Rhiannon Burruss.

I'd also like to thank Mary Claire Kendall for her writerly advice and valuable work.

I'd like to thank my literary agent, Richard Pine, and the rest of the team at Inkwell Management, and my television agent, Ian Kleinert, at Objective Entertainment.

My editor at St. Martin's Press, George Witte, deserves my special thanks. A published poet, he brought his unique eye to this book and it has enormously benefited as a result.

I would also like to thank the following:

David Martosko, who trained to conduct orchestras, but now conducts reporters at *The Daily Caller* as executive editor. He read the entire manuscript and made many helpful additions and subtractions, thus multiplying the manuscript's clarity and impact.

At the International Spy Museum in Washington, D.C., Peter Earnest, President, and at the National Navy UDT-SEAL Museum in Fort Pierce, Florida, Rolf Snyder.

Additional thanks are due to: Matthew Boyle at *The Daily Caller;* John Tamny at *Forbes;* Wayne Laugesen at the *Colorado Springs Gazette;*

Tunku Varadarajan and Tina Brown at *Newsweek/The Daily Beast;* John Fund at *The American Spectator;* James Taranto of *The Wall Street Journal,* and, on Capitol Hill, the ever-enterprising Jacki L. Pick.

NOTES

Introduction

1. Barack Obama, *Dreams from My Father* (New York: Three Rivers Press, 1995), 4.
2. See *Official White House Photo* by Pete Souza, February 1, 2009. The Steelers beat the Arizona Cardinals 27–23, earning their sixth Super Bowl win.
3. Obama, *Dreams from My Father,* 3.
4. Janny Scott, *A Singular Woman: The Untold Story of Barack Obama's Mother* (New York: Riverhead Books, 2011).
5. Author interview with Illinois state lawmaker who served with Obama.
6. Author interview with Crowley.

Chapter 1: The Women

1. Janny Scott, *A Singular Woman: The Untold Story of Barack Obama's Mother* (New York: Riverhead Books, 2011), 42.
2. Paul Watson, "As a Child, Obama Crossed a Cultural Divide in Indonesia," *Los Angeles Times,* March 15, 2007.
3. "'Meet the 'chubby boy with curly hair': New photographs of Barack Obama's childhood in Indonesia emerge," *Daily Mail,* March 18, 2010.

4. Barack Obama, *Dreams from My Father* (New York: Three Rivers Press, 1995).

5. Chip Reid and Robert Hendin, "In Indonesia, A Glimpse into Obama's Childhood," CBS News, November 9, 2010.

6. Kelly Heffernan-Tabor, "Indonesia: Obama's Childhood Friends and Teachers Share Memories," CBS News, November 7, 2010.

7. " 'Barry' Obama's childhood with transvestite gay nanny revealed by visit to Indonesia," *Daily Mail,* November 10, 2010.

8. Dan Amira, "President Obama Wanted to Be Prime Minister of Indonesia," *New York Magazine,* April 20, 2011.

9. Heffernan-Tabor, "Indonesia: Obama's Childhood Friends and Teachers Share Memories."

10. Scott, *A Singular Woman,* 158.

11. Ibid.

12. Ibid., 159.

13. "Barack Obama: The Road to the White House," *New York Times* at http://topics.nytimes.com/topics/reference/timestopics/subjects/b/barack_obama_the_road_to_the_white_house/index.html (accessed January 12, 2012).

14. Ibid.

15. "Senior Advisor Valerie Jarrett," *The Administration: White House Staff,* WhiteHouse.gov (retrieved January 29, 2009).

16. M. J. Stephey and Claire Suddath, "Valerie Jarrett," *Time,* November 11, 2008.

17. Jonathan Van Meter, "Valerie Jarrett: Barack's Rock, *Vogue,* October 1, 2008.

18. Ibid.

19. David Remnick, *The Bridge: The Life and Rise of Barack Obama* (New York: Random House, 2010), 273.

20. Ibid.

21. John Easton, "James Bowman, expert on pathology and blood diseases, 1923–2011," *UChicago News,* September 29, 2011.

22. Ibid.

23. Elwood Watson, "Jarrett, Valerie (1956–)," *The Black Past: Remembered and Reclaimed,* 2007.

24. Paul Kengor, "Letting Obama Be Obama, *American Spectator,* July/August 2011.

25. Don Terry, "In the Path of Lightning: Valerie Jarrett is known as the other side of Barack Obama's brain. Can this tough-minded adviser, who is guided by aphorisms and gut instinct, help him reach the White House?," *Chicago Tribune,* July 27, 2008.

26. Ibid.

27. Robert Draper, "The Ultimate Obama Insider," *New York Times Magazine,* July 21, 2009.

28. "Senior Advisor Valerie Jarrett," *The Administration.*

29. Wilma Randle, "Aide Brings Own Vision to City Post," *Chicago Tribune,* December 8, 1991.

30. Van Meter, "Valerie Jarrett: Barack's Rock."

31. Ibid.

32. John D. McKinnon and T. W. Farnam, "Hedge Fund Paid Summers $5.2 Million in Past Year," *Wall Street Journal,* April 5, 2009.

33. Ibid.

34. "USG Corp.," Industrials Sector, Building Products Industry, *Bloomberg Businessweek* (retrieved December 2, 2011).

35. McKinnon and Farnam, "Hedge Fund Paid Summers $5.2 Million in Past Year."

36. "Valerie Jarrett Profile," Forbes.com, August 23, 2008.

37. "Obama's Senior Advisor Valerie Jarrett: The Point of Government Is to Give People a Livelihood so They Can Provide for Their Families," *The Blaze,* September 29, 2011. Video post: http://www.youtube.com/watch?v=3uqjIG5m-MI (accessed May 25, 2012).

38. Binyamin Appelbaum, "Grim Proving Ground for Obama's Housing Policy," *Boston Globe,* June 27, 2008.

39. Ibid.

40. "City Receives $30.5 Million Grant to Revitalize Woodlawn Neighborhood," *CBS Chicago News,* August 31, 2011.

41. Tim Novak and Chris Fusco, "U. of C. Shunning Poor Patients? Hospital Dispute: Obama's wife, 3 aides tied to plan to free up space," *Chicago Sun-Times,* August 23, 2008.

42. Jason Grotto and Bruce Japsen, "Are Hospitals Passing Off Their Low-Profit Patients?," *Chicago Tribune,* April 10, 2009.

43. Thomas Gionis, Carlos A. Camargo Jr. and Anthony S. Zito Jr., *The Intentional Tort of Patient Dumping,* December 12, 2002.

44. Office of Inspector General, U.S. Department of Health & Human Services, Patient Dumping Archive, http://oig.hhs.gov/reports-and -publications/archives/enforcement/patient_dumping_archive.asp (accessed December 30, 2011).

45. "Barack Obama: The Road to the White House."

46. Draper, "The Ultimate Obama Insider."

47. Ibid.

48. Ibid.

49. Ibid.

50. Terry, "In the Path of Lightning."

51. Draper, "The Ultimate Obama Insider."

52. Jodi Kantor, *The Obamas* (New York: Little, Brown & Company, 2012), 66.

53. Ibid.

54. Ibid.

55. Ibid.

56. Ibid.

57. Ibid.

58. Jason Horowitz, "Valerie Jarrett's Latest Role: Shoring Up Obama's Support Base," *Washington Post,* October 25, 2011.

59. Horowitz, "Valerie Jarrett's Latest Role."

60. Kantor, *The Obamas,* 237.

61. Ibid., 253.

62. Ibid., 254.

63. Peter Baker and Jeff Zeleny, "For Obama, an Unsuccessful Campaign," *New York Times,* October 2, 2009.

64. Peter Roff, "Obama's Olympic Sales Pitch Oils the Daley Political Machine," *US News & World Report,* September 28, 2009.

65. John McCormick, "Michelle Obama Plans Dramatic Pitch for Olympics, Jarrett Says," *Bloomberg News,* September 17, 2009.

66. Ed Hula III, "Q&A with Valerie Jarrett, White House Olympic Chief," *Around the Rings,* September 18, 2009.

67. "Obama to Front Chicago's Olympics Bid," CBS News, September 28, 2009.

68. McCormick, "Michelle Obama Plans Dramatic Pitch for Olympics, Jarrett Says."

69. Baker and Zeleny, "For Obama, an Unsuccessful Campaign."

70. Author interview with source.

71. "Michelle Obama," Biography.com, http://www.biography.com /people/michelle-obama-307592 (accessed January 5, 2012).

72. Ibid.

73. Michael Powell and Jodi Kantor, "After Attacks, Michelle Obama Looks for a New Introduction," *New York Times,* June 18, 2008.

74. Sally Jacobs, "Learning to Be Michelle Obama: At Princeton, she came to terms with being a black achiever in a white world," *Boston Globe,* June 15, 2008.

75. Jeffrey Ressner, "Michelle Obama Thesis Was on Racial Divide." *Politico,* February 23, 2008.

76. Michelle LaVaughn Robinson, "Princeton-Educated Blacks and the Black Community," Princeton, 1985.

77. Ibid.

78. Ibid.

79. Richard Wolffe, "Barack's Rock," *Newsweek,* February 25, 2008.

80. Liza Mundy, "When Michelle Met Barack," *Washington Post,* October 5, 2008.

81. Ibid.

82. Ibid.

83. Ibid.

84. Ibid.

85. Powell and Kantor, "After Attacks, Michelle Obama Looks for a New Introduction."

86. David Mendell, *Obama: From Promise to Power* (New York: HarperCollins, 2007).

87. Katie Couric, "Michelle Obama on Love, Family & Politics," *CBS Evening News,* February 18, 2008.

88. Cassandra West, "Her Plan Went Awry, But Michelle Obama Doesn't Mind," *Chicago Tribune,* September 1, 2004.

89. "Bio of Michelle Obama," http://www.treehousefoods.com/bio _michelle_obama.html (retrieved December 30, 2011).

90. Judy Keen, "Michelle Obama: Campaigning Her Way," *USA Today,* May 11, 2007.

91. Ibid.

92. Kantor, *The Obamas,* 79.

93. Ibid, 82.

94. Linda Hervieux, "Michelle Obama enjoys Paris privilege barred to millions in France: Sunday Shopping," *New York Daily News,* June 30, 2009.

95. Julie Bosman, "Politics Can Wait: The President Has a Date." *New York Times,* May 31, 2009.

96. Kenneth T. Walsh, "The Political Cost of the Obamas' Date Night," *U.S. News & World Report,* June 9, 2009.

97. Brian Montopoli, "Obama: Complaints About Date Night 'Annoyed' Me," CBS News, October 29, 2009.

98. Lynn Sweet, "Obamas Rent Lavish Farm for Martha's Vineyard Vacation: Michelle, daughters to arrive early," *Chicago Sun-Times,* August 11, 2009.

99. "Michelle Obama's Spain Trip Sparks Debate," *Huffington Post,* August 6, 2010.

100. "Michelle Obama's Africa Trip Cost More Than $424,142," *U.S. News & World Report,* October 4, 2011.

101. Markos Moulitsas Zúniga, "Update III: Michelle, Our Belle, Grabs the Cover of *US Weekly,* Co-Hosts *The View, NY Times* Splash . . ." *The Daily Kos,* June 17, 2008.

102. Mark Leibovich, "Letters Offer a View into the Mind of Hillary Rodham as a College Student," *New York Times,* July 29, 2007.

103. Bill Dedman, "Reading Hillary Clinton's Hidden Thesis," MSNBC, May 9, 2007.

104. Ibid.

105. Hillary Rodham, "There Is Only the Fight: An Analysis of the Alinsky Mode," Wellesley, Massachusetts, May 2, 1969.

106. Barbara Olson, "Hil's College Thesis Reveals Her Mind," *Free Republic,* January 17, 2000.

107. Michael Tomasky, *Hillary's Turn: Inside Her Improbable, Victorious Senate Campaign* (New York: Free Press, 2001), 10.

108. JoAnn Bren Guernsey, *Hillary Rodham Clinton* (New York: Lerner Publications, 2005), 46.

109. Todd S. Purdum, "The Clinton Pardons: The Brothers; Siblings Who Often Emerge In an Unflattering Spotlight," *New York Times,* February 23, 2001.

110. Ibid.

111. Ibid.

112. David Maraniss and Susan Schmidt, "Hillary Clinton and the Whitewater Controversy: A Close-Up," *Washington Post,* June 2, 1996.

113. Stephen Labaton, "Rose Law Firm, Arkansas Power, Slips as It Steps Onto a Bigger Stage," *New York Times,* February 26, 1994.

114. Michael Weisskopf and David Maraniss, "The Uncertain Intersection: Politics and Private Interests—Hillary Clinton's Law Firm Is Influential with State," *Washington Post,* March 15, 1992.

115. Mary Voboril, " 'Elect Him, You Get Hillary' Hillary Clinton Will Stand By Her Man, All Right, But She Has An Agenda. Love Her Or Hate Her For It." *Philadelphia Inquirer,* May 4, 1992.

116. Steve Kroft interview, "The Clintons," *60 Minutes,* January 26, 1992.

117. Barbara C. Burrell, *Public Option, the First Ladyship, and Hillary Rodham Clinton* (New York: Taylor & Francis, 2001), 26.

118. Ted Koppel and Jackie Judd, "Making Hillary Clinton An Issue," *Nightline,* March 26, 1992.

119. Maureen Dowd, "The 1992 Campaign: Candidate's Wife; Hillary Clinton as Aspiring First Lady: Role Model, or a 'Hall Monitor' Type?" *New York Times,* May 18, 1992.

120. Marian Burros, "Now Is the Time to Come to the Aid of Your Favorite Cookies," *New York Times,* July 15, 1992.

121. Al Kamen, "The Bobby Kennedy Law and Hillary Clinton," *Washington Post,* December 1, 1992.

122. Susan Baer, "Hillary Clinton's Office, Near Seat of Power, Signals Her Influential Role," *Baltimore Sun,* January 22, 1993.

123. Cal Thomas, "Hillary Getting Ready to Grab Reins of Power," *Buffalo News,* December 29, 1992.

124. Bill Clinton, "Statement of President Clinton," The White House, January 25, 1993.

125. "Hillary Clinton Launches White House Bid: 'I'm In'," CNN, January 20, 2007.

126. Gail Sheehy, *Hillary's Choice* (New York: Random House, 1999).

127. Adam Hanft, 'The Curious Myth of Hillary Clinton's Senate Effectiveness," *Huffington Post,* February 20, 2008.

128. Gail Sheehy, "Hillaryland at War," *Vanity Fair,* August 2008.

129. Alexander Bolton, "Clinton Was Brain Behind the War Room," *The Hill,* May 13, 2008.

130. *This Week with George Stephanopoulos,* ABC News, December 30, 2007.

131. Peter Nicholas and Peter Wallsten, "Romney, Clinton Shake Up Tactics as Their Leads Vanish in Iowa: He plans to speak on his religion while she seeks to point up her differences with Obama," *Los Angeles Times,* December 3, 2007.

132. Sheehy, "Hillaryland at War."

133. Helen Kennedy, "Hillary Clinton attack on Barack Obama comes after she loses Iowa lead," *New York Daily News,* December 3, 2007.

134. Sheehy, "Hillaryland at War."

135. Gil Kaufman, "Hillary Clinton, Barack Obama Get Personal At Testy Debate," *MTV News,* January 27, 2008.

136. Sheehy, "Hillaryland at War."

137. "Bill Clinton says race, gender to decide S.C. vote," *USA Today,* January 24, 2008.

138. John Heilemann and Mark Halperin, *Game Change* (New York: HarperCollins, 2010).

139. Susan Milligan, "Ted Kennedy Endorsing Obama," *Boston Globe,* January 27, 2008.

140. Sheehy, "Hillaryland at War."

141. Chris Cillizza, "Clinton's '3 a.m. Phone Call' Ad," *Washington Post,* February 29, 2008.

142. John Swaine, "Birther Row Began with Hillary Clinton," *Daily Telegraph,* April 27, 2011.

143. Richard Berg-Andersson,"Pennsylvania Democrat Presidential Nominating Process," *Green Papers* (retrieved January 10, 2011).

144. Adam Nagourney and Jeff Zeleny, "Clinton Ready to End Bid and Endorse Obama," *New York Times,* June 5, 2008.

145. Al Kamen and Philip Rucker, "Hillary Clinton, Secretary of State?," *Washington Post,* November 13, 2008.

146. Patrick H. Caddell and Douglas E. Schoen, "The Hillary Moment," *Wall Street Journal,* November 21, 2011.

Chapter 2: Health Care, by Hook or Crook

1. Carolyn Lochhead, "Pelosi: Pole Vaults and Parachutes," *San Francisco Chronicle,* January 28, 2010.

2. David Corn, *Showdown: The Inside Story of How Obama Fought Back Against Boehner, Cantor, and the Tea Party* (New York: William Morrow, 2012), 3–4.

3. Lee Igel, "The History of Health Care as a Campaign Issue," *Physician Executive,* May–June 2008.

4. Bob Cohn and Eleanor Clift, "The Lost Chance," *Newsweek,* September 19, 1994.

5. John Bresnahan, "Pelosi Lays Down the Law with Rahm," *Politico,* December 16, 2008.

6. Ibid.

7. Ibid.

8. Ibid.

9. Ibid.

10. Michelle Cottle, "House Broker: Nancy Pelosi doesn't like to be threatened," *New Republic,* June 11, 2008.

11. Ibid.

12. Jonathan Alter, *The Promise: President Obama, Year One* (New York: Simon & Schuster, 2010).

13. Ibid.

14. Ibid.

15. Richard Wolffe, "New Obama Book's Revelations," *Daily Beast,* November 15, 2010.

16. Alter, *The Promise: President Obama, Year One.*

17. Jane Hamsher, "Rahm goes Apeshit on Liberals in the Veal Pen," *FireDogLake,* a liberal blog, August 7, 2009. Hamsher claimed she had sources directly in the meeting and there is no reason to doubt her.

18. Sheryl Gay Stolberg, Jeff Zeleny, and Carl Hulse, "Health Vote Caps a Journey Back from the Brink," *New York Times,* March 20, 2010.

19. Alexander Bolton, "Harkin: Health deal was reached days before Brown's Senate victory," *The Hill,* January 30, 2010.

20. Carrie Budoff Brown and Glenn Thrush, "Nancy Pelosi Steeled White House for Health Push," *Politico,* March 20, 2010.

21. Ibid.

22. Ibid.

23. Wolffe, "New Obama Book's Revelations."

24. Brown and Thrush, "Nancy Pelosi Steeled White House for Health Push."

25. Stolberg, Zeleny, and Hulse, "Health Vote Caps a Journey Back from the Brink."

26. Rachel Morris, "Healthcare reform? Thank Nancy Pelosi," *Guardian,* March 23, 2010.

27. Ibid.

28. Brown and Thrush, "Nancy Pelosi Steeled White House for Health Push."

29. Stolberg, Zeleny, and Hulse, "Health Vote Caps a Journey Back from the Brink."

30. Ibid.

31. Author interview with senate staffer involved in negotiations between Reid and Pelosi. The source is apparently referring to Brigadier Gen. George Armstrong Custer, who rallied Union forces to close ranks and repel a confederate advance, turning the Battle of Gettysburg from a rout to a victory for federal troops. See "Report of Brigadier Gen. George A. Custer," September 9, 1863.

32. Dick Morris and Eileen McGann, "Pelosi and Reid Plot Secret Plan for Obamacare," *DickMorris.com,* January 25, 2010.

33. Lochhead, "Pelosi: Pole Vaults and Parachutes."

34. Noam N. Levy, "Pelosi Suggests Maneuver to Pass Healthcare Overhaul," *Los Angeles Times,* January 28, 2010.

35. Brown and Thrush, "Nancy Pelosi Steeled White House for Health Push."

36. Stolberg, Zeleny, and Hulse, "Health Vote Caps a Journey Back from the Brink."

Chapter 3: Nothing Is Sure but Debt and Taxes

1. David Corn, *Showdown: The Inside Story of How Obama Fought Back Against Boehner, Cantor, and the Tea Party* (New York: William Morrow, 2012), 43.

2. Lucy Madison, "Obama's 2010 'Shellacking' is Like Bush's 2006 'Thumping,'" CBS News, November 3, 2010.

3. Corn, *Showdown,* 48–49.

4. Ibid., 18.

5. Ibid., 32.

6. Ibid., 31.

7. Sunlen Miller, "Obama Says Republicans Cannot Have the Keys Back to the Car: 'No! You Can't Drive,'" ABC News, May 13, 2010.

8. Corn, *Showdown,* 20.

9. Jared A. Favole, "Obama Blames Bush and GOP," *Wall Street Journal,* August 2, 2010.

10. Corn, *Showdown,* 43.

11. Ibid., 45.

12. Ibid., 47.

13. Ibid., 48–49.

14. Executive Order 13531, "National Commission on Fiscal Responsibility and Reform," The White House, February 18, 2010.

15. Jackie Calmes, "Deficit Reduction Plan Draws Scorn From Left and Right," *New York Times,* November 11, 2010.

16. Matt Bai, "Obama vs. Boehner: Who Killed the Debt Deal?," *New York Times,* March 28, 2012.

17. Ibid.

18. Fred Kaplan, "Obama's 'Sputnik Moment,'" *Slate,* January 25, 2011.

19. "Republicans Say Obama Budget Plan Not Serious," Fox News, February 15, 2011.

20. Dana Milbank, "In His New Budget, Obama Kicks the Can One More Time," *Washington Post,* February 15, 2011.

21. Jackie Calmes, "The Obama Budget," *New York Times,* February 14, 2011.

22. Perry Bacon Jr., "Obama's Budget Speech Has Partisan Tone," *Washington Post,* April 13, 2011.

23. Margaret Talev and Mike Dorning, "Obama's Grand Deficit Bargain Lost Out to 2012 Politics," *Bloomberg News,* August 1, 2011.

24. Bill Hemmer, "Boehner: Budget Deal Was First Step in the Right Direction," Fox News, April 11, 2011.

25. Sam Stein, "Reid: The Senate Will Vote On Paul Ryan's Budget," *Huffington Post,* April 27, 2011.

26. Carrie Dann and Libby Leist, "Senate Rejects Ryan Budget; Vote Puts GOP on the Spot," MSNBC, May 25, 2011.

27. Timothy Geithner, Letter to Sen. Michael Bennett of Colorado, May 12, 2011.

28. Carl Hulse, "Boehner Outlines Demands on Debt Limit Fight," *New York Times,* May 9, 2011.

29. Alan Silverleib, "Biden hosts budget talks as debt limit nears," CNN, May 5, 2011.

30. Ibid.

31. Ibid.

32. Dennis Jacobe, "Americans Oppose Raising Debt Ceiling, 47% to 19%," Gallup, May 13, 2011.

33. Andy Sullivan, "Debt-Limit Hike Fails in House in Symbolic Vote," *Reuters,* May 31, 2011.

34. Ibid.

35. Janet Hood and Carol E. Lee, "Budget Face-Off at the White House," *Wall Street Journal,* June 1, 2011.

36. Devin Dwyer, "A 'Frosty' and 'Frank' Meeting Between President Obama and House GOP," ABC News, June 1, 2011.

37. Virginia Foxx at @virginiafoxx. https://twitter.com/#!/virginiafoxx, Twitter, June 1, 2011.

38. Mark Knoller, "Obama, House GOP Hold 'Very Frank' Meeting on Debt Limit," CBS News, June 1, 2011.

39. Jennifer Bendery, "House GOP Signals Little Progress In 'Frosty' Deficit Meeting With Obama," *Huffington Post,* June 1, 2011.

40. Dwyer, "A 'Frosty' and 'Frank' Meeting Between President Obama and House GOP."

41. Ibid.

42. Ibid.

43. John Brummett, "The Audacity of Paul Ryan's Whining," *Las Vegas Review Journal,* June 5, 2011.

44. Bai, "Obama vs. Boehner: Who Killed the Debt Deal?"

45. Eric Cantor, "Leader Cantor Statement on Biden Debt Limit Talks," Office of the U.S. House of Representatives Majority Leader, June 23, 2011.

46. Dwyer, "A 'Frosty' and 'Frank' Meeting Between President Obama and House GOP."

47. *Political Capital with Al Hunt,* Bloomberg Television, June 25, 2011.

48. Heidi Przybyla, "Obama Wants to Scrap $72-Billion Business Tax Break as Republicans Balk," *Bloomberg,* June 27, 2011.

49. Bai, "Obama vs. Boehner: Who Killed the Debt Deal?"

50. Brian Montopoli, "Obama: 'Real Differences' Remain on Debt Deal," CBS News, July 5, 2011.

51. "Obama, Hill leaders hold 'constructive' debt talks, schedule more," CNN, July 7, 2011.

52. Bai, "Obama vs. Boehner: Who Killed the Debt Deal?"

53. Jonathan Allen and Jake Sherman, "Obama Abruptly Walks Out of Talks," *Politico,* July 13, 2011.

54. Ibid.

55. Michael D. Shear, "What Happened Between Cantor and Obama?," *New York Times,* July 14, 2011.

56. Andy Sullivan, "Obama says has reached his limit in debt talks— aide," *Reuters,* July 13, 2011.

57. Allen and Sherman, "Obama Abruptly Walks Out of Talks."

58. Ibid.

59. Paul Smalera, "Cantor Describes Obama Walking Out of Debt Talks," *Reuters,* July 13, 2011.

60. Jeff Mason and Andy Sullivan, "Moody's adds pressure to stalled debt talks," *Reuters,* July 13, 2011.

61. "Moody's Report Reinforces Need for White House to Cut Spending," Office of the Speaker of the House John Boehner, July 13, 2011.

62. Bai, "Obama vs. Boehner: Who Killed the Debt Deal?"

63. Talev and Dorning, "Obama's Grand Deficit Bargain Lost Out to 2012 Politics."

64. Eric Alterman, "Obama's Next Budget Deal Cave-In," *Daily Beast,* April 12, 2011.

65. Peter Wallsten, Lori Montgomery, and Scott Wilson, "Obama's Evolution: Behind the Failed 'Grand Bargain' on the Debt," *Washington Post,* March 17, 2011.

66. Jennifer Bendery, Ryan Grim, and Sam Stein, "Obama: Debt Ceiling Talks Fell Apart, Boehner Walked Out," *Huffington Post,* July 22, 2011.

67. Jay Newton-Small, "The Inside Story of Obama and Boehner's Second Failed Grand Bargain," *Time,* July 23, 2011.

68. Bai, "Obama vs. Boehner: Who Killed the Debt Deal?"

69. Newton-Small, "The Inside Story of Obama and Boehner's Second Failed Grand Bargain."

70. Wallsten, Montgomery, and Wilson, "Obama's Evolution: Behind the Failed 'Grand Bargain' on the Debt."

71. Ibid.

72. Bai, "Obama vs. Boehner: Who Killed the Debt Deal?"

73. Trish Turner, "Support for Senate 'Gang' Plan Could Signal Breakthrough on Debt Reduction Deal," Fox News, July 19, 2011.

74. Ibid.

75. Thomas Ferraro and Laura MacInnis, "New Plan Offers Hope for Debt Talk Progress," *Reuters,* July 19, 2011.

76. Kwame Holman, " 'Gang of 6' Debt Plan Gains Momentum as Aug. 2 Deadline Looms," *PBS NewsHour,* July 19, 2011.

77. Linda Feldmann, " 'Gang of Six' Revives Hope for Big Deal in Stalled Debt-Ceiling Talks," *Christian Science Monitor,* July 19, 2011.

78. Wallsten, Montgomery, and Wilson, "Obama's Evolution: Behind the Failed 'Grand Bargain' on the Debt."

79. Barack Obama, "Remarks by the President on the Status of Efforts to Find a Balanced Approach to Deficit Reduction," The White House, July 19, 2011.

80. Wallsten, Montgomery, and Wilson, "Obama's Evolution: Behind the Failed 'Grand Bargain' on the Debt."

81. Ibid.

82. Peter Nicholas and Lisa Mascaro, "How the Obama-Boehner Debt Talks Collapsed," *Los Angeles Times,* July 22, 2011.

83. Barack Obama, "Remarks by the President," The White House, July 21, 2011.

84. Jonathan Karl, et al, "House Passes Debt Ceiling Bill; Gabrielle Giffords Votes," ABC News, August 1, 2011.

85. Lucy Madison, "Senate Passes Bill to End Debt Showdown," CBS News, August 2, 2011.

86. Frank Newport, "Obama's Weekly Job Approval at 40%, Lowest of Administration," Gallup, August 15, 2011.

87. Maureen Dowd, "Tempest in a Tea Party," *New York Times,* July 30, 2011.

Chapter 4: Killing bin Laden Loudly

1. David Remnick, "Behind the Curtain," *New Yorker,* September 5, 2011.

2. Bill Keller, "Fill in the Blanks," *New York Times,* September 18, 2011.

3. Darlene Superville, "Obama Golf Shoes Could Have Been Clue to bin Laden," Associated Press, May 4, 2011.

4. Author interview with intelligence officer, May 2003.

5. Jose A. Rodriguez, "The Path to bin Laden's Death Didn't Start with Obama," *Washington Post,* April 20, 2012.

6. Ibid.

7. Sam Greenhill, David Williams, and Imtiaz Hussain, "How a 40-minute raid ended ten years of defiance, as American troops' head cameras relayed every detail to the President," *Daily Mail,* May 3, 2011.

8. Mark Memmott, "Bin Laden's Courier, Abu Ahmed al-Kuwaiti, Had Several Responsibilities," NPR, May 4, 2011.

9. Luis Martinez and Teri Finneman, "Panetta Sworn in As New CIA Director," ABC News, February 19, 2009.

10. Leon Panetta, "Lawyers Who Lead, Santa Clara Law Alumni Profiles" (accessed December 20, 2011).

11. "Obama names Panetta for CIA," Associated Press, January 9, 2009.

12. Mary Lu Carnevale, "Leon Panetta Gets a Rock Star Welcome at CIA Headquarters," *Wall Street Journal,* February 19, 2009.

13. Peter Bergen and Katherine Tiedemann, "The Drone War," *New Republic,* June 3, 2009.

14. Bill Dedman, "How the US Tracked Couriers to Elaborate bin Laden Compound," MSNBC, May 3, 2011.

15. "Shot dead 'with money sewn into his clothes': Bin Laden was captured alive and then executed, 'claims daughter, 12,'" *Daily Mail,* May 4, 2011.

16. Mushtaq Yusufzai, "Bin Laden's daughter confirms her father shot dead by US Special Forces in Pakistan," *Al-Arabiya News,* May 4, 2011.

17. Greenhill, Williams, and Hussain, "How a 40-minute raid ended ten years of defiance, as American troops' head cameras relayed every detail to the President."

18. Ibid.

19. Greg Miller, "CIA Spied on bin Laden from Safe House," *Washington Post,* May 5, 2011.

20. Ibid.

21. Ibid.

22. Mark Mazzetti, Helene Cooper, and Peter Baker, "Behind the Hunt for bin Laden," *New York Times,* May 2, 2011.

23. Miller, "CIA Spied on bin Laden from Safe House."

24. Nicholas Schmidle, "Getting bin Laden: What Happened that Night in Abbottabad," *New Yorker,* August 8, 2011.

25. Greenhill, Williams, and Hussain, "How a 40-minute raid ended ten years of defiance, as American troops' head cameras relayed every detail to the President."

26. Jake Tapper, "In March, President Obama Authorized Development of Plan to Bomb Compound but Wanting Evidence of OBL's Death, Did Not Execute," ABC News, May 2, 2011.

27. Mazzetti, Cooper, and Baker, "Behind the Hunt for bin Laden."

28. Miller, "CIA Spied on bin Laden from Safe House."

29. Ibid.

30. Mazzetti, Cooper, and Baker, "Behind the Hunt for bin Laden."

31. Ibid.

32. Author interview with Crowley, April 2012.

33. Fred Kaplan, "The Transformer," *Foreign Policy Magazine,* September/October 2010.

34. Jason Ukman, "Gates, on Eve of Retirement, Is Sent Off in Fashion," *Washington Post,* June 30, 2011.

35. "JTF-GTMO Detainee Assessment of Abu al-Libi," September 10, 2008, Department of Defense (retrieved from Wikileaks/Switzer land Site 12/30/2011: http://wikileaks.ch/gitmo/pdf/ly/us9ly -010017dp.pdf).

36. Schmidle, "Getting bin Laden."

37. Mazzetti, Cooper, and Baker, "Behind the Hunt for bin Laden."

38. Ibid.

39. Keith Koffler, "Obama Golfs for the Fifth Weekend in a Row," White House Dossier, May 1, 2011.

40. Jeremy Scahill, "Osama's Assassins," *Nation,* May 4, 2011.

41. Superville, "Obama Golf Shoes Could Have Been Clue to bin Laden."

42. Mazzetti, Cooper, and Baker, "Behind the Hunt for bin Laden."

43. Dana Hughes, "Hillary Clinton on Bin Laden Death: No One Watching 'Could Breathe for 35 Minutes,'" *ABC News Blogs,* April 11, 2012.

44. Schmidle, "Getting bin Laden."

45. Author interview with an intelligence source with knowledge of the operation.

46. Schmidle, "Getting bin Laden."

47. Office of the Press Secretary, "Remarks by the President on Osama bin Laden," The White House, May 1, 2011.

48. George H. W. Bush, "Address to a Joint Session of Congress and the Nation," September 20, 2001.

49. Mark Landler and Mark Mazzetti, "Account Tells of One-Sided Battle in Bin Laden Raid," *New York Times,* May 4, 2011.

50. Matt Negrin and M. J. Lee, "Carney: 'Even I'm Getting Confused,' " *Politico,* May 3, 2011.

51. James Rosen, "Bin Laden Killing: How the White House, Pentagon and CIA Botched the Storyline," Fox News, May 6, 2011.

52. Ibid.

53. Yusufzai, "Bin Laden's daughter confirms her father shot dead by US Special Forces in Pakistan."

54. Lynn Sweet, "Bin Laden Raid: U.S. Has Plan to Take Him Alive. Hiding in Plain Sight?" *Chicago Sun-Times,* May 2, 2011.

Chapter 5: Iran's Bomb, Israel's Dilemma

1. Julian Borger, "Sarkozy: 'Netanyahu's a "Liar," ' " *Guardian,* November 8, 2011.

2. Peter Beinart, *The Crisis of Zionism* (New York: Times Books, 2012), 92.

3. "Mr. Obama's Neighborhood," *Jerusalem Post Magazine,* February 15, 2010.

4. Beinart, *The Crisis of Zionism,* 95.

5. Ibid., 92.

6. Ibid.

7. Ibid., 80.

8. Ibid.

9. Ibid., 81–82.

10. Dave Newbart, "Prominent Rabbi, Friend of Obama Dies at 84," *Chicago Sun-Times,* December 24, 2008.

11. Beinart, *The Crisis of Zionism,* 84.

12. "Mr. Obama's Neighborhood."

13. Beinart, *The Crisis of Zionism,* 88.

14. "About NIF," New Israel Fund, February 2010.

15. *This Week,* ABC News, March 14, 2010.

16. Barack Obama, *The Audacity of Hope* (New York: Three Rivers Press, 1995).

17. David Remnick, "The Spirit Level," *New Yorker,* November 8, 2004.

18. Amos Oz, *How to Cure a Fanatic* (Princeton: Princeton University Press, reprinted January 2006).

19. Mark Weisbrot, " 'The Audacity of Hope' Waits to Sail for Gaza," *Al Jazeera,* June 30, 2011.

20. Gabrielle Birkner, "Rabbi Arnold Wolf, 84, Was Progressive Leader," *Jewish Daily Forward,* December 26, 2008.

21. "Mr. Obama's Neighborhood."

22. Ibid.

23. Ibid.

24. Ibid.

25. Ibid.

26. Ibid.

27. Beinart, *The Crisis of Zionism,* 124.

28. Andrea Stone, "Mideast Envoy George Mitchell Resigns, 'Hit a Brick Wall' On Israeli-Palestinian Peace Talks," *Huffington Post,* May 13, 2011.

29. Toby Harnden, "Barack Obama: Israel must recognise 1967 borders," *Telegraph,* May 20, 2011.

30. Stone, "Mideast Envoy George Mitchell Resigns."

31. Ibid.

32. Harnden, "Barack Obama."

33. Huma Kahn, "In Oval Office, Bibi Offers History Lessons to Obama," ABC News, May 20, 2011.

34. Benjamin Netanyahu Biography, www.netanyahu.org (accessed April 28, 2012).

35. Benjamin Netanyahu, *A Durable Peace: Israel and Its Place Among Nations* (New York: Warner Books, 1993), xi.

36. Kahn, "In Oval Office, Bibi Offers History Lessons to Obama."

37. Netanyahu, *A Durable Peace,* xiii.

38. Edward Luce and Andrew Ward, "Obama Fails to Coax Netanyahu," *Financial Times,* May 19, 2009.

39. Scott Wilson, "At White House, Obama and Israel's Netanyahu Differ on Mideast Emphasis," *Washington Post,* May 19, 2009.

40. Beinart, *The Crisis of Zionism,* 129.

41. Ibid., 136.

42. Ibid., 124.

43. Ian Black, "Barack Obama pledges new beginning between US and Muslims," *Guardian,* June 4, 2009.

44. Benjamin Netanyahu, Full Text of the Prime Minister's Speech at Bar-Ilan University, June 14, 2009.

45. Beinart, *The Crisis of Zionism,* 136.

46. Ibid., 138–39.

47. Ibid., 152.

48. Ibid., 145–46.

49. Ibid., 151.

50. Ibid., 152.

Chapter 6: Fast and Loose and Furious

1. "Attorney General Eric Holder Speaks at the National Action Network 14th Annual Convention Washington, D.C.—Wednesday, April 11, 2012," prepared remarks, U.S. Department of Justice, Justice News, http://www.justice.gov/iso/opa/ag/speeches/2012/ag-speech-120411.html (accessed May 25, 2012).

2. Andrew Longstreth, "Making History with Obama," *American Lawyer,* June 5, 2008.

3. Ibid.

4. *No. 454, Justice Undone: Clemency Decisions in Clinton White House,* U.S. House of Representatives, Washington, D.C.: U.S. Government Printing Office, 2004.

5. Ibid.

6. Longstreth, "Making History with Obama."

7. Leo W. Banks, "Smugglers' Paradise: Perhaps Janet Napolitano

should visit the Peck Canyon Corridor outside of Nogales—with an armed escort," *Tucson Weekly,* November 25, 2010.

8. Son Lisaius, "The Murder of Agent Brian Terry: One Year Later," KOLD-TV, December 24, 2011.

9. Ibid.

10. J. B. Miller, "Border Patrol Apprehends Suspected 'Rip Crew,'" *Nogales International,* March 30, 2012.

11. Affidavit of Special Agent Scott Hunter of the Federal Bureau of Investigations, filed on December 29, 2010.

12. Ibid.

13. Jerry Seper, "Armed Illegals Stalked Border Patrol: Mexicans Were 'Patrolling' When Agent Was Slain, Indictment Says," *Washington Times,* November 22, 2011.

14. Office of the Medical Examiner, Pima County, Arizona, "Autopsy of Agent Brian A. Terry," March 3, 2010.

15. Seper, "Armed Illegals Stalked Border Patrol."

16. Tim Steller, "Case of Slain Border Agent's Killers Sealed in Court," *Arizona Daily Star,* November 15, 2011. Office of the Medical Examiner, Pima County, Arizona, "Autopsy of Agent Brian A. Terry," March 3, 2010.

17. Devin Dwyer, "Bean Bags Fired First in Arizona Shootout Killing Border Patrol Agent," ABC News, March 4, 2011.

18. Sharyl Attkisson, "Gunrunning Scandal Uncovered at the ATF," CBS News, February 23, 2011.

19. David Voth, ATF Group Supervisor, Phoenix Group VII, Letter to "redacted," U.S. Department of Justice, Bureau of Alcohol, Tobacco, Firearms and Explosives, June 1, 2010.

20. Attkisson, "Gunrunning Scandal Uncovered at the ATF."

21. Joint Press Conference with President Barack Obama and President Felipe Calderón of Mexico, Los Pinos, Mexico City, Mexico, April 6, 2009.

22. E-mail from Mark R. Chait to William D. Newell, Subject: SIR, Date: July 14, 2010.

23. Sharyl Attkisson, "ATF Manager Says He Shared Fast and Furious Info with White House," CBS News, July 26, 2011.

24. Transcript Testimony by former Phoenix Field Division Special Agent in Charge William Newell to the House Oversight Committee on Government, July 26, 2011.

25. Remarks of Attorney General Eric Holder at the Mexico/United States Arms Trafficking Conference, Cuernavaca, Mexico, April 2, 2009.

26. Sharyl Attkisson, "ATF Fast and Furious: New Documents Show Attorney General Eric Holder Was Briefed in July 2010," CBS News, October 3, 2011.

27. Attkisson, "Gunrunning Scandal Uncovered at the ATF."

28. Richard A. Serrano, "Gun Store Owner Had Misgivings about ATF Sting," *Los Angeles Times,* September 11, 2011.

29. William Lajeunesse, "'Fast and Furious' Whistleblowers Struggle Six Months After Testifying Against ATF Program," Fox News, November 30, 2011.

30. Dennis Wagner, "Sen. Chuck Grassley: Guns in ATF Sting Tied to Agent's Death," *USA Today,* February 1, 2011.

31. Letter from Charles Grassley, U.S. Senate to Kenneth E. Melson, Acting Director of the Bureau of Alcohol, Tobacco, Firearms and Explosives, Washington, D.C., January 27, 2011.

32. Letter from the Honorable Charles Grassley, U.S. Senate to Kenneth E. Melson, Acting Director of the Bureau of Alcohol, Tobacco, Firearms and Explosives, Washington, D.C., January 31, 2011.

33. Dennis Wagner, "Claims Tie ATF Sting to Guns in Shootout," *Arizona Republic,* February 1, 2011.

34. Letter from Assistant Attorney General Ronald Weich, U.S. Department of Justice, Office of Legislative Affairs, U.S. Department of Justice to the Honorable Charles Grassley, U.S. Senate, February 4, 2011.

35. Jorge Ramos, "Interview with U.S. President Barack Obama," Univision, March 23, 2011.

36. Testimony by U.S. Attorney General Eric Holder before the Committee on the Judiciary, Oversight Hearing on the United States Department of Justice, Rayburn Building, Washington, D.C., May 3, 2011.

37. Testimony by Assistant Attorney General Ronald Weich before the

Committee on the Judiciary, Oversight Hearing on the United States Department of Justice, Rayburn Building, Washington, D.C., June 15, 2011.

38. "Clemens Hires Clinton's High-Powered Washington Lawyer," *Houston Chronicle* at http://blog.chron.com/legaltrade/2008/01 /clemens-hires-clintons-high-powered-washington-lawyer-updated / (accessed May 25, 2012).

39. E-mail from James Trusty to Kevin Carwile, Subject: How did the meeting go with Lanny?, Sent: April 19, 2011.

40. E-mail from Jason Weinstein to Lanny A. Breuer, Subject: Operation Wide Receiver, Sent: April 20, 2010.

41. "Documents Show Justice's Breuer Misled On 'Furious,'" *Investor's Business Daily,* December 14, 2011.

42. Carrie Johnson, "Justice Withdraws Inaccurate 'Fast And Furious' Letter It Sent to Congress," NPR, December 2, 2011.

43. Testimony by U.S. Attorney General Eric Holder before the Committee on the Judiciary, Oversight Hearing on the United States Department of Justice, Rayburn Building, Washington, D.C., December 8, 2012.

44. Chairman Darrell Issa Hearing Preview Statement, Hearing of the House Committee on Oversight and Government Reform to examine the effects of the Bureau of Alcohol, Tobacco, and Firearms (ATF) program dubbed Operation Fast and Furious, July 26, 2011.

45. Sharyl Attkisson, "New Fast and Furious Docs Released by White House," CBS News, September 30, 2011.

46. Serrano, "Gun Store Owner Had Misgivings about ATF Sting."

47. William Lajeunesse, "Lawmakers Claim Justice Inspector Obstructed Probe Into 'Fast and Furious,'" Fox News, September 21, 2011.

48. Tim Mak, "Issa: DOJ compromised gun probe," *Politico,* September 22, 2011.

49. Josh Gerstein and Tim Mak, "Sparks Fly Between Holder, Issa," *Politico,* December 8, 2011.

50. Charlie Savage, "A Partisan Lightning Rod Is Undeterred," *New York Times,* December 17, 2011.

51. Serrano, "Gun Store Owner Had Misgivings about ATF Sting."

52. Sharyl Attkisson, "Another Murder Linked to US Gunwalker Case," CBS News, June 23, 2011.

53. Frank Miniter, "Inside President Obama's War On The Fast & Furious Whistleblowers," *Forbes,* December 7, 2011.

54. Josh Gerstein, "Eric Holder: Black Panther Case Focus Demeans 'My People,'" *Politico,* March 1, 2011.

55. Jane Mayer, "The Trial: Eric Holder and the battle over Khalid Sheikh Mohammed," *New Yorker,* February 15, 2010.

56. Richard A. Serrano, "Obama Defends Atty. Gen. Eric Holder Amid Fast and Furious Probe," *Los Angeles Times,* October 6, 2011.

57. Eric Umansky, "Obama Details Promises for Transparency," *ProPublica,* November 7, 2008.

ABOUT SOURCES AND METHODS

Inevitably, when writing about presidents of the United States—who simultaneously hold the most public and most private office in the world—and focusing your investigation on the president's leadership qualities, especially in the run-up to what is widely expected to be the most consequential election in a generation, there are two kinds of sources that are both plentiful and unhelpful. I, of course, refer to partisans who either devoutly defend or ceaselessly criticize the current president. Just as the economy mirrors the distress of the 1930s and the late 1970s, so does the partisanship of those two eras repeat in our own time.

In considering the qualities of any leader as president, it is essential to get close to people who have actually worked closely with him in the White House and, to a lesser extent, in lower offices. These people have a broad knowledge of the president's abilities as a leader, but because their words may negatively impact both their own job security and that of the president's, they usually decline to speak either on or off the record. A future historian will have an easier time interviewing participants because political passions will have cooled and the outcome of the presidential election will not be hanging like a sword of Damocles over their heads. So, the sources for this book are necessarily limited and the account subject to revision and extension. Such is the fate of all books like this one written in real time, as events unfold.

Another kind of useful source is one who makes it his profession to keep and hold the nation's secrets: intelligence and military officers, diplomats, and bureaucrats. Given the strict national security confidences they hold, many of these sources insist on being anonymous, for professional or personal reasons. Any work of this kind naturally has to rely on such sources. Without anonymity, these sources would simply not talk to a reporter at all.

Fortunately, many people agreed to sit for interviews and to supply documents—ranging from official reports to private notes—that enabled me to tell this story. I appreciate their time and trust. Even within the same political party, there are ideological, personal, and institutional crosscurrents that can motivate some sources to talk to a reporter. The divisions among the Pentagon, State Department, and the White House were an unusually rich vein to mine. Additionally, the people who came into politics with Hillary Clinton have not always found a happy home in the Obama administration. Finally, as in previous administrations, the West Wing of the White House remains an O.K. Corral of rivalries.

I also interviewed experts who could provide perspective, analysis, and insight into events and participants.

Particularly useful was the long-form journalism of Ryan Lizza of *The New Yorker* and Noam Scheiber of *The New Republic*. Jodi Kantor's work for *The New York Times* and her book, *The Obamas,* provided useful leads on longtime friends and neighbors of the Obama family, who have generally not talked to the press. *The New York Times* also maintains an important online database of documents, including Department of Justice memos on interrogation practices. This was very useful for a key part of chapter 4, "Killing bin Laden Loudly." Lexis, Nexis, and Factiva are the key databases to search. Factiva is generally better than Lexis, as it includes *The Wall Street Journal* and the *Financial Times*. The World News Connection is less well-known than Lexis or Factiva, but is nonetheless invaluable. Produced by the CIA's Foreign Broadcast Information Service, World News Connection includes many translations of articles from foreign newspapers, along with radio and television broadcasts. It is the primary source of translated articles from the Arab press. It's only available, in limited release, in some university libraries.

BIBLIOGRAPHY

Alter, Jonathan. *The Promise: President Obama, Year One.* New York: Simon & Schuster, 2010.

Beinart, Peter. *The Crisis of Zionism.* New York: Times Books, 2012.

Bin Laden, Najwa and Omar bin Laden with Jean Sasson. *Growing Up bin Laden: Osama's Wife and Son Take Us Inside Their Secret World.* New York: St. Martin's Griffin, 2009.

Burrell, Barbara C. *Public Option, the First Ladyship, and Hillary Rodham Clinton.* New York: Taylor & Francis, 2001.

Corn, David. *Showdown: The Inside Story of How Obama Fought Back Against Boehner, Cantor, and the Tea Party,* New York: William Morrow, 2012.

Fury, Dalton. *Kill Bin Laden.* New York: St. Martin's Griffin, 2008.

Guernsey, JoAnn Bren. *Hillary Rodham Clinton.* New York: Lerner Publications, 2005.

Heilemann, John and Mark Halperin. *Game Change.* New York: HarperCollins, 2010.

Holcomp, Raymond W., with Lillian S. Weiss. *Endless Enemies: Inside FBI Counter-Terrorism.* Washington: Potomac Books, Inc., 2011.

Hull, Edmund J. *High-Value Target.* Dulles: Potomac Books, Inc., 2011.

Kantor, Jodi. *The Obamas.* New York: Little, Brown & Company, 2012.

Kurtz, Stanley. *Radical-in-Chief: Barack Obama and the Untold Story of American Socialism.* New York: Threshold Editions, 2010.

Mendell, David. *Obama: From Promise to Power.* New York: Harper-Collins, 2007.

Netanyahu, Benjamin. *A Durable Peace: Israel and Its Place Among the Nations.* New York: Grand Central Publishing, 1999.

Obama, Barack. *The Audacity of Hope.* New York: Three Rivers Press, 2006.

———. *Dreams from My Father.* New York: Three Rivers Press, 1995.

Oz, Amos. *How to Cure a Fanatic.* Princeton University Press, 2006.

Peterson, Scott. *Let the Swords Encircle Me.* New York: Simon & Schuster, 2010.

Pfarrer, Chuck. *SEAL Target Geronimo.* New York: St. Martin's Press, 2011.

Remnick, David. *The Bridge: The Life and Rise of Barack Obama.* New York: Random House, 2010.

Scheiber, Noam. *The Escape Artists: How Obama's Team Fumbled the Recovery.* New York: Simon & Schuster, 2012.

Scott, Janny. *A Singular Woman: The Untold Story of Barack Obama's Mother.* New York: Riverhead Books, 2011.

Sheehy, Gail. *Hillary's Choice.* New York: Random House, 1999.

Suskind, Ron. *Confidence Men.* New York: HarperCollins, 2011.

Tomasky, Michael. *Hillary's Turn: Inside Her Improbable, Victorious Senate Campaign.* New York: Free Press, 2001.

Weisman, John. *Kill Bin Laden.* New York: William Morrow, 2011.

INDEX

Abbottabad compound, Pakistan, 132–33, 149
  intelligence from, 152–53, 159–62
  surveillance, 133
abortion, 72
Abu Ahmed al-Kuwaiti, 127–29
  search for, 131–32
Abu Faraj al-Libi, 128, 143
Abu Musab al-Zarqawi, 127, 160
Alterman, Eric, 105
Arab Spring, 196
ATF. *See* Bureau of Alcohol, Tobacco, Firearms, and Explosives
The Audacity of Hope (Obama, B.), 179
Avila, Jaime, 224
Axelrod, David, 74, 83–84
  Israel and, 177–78, 195
  Pelosi and, 82

Baucus, Max, 68, 96
Ben-Ami, Jeremy, 176–77
Biden, Joseph, 57, 96, 161
  national debt and, 99–100
bin Laden, Osama, 45
  Clinton, B., and, 117, 121
  communication methods used by, 125–26
  death of, 115–16, 153–61
  locating, 116
  Pakistan and, 116
  search for, 119–21, 123–24
  September 11 attacks and, 122
  wives, 163–64
bin Laden operation (Neptune's Spear), 115–67
  Bush, G. W., and, 116
  cancellation of, 118
  CIA and, 123–24, 145–46
  Clinton, H., and, 118, 136, 141–43
  credit for, 162

bin Laden operation (*continued*)
    FBI and, 123
    foreign intelligence services and,
      123–24
    Gates and, 136
    intelligence, 123–24, 134–36
    Jarrett and, 118, 135–36, 143
    as kill mission, 164–65
    McRaven and, 145–48
    military options, 137–39
    narrative, 162–63, 165
    Obama, B., and approval of,
      147
    Obama, B., and involvement in,
      118–19, 135, 154–60
    Pakistan and, 139–40
    Panetta and, 131–33, 136,
      144–45
    Petraeus and, 142–43
    planning, 117–18, 138–39
    Razor 1 helicopter crash,
      150–51
    Rodriguez and, 127–28
    secrecy and, 159–62
    shootout, 164
    untruths regarding, 163–65
Boehner, John, 94–95
    national debt crisis and, 104–7
    national debt plan, 105–12,
      239
    Obama, B., and, 101, 239
Brennan, John, 146, 153
Breuer, Lanny, 221–22
Brown, Scott, 67, 72
Bruni, Carla, 25–26

budget
    cuts, 99
    deficit, 87
budget plans, 89–90, 98, 105–8
    Boehner's, 105–12, 239
    Cantor and, 105–10
    Gang of Six, 108–10
    Ryan's, 90
Bureau of Alcohol, Tobacco,
    Firearms, and Explosives
    (ATF), 207–16
    allegations against, 217–18
    demand letter and, 212–13
    negligence of, 217
Bush, George H. W., 92
Bush, George W., 4, 113, 160
    bin Laden operation and, 116
    counterterrorism techniques,
      127
    decision-making process, 6
    Israel and, 184
    Wide Receiver, 222
Bush-era tax cuts, 95–96

Calderón, Felipe, 212
Cantor, Eric, 96, 98
    national debt and, 99–100,
      102–4
    national debt crisis and, 105–7
    national debt plan and, 105–10
    Obama, B., and, 102–4
Carter, Jimmy, 84, 185
Cartwright, James, 139
Celis-Acosta, Manuel Fabian, 207

Chambliss, Saxby, 88, 165

CIA
  bin Laden operation and, 145
  bin Laden search and, 123–24
  black sites, 127
  military and, 145

Citizens United case, 82

Clinton, Bill, 4, 113
  bin Laden and, 117, 121
  Clinton, H., and, 39–40, 42
  decision-making process, 6
  health care reform and, 35, 40, 48,
    56–57
  Panetta and, 130–31
  presidential campaign, 39–40

Clinton, Hillary, 6, 22
  bin Laden operation and, 118,
    136, 141–43
  Clinton, B., and, 39–40, 42
  as first lady, 35
  health care reform and, 40
  influence during Clinton
    administration, 39–40
  Israel and, 184, 195
  Obama, B., and, 37–43, 141
  Panetta and, 130
  Pelosi and, 55–56
  Petraeus and, 142
  politics, 37–38
  presidential campaign, 41–43
  as secretary of state, 43
  in Senate, 40–41
  as wife, 39

Clyburn, Jim, 53, 96

Coburn, Tom, 88, 108

Cole, James, 219–20

Common Purpose Project, 59–60

Congress
  Democratic Congressional
    Campaign Committee, 52–53
  lame duck, 84–85
  National Commission on Fiscal
    Responsibility and Reform, 88

Corn, David, 46, 80

counterterrorism techniques, 127

credit downgrade, 93, 104, 113

Crowley, P. J., 6, 141

Cut, Cap and Balance bill, 111

Daley, Bill, 106, 145

Daley, Richard, 15, 18

Daschle, Tom, 23, 40–41

Democratic Congressional
    Campaign Committee, 52–53

Democratic Party
  health care reform and, 47, 49
  House majority held by, 52, 75
  midterm elections and, 78–79

DeParle, Nancy-Ann, 57

Dermer, Ron, 188, 191

Dodson, John, 210–11, 214–15,
    218

Dreams from My Father (Obama,
    B.), 235

Dunham, Stanley Ann, 9–14

*A Durable Peace: Israel and Its Place
    Among the Nations*
    (Netanyahu), 189

dynamic scoring, 107

earmark ban, 54–55

economy. *See also* budget; national debt

dynamic scoring, 107

growth, 107

stimulus bill, 79–80

Emanuel, Rahm, 19–20

health care reform and, 50, 56, 60–61

Jarrett and, 24–25

Pelosi and, 52–54

European Union, national debt, 86

FBI, bin Laden operation and, 123

Feinstein, Dianne, 88

Ford, Gerald, 185

Franken, Al, 74

Gang of Six, 88

debt plan, 108–10

Gates, Robert, 118, 139

bin Laden operation and, 136

Obama, B., and, 143

Gaza Strip, 176

Geithner, Timothy, 93–94, 106, 107

Gibbs, Robert, 77, 80

Jarrett and, 25–27

Obama, M., and, 26–27

Sher and, 27

Gingrich, Newt, 113

government shutdown, 91

Grassley, Charles E., 216–18, 222

Grossman, David, 178–79

Guantánamo Bay, 126–27, 237–38

gun regulation, 212

gun sales, 207–8. *See also* Operation Fast and Furious

Habitat Company, The, 19

Hamilton, Lee, 191–92

health care reform

Clinton administration, 35, 40, 48, 56–57

Common Purpose Project and, 60

costs, 58–59

Democratic Party and, 47, 49

Emanuel and, 50, 56, 60–61

fight over, 50–51

fixes, 73

in House of Representatives, 68, 71–72

insurance exchanges, 61

insurance industry and, 66

international programs, 51

issue of, 47

legislation, 64

Obama, B., and, 45–46, 49–52, 70–71

Obama, B., and passage of, 68–70, 74–75

opposition to, 57–59, 62–63

passing, 49–50, 57–58, 68–70, 73–75

Pelosi and, 45, 49–52, 56–57, 65–66, 71

Pelosi and passage of, 68–70, 73–74

Reid and, 71, 73
Sebelius and, 50
Senate bill, 65
single payer, 60–61
state plans, 49
two-step passage of, 70, 71
health care summit, 75
Heschel, Abraham Joshua, 173–74
HillaryCare, 56. *See also* health
    care
Hillary's Turn (Tomasky), 38
Holder, Eric, 4
    Jarrett and, 202–3
    job performance, 202
    KSM trial and, 230
    Obama, B., and, 201–4, 235, 241
    Operation Fast and Furious, 7,
        204, 214, 219–21
    opposition to, 235
    race and, 230
    subpoenas, 227
    testimony, 223, 227
House of Representatives
    Democratic majority in, 52, 75
    health care reform in, 68, 71–72
    midterm elections and, 84
Howard, Andre, 224–26

Ibrahim, Raymond, 124–25
Inouye, Daniel, 96
insurance
    exchanges, 61
    industry, 66
    unemployment, 48–49

integration, 30–31
interrogation techniques, 127,
    237–38
Iran, nuclear weapons, 191
Israel
    America's policy toward, 181–85
    Axelrod and, 177, 195
    borders, 182–85, 196–99
    Bush, G. W., and, 184–85
    Clinton, H., and, 184, 195
    Jewish state and, 192–93
    Obama, B., and, 170–73, 178–80,
        188–89
    Oslo Peace accords and, 172
    Palestine and, 171–72, 182–83
    red lines, 189
    settlements, 192–95
    statehood, 182
Issa, Darrell E., 219–21, 223

J Street, 176–77
Jackson, Jesse, 170
Jarrett, Valerie, 3
    bin Laden operation and, 118,
        135–36, 143
    career, 17–19
    Emanuel and, 24–25
    family, 16–17
    Gibbs and, 25–27
    at The Habitat Company, 18–19
    Holder and, 202–3
    influence of, 25
    misuse of power by, 25–27
    Obama, B., and, 15–28

Jarrett, Valerie (*continued*)
Obama, M., and, 15–16, 34, 37
plight of the poor and, 19–20
Plouffe and, 23
presidential campaign role of, 23–24
Rouse and, 24
social network, 19
2016 Olympic Games bid and, 27–28
on University of Chicago Medical Center and, 20–21
White House role, 24–25
Jewish state, 192–93
Johnson, Lyndon, 47, 185

Kennedy, Ted, 42, 62
Khalidi, Rashid, 176
Klutznick, Philip, 177
KSM. *See* Mohammed, Khalid Shaikh
al-Kuwaiti, Omar, 151

labor unions, 48–49
Levin, Jack, 179–80
Lew, Jack, 105, 110
Lieberman, Joe, 108
Loper, Brett, 107–8

MacAllister, Hope, 207, 225–26
Martin, Trayvon, 242
McCarthy, Kevin, 99, 100

McConnell, Mitch, 89, 112
McDonough, Denis, 146, 192
McRaven, Bill, 136–37, 139
bin Laden operation and, 145–48
Medicaid, 102
Medicare, 48, 102
Mexico, Operation Fast and Furious and, 212, 228
midterm elections, 77–78
House of Representatives and, 84
Senate and, 84
Mikva, Abner, 177
military
bin Laden operation and, 145
secrecy and, 159
Minow, Newton, 176
Mitchell, George, 181–82, 191
Mohammed, Khalid Shaikh (KSM), 128
capture, 160
trial, 230
Morales, Marisela, 228
Moseley-Braun, Carol, 21–22

Nabors, Rob, 107–8
National Commission on Fiscal Responsibility and Reform, 86–88
national debt
Biden and, 99–100
budget deficit and, 87
Cantor and, 99–100, 102–4
credit downgrade and, 93, 104, 113

defaulting on, 93–94
economic growth and, 107
in European Union, 86
increasing, 95, 97–98
limit, 95
Obama administration, 85–86,
97
national debt crisis of 2011, 7
Boehner and, 104–7
Cantor and, 105–7
Obama, B., and, 81–82,
244–45
Neptune's Spear. *See* bin Laden
operation
Netanyahu, Benjamin
*A Durable Peace: Israel and Its
Place Among the Nations,*
189
history, 187–88
Obama, B., and, 169–70, 172–73,
181, 234–35
Obama, B., and meeting with,
185–87, 189–91
settlement freeze and, 194–95
Newell, Bill, 213–14, 216, 223
Norquist, Grover, 59–60

Obama, Barack
aloofness, 5, 14
approval rating, 113
The Audacity of Hope, 179
bin Laden operation and
involvement of, 118–19, 135,
151–60
bin Laden operation approved by,
147
bin Laden's death and, 115–16,
151–59
birth certificate, 42
Boehner and, 101, 239
budget proposal, 89–90
Cantor and, 102–4
career prior to presidency,
5–6
Clinton, H., and, 37–43, 141
compromise and, 238–39
in crisis, 7
decision-making style, 4–6,
240–41
Dreams from My Father, 235
failures of, 79–80, 234
family life, 14
father, 10
Gates and, 143
grandparents, 13–14
gun regulation and, 212
half sister, 13
in Hawaii, 12
health care reform and, 45–46,
49–52, 70–71
health care reform passage and,
68–70, 74–75
Holder and, 201–4, 235, 241
identity of, 11
in Indonesia, 11–12
Israel and, 170–73, 178–80,
188–89
Jarrett and, 15–28
Jewish community and, 180–81

Obama, Barack (*continued*)
  lame duck Congress used by,
      84–85
  leadership abilities, 1–2, 76
  leadership failures, 79–80
  leadership style, 14, 233–45
  life story, 235–36
  midterm elections and, 78–79
  mother, 9–14
  National Commission on Fiscal
      Responsibility and Reform,
      86–87
  national debt and, 85–86, 97
  national debt crisis and, 81–82,
      244–45
  Netanyahu and, 169–70, 172–73,
      181, 234–35
  Netanyahu's meeting with,
      185–87, 189–91
  Panetta and, 134
  Pelosi and, 50, 54–55
  presidential campaign, 23–24
  principles of, 236–38
  privacy and, 14
  racial identity of, 11
  racism and, 241–42
  religious identity of, 11–12
  risks taken by, 239–40
  Rouse and, 23
  in Senate, 5, 22–23
  social circle, 3
  solitariness, 2–5
  spending, 88–90
  stimulus bill, 79–80

  successes, 234
  tax increases, 99–100
  2016 Olympic Games bid, 27–28
  vision of, 240
  Wolf and, 175–76, 179
Obama, Michelle, 28–37
  Bruni and, 25–26
  family, 29
  as first lady, 34–37
  Gibbs and, 26–27
  Jarrett and, 15–16, 34, 37
  legal career of, 31–32
  at Princeton, 29–30
  public image, 36–37
  racial identity of, 30–31
ObamaCare, 45–46. *See also* health
      care
The Obamas (Kantor), 26
Olson, Barbara, 38
Omar, Mullah, 126
O'Neill, Tip, 103, 113
Operation Fast and Furious
  agents testifying on, 218–19
  arrests and, 211–12
  authorization of, 219–20, 223
  bureaucrats in charge of, 229
  coverup, 216–17
  crimes linked to, 228–29
  flaws in, 208–9
  gun-tracking in, 208–9, 228
  Holder and, 7, 204, 214, 219–21
  Mexico and, 228
  origin of, 206–7
  Terry and, 204–6, 228

O'Reilly, Kevin, 213–14, 223
Oslo Peace accords, 172
Oz, Amos, 178–79

Pakistan
    Abbottobad compound, 132–33,
        149, 152–53, 160–61
    bin Laden in, 116
    bin Laden operation and, 139–40
Palestine
    Israel and, 172, 182–83
    U. N. resolution and, 196–97
Palestine Liberation Organization,
    172
Panetta, Leon, 118, 129–30
    bin Laden operation and, 131–33,
        136, 144–45
    Clinton, B., and, 130–31
    Clinton, H., and, 130
    Obama, B., and, 134
Pareira, Israella, 11
The Patient Protection and
    Affordable Care Act, 51–52
Pelosi, Nancy, 113
    Axelrod and, 82
    campaign for speaker, 52–53
    Clinton, H., and, 55–56
    Emanuel and, 52–54
    health care reform and, 45, 49–52,
        56–57, 65–66, 71
    health care reform passage and,
        68–70, 73–74
    Obama, B., and, 50, 54–55

Perino, Dana, 165
Petraeus, David, 142–43
Pitts, Adrienne, 18
Plouffe, David, 23
Poe, Ted, 228–29
Pollack, Ron, 69–70
Pressler, Larry, 122
Pritzker, Penny, 23

Qaddafi, Muammar, 43
al-Qaeda, 125–26. *See also* bin
    Laden, Osama
    intelligence on, 153
al-Qosi, Ibrahim, 119

racial identity
    Obama, B., and, 11
    Obama, M., and, 30–31
racism, 30–31
    Obama, B., and, 241–42
Razor 1 helicopter crash, bin Laden
    operation, 150–51
Reagan, Ronald, 5, 92, 103, 113,
    174–75
Reid, Harry, 53, 63
    health care reform and, 71, 73
    Ryan budget and, 90
Remnick, David, 16
Republican Party
    Cut, Cap and Balance bill, 111
    midterm elections and, 78
Rhodes, Ben, 146–47, 154, 182

Robinson, Marian Shields, 14

Robinson, Michelle LaVaughn. *See*
    Obama, Michelle

Rodriguez, Jose A., 127–28

Rodriguez, Mario Gonzalez, 228

Roosevelt, Franklin Delano, 47, 93

Roosevelt, Teddy, 47

Rosenberg, Lee, 171

Rostenkowski, Dan, 61–62

Rouse, Pete, 4, 23
    Jarrett and, 24

Rove, Karl, 24

Rumsfeld, Donald, 121

Ryan, Paul, 90, 98

Said, Edward, 170

Saltzman, Bettylu, 177

Sarkozy, Nicolas, 25

Schedar, Cynthia, 223–24, 226–27

SEAL Team Six, 137. *See also* bin
    Laden operation
    training, 145–46

Sebelius, Kathleen, 55
    health care reform and, 50

Senate
    Clinton, H., in, 40–41
    health care reform, 65
    midterm elections and, 84
    National Commission on Fiscal
        Responsibility and Reform, 88
    Obama, B., in, 5, 22–23

September 11 attacks, 117
    bin Laden and, 122

Sharpton, Al, 243

Sher, Susan, 15, 22
    Gibbs and, 27

al-Shibh, Ramzi bin, 160

Simpson-Bowles commission. *See*
    National Commission on
    Fiscal Responsibility and
    Reform

Social Security, 49, 101, 106

spending
    cuts, 91, 113
    Obama administration, 88–90

stimulus bill, 79–80

taxes
    Bush-era tax cuts, 95–96
    increases, 92, 99–100
    revenue, 107
    on rich, 88, 95–96

Taylor, Robert, 16–17

tea party, 62–63

Terry, Brian A., 204–6, 228

Tomasky, Michael, 38

2016 Olympic Games bid, 27–28

U.N. *See* United Nations

unemployment insurance, 48–49

United Nations (U.N.), 196–97

University of Chicago Medical
    Center, 20–21

Van Hollen, Chris, 81, 96

Voth, David, 210, 215, 216

Washington, Harold, 17, 22, 83
Weich, Ronald, 218, 221
West Bank, 190
White, Quincy, 31–32
Wide Receiver (operation), 222
WikiLeaks, 143
Winfrey, Oprah, 3
   2016 Olympic Games bid, 28

Wolf, Arnold Jacob, 174–76
   Obama, B., and, 175–76, 179
Wright, Jeremiah, 170, 203

Zapata, Jaime, 229
al-Zawahiri, Ayman, 125
Zimmerman, George, 242